IN THE ABSENCE
OF POWER

ALSO BY HAYNES JOHNSON

The Working White House (1975)
The Bay of Pigs (1964)
Dusk at the Mountain (1963)
Lyndon (1973) with Richard Harwood
The Unions (1972) with Nick Kotz
Army in Anguish (1972) with George C. Wilson
Fulbright: The Dissenter (1968) with Bernard M. Gwertzman

IN THE ABSENCE
OF POWER
GOVERNING AMERICA

HAYNES JOHNSON

THE VIKING PRESS □ NEW YORK

First published in 1980 by The Viking Press
625 Madison Avenue, New York, N.Y. 10022
Published simultaneously in Canada by
Penguin Books Canada Limited

Library of Congress Cataloging in Publication Data
Johnson, Haynes Bonner, 1931–
   In the absence of power.
   Includes index.
1. United States—Politics and government—1977–
2. Carter, Jimmy, 1924–   I. Title.
E872.J63   320.9'73'0926   79-3625
ISBN 0-670-20548-6

Printed in the United States of America
Set in CRT Baskerville

FOR MIKE,
WHO WOULD HAVE TOLD
THE STORY BETTER

AUTHOR'S NOTE

A word about sources, source materials, and their uses: While I was not present at most of the private sessions described in these pages, particularly those between the president and the congressional leaders, I'm confident that what appears herein accurately reports what was said. Much as I dislike the use of "blind quotes," it has been necessary at times to grant certain people the privilege of anonymity. On occasion, also, where people's thoughts are recalled, they stem from what the person said he *remembered* thinking at the time. In most cases when individuals are directly quoted by name, such as Hubert Humphrey, their words are taken from transcripts of tape-recorded interviews.

CONTENTS

"Do I understand you," I said, "and is your
meaning that you teach the art of politics,
and that you promise to make men good citizens?"
"That, Socrates, is exactly the profession
which I make."
"Then," I said, "you do indeed possess a
noble art, if there is no mistake about this,
for I will freely confess to you, Protagoras,
that I have a doubt whether this art is capable
of being taught."

—THE DIALOGUES OF PLATO

PROLOGUE

THE NARRATOR

TWENTY-TWO years ago I arrived in Washington. It was a sultry day, and the Capitol loomed ahead through an August haze. The trolley was running then, and I took it from Union Station down Pennsylvania Avenue, past the rows of seedy shops on one side and massive gray government structures on the other, until it stopped in front of a newspaper office halfway between the Hill and the White House. I was twenty-five, I had a master's degree in American history, and I was about to start my journalistic career in the capital.

Other than a half-remembered boyhood visit to a city sleeping in the summer sun, a place of wide and empty avenues offering glimpses of marble monuments, I knew Washington only from the pages of my books. These, I have discovered, are almost all false. The memoirs, the biographies, the narrative histories of a presidency or political epoch, as well as the government's written records of how events supposedly occurred and what role the mighty figures played in them, bear little resemblance to reality as I've found it.

Since I've come to Washington I've witnessed the workings of six presidents, assassinations, riots, and other political convulsions. The experience has changed me: close observation of politics tempers one's innocence with reality and offers one an appreciation of the unstable nature of power. If our politics seems sterile to me now, our leaders impotent, our people disaffected from the process in their capital, it's hardly unexpected.

But more than this, it's the operation of government that most concerns me. I know many Americans share my disquiet. My contention, and the reason for this book, is that in the last decades of the twentieth century the United States has become a nation in danger of being unable or unwilling to govern itself, and that the experience of Jimmy Carter—a singularly different president who has presided, however briefly, over its destinies—offers clues to the outcome of that proposition. Furthermore, while the place to observe the struggle is Jimmy Carter's Washington, the only way to understand it is to take into full account the reaction of the rest of the country to the events and personalities dominating the capital.

Readers have a right to know, and be wary of, the biases and background of the narrator who proposes to take them on such a journey. Here, too, a confession and warning: As Scott Fitzgerald once said of himself, I find I've done little serious thinking, other than within the problems of my craft, for years. The journalistic deadlines, however difficult, were always met; the book manuscripts, with their simple narrative themes—the injustice against blacks, the wrongness of a war, the tragedy of a clandestine military operation—always delivered. But *really* thinking about the sum of all these events, about how they were affecting me and people I met around the country, was conveniently avoided. Daily journalism, with its strictures of bland objectivity, offers sanctuary from doubt and introspection. As a rule we newspapermen pretend to know more than we do, and yet we report less than we see and hear. Walter Lippmann understood this all too well: We are captives of what he called the pictures in our heads—our belief that the world we know is the world that exists. And the world that will be.

□ □ □

When I arrived in Washington, Eisenhower was beginning his second term. I believed he was not exercising the powers of the presidency aggressively enough. Like many of my generation, I had grown up convinced of certain political "facts." Franklin Roosevelt was my hero, the Democrats were my party, and liberalism was my ideology. A strong central government was essential, I believed, and we the people could rely on that government to exercise its powers to insure that the greatest number derived the greatest benefits. *Vox populi,* democracy in action. Ike was weak.

That America of a generation ago has vanished. Then, there were no great issues, no dissent, no marches, no protests, no climate of violence, not even many doubts. It was possible to believe, and many did, that there were no real problems, certainly none we couldn't solve, except perhaps the ever-present one of communism, and we could handle that. Ike fit the confident public mood perfectly. As the 1960s began he told the Congress that the year ahead would be the best in our history, and soon he was forecasting a budget surplus of more than $4 billion. On television he was telling us we had "forged an indestructible force of incalculable power." When he routinely asked Congress to authorize nearly $5 billion for U.S. economic and military foreign aid, Congress routinely approved. There was no public outcry when he vetoed a bill to control river pollution because it would require spending too many federal funds, and days later he vetoed another that would have given U.S. money to economically depressed areas. To some of us, then, these were signs of Ike's benign but ineffectual leadership.

In my graduate-school days, I remember, I studied the debates over adopting our Constitution. John Marshall, who believed in a strong central government, was pitted against Patrick Henry, who feared that such concentrated power could be used to destroy liberty. Marshall believed that public faith and strict observance of justice would be maintained by having the best citizens entering the government. He could conceive of no other possibility—certainly not that those good men would abuse their power and threaten the liberties of others. Those early debates, probably the most critical in our national experience, set the tone for American political discourse. Two strands run through American history—the necessity for a strong government and the equal necessity for the protection of the individual against the encroachments of the state. I always came down on Marshall's side.

Certainly my initial experience in the 1960s strengthened those

beliefs. I welcomed the Kennedy era. There at last, I believed, was
an example of aggressive action and vitality, of a president using
the full force of his office for the best public interest.

Only one nagging concern intruded, and that was over the role
of the Central Intelligence Agency in the Bay of Pigs invasion. To
me, the CIA was a powerful, secret arm of the government, unchecked, unaccountable to anyone including the president, deciding on its own what was right and what was wrong. I wrote a book
strongly criticizing the CIA and in turn was accused by Allen Dul-
les, then its director, of coming close to being a traitor for disclos-
ing what he conceded were accurate accounts of his agency's
actions. In my naïveté I believed that it was the bureaucracy, not
the presidency, that was mainly at fault. The record now available
clearly establishes other responsibility—rogue elephant at times
the CIA may have been, but its depredations (and, yes, those of
the FBI) were sanctioned by higher governmental authority, often
directly from the Oval Office itself.

Any doubts I had about the need for a strong central government were, however, swept away by the ensuing civil-rights struggles across the South. Oxford, Mississippi, Birmingham, and Selma, Alabama, were proof that blacks could look only to the powers
of the federal government to protect their rights; for local and
state governments could not or would not do so. Good and evil
were starkly defined: the federal government was good, the bul-
wark of liberty, and the president was its most effective symbol.

But personal disillusionment quickly followed. Immediately
after Selma came Lyndon Johnson's dispatch of troops to the
Dominican Republic in April 1965. As a reporter present at the
scene, I looked across the harbor at Santo Domingo and saw the
might of the U.S. Navy at its battle stations. And for what? To sup-
press a handful of rebels against the Dominican government, to
prevent a "Communist" takeover. This, it seemed to me, was a naked case of military power being used improperly at the behest of
the president. Under presidential direction, the CIA and FBI and
the State Department were leaking documents to the press so as to
justify the action and prove a case of subversion against the Dominican government. Their case was false.

In Washington, in his Oval Office out of sight of the television cameras, Lyndon Johnson would storm and rage, pull classified documents from his pockets to "prove" his points. On one memorable occasion, the day after I had returned from Santo Domingo, he described to me and to other journalists how masses of Dominicans had been slaughtered and their severed heads impaled on poles. It was not true.

Covering the war between India and Pakistan in that same stormy year of 1965 left another impression. On the Pak side and then on the Indian, you would come across ammunition cases bearing the emblem of the United States and marked by two hands clasped in friendship. They were gifts from the people of the United States, gifts used first to arm and then to kill the people of two allied nations. After a large tank battle on the plains of Punjab, one saw a landscape littered with wreckage: American tanks destroyed by American planes and shells. I have not felt the same about military foreign aid since.

Later it was Greece and Turkey, and again American arms were used against American allies. By the end of the 1970s, a decade in which we simultaneously armed Arabs and Israelis in the Middle East and turned a corrupt regime in Iran into one of the greatest storehouses of weaponry in the world, only to see it and them disintegrate in bloody revolution, we saw our own captured weapons employed in a massive invasion from Vietnam into Cambodia— and then used to fight our former enemy, the Chinese, when *they* invaded Vietnam.

The same kinds of mad scenes and official justifications became standard during the long years in Vietnam. We had to destroy the village in order to save it, explained the American officer. Of course. Even now, I find Vietnam too painful to put into any kind of proper perspective.

Again like many of my generation, the greatest single influence of my youth had been World War II. I dreamed childish dreams of daring in darkened movie houses watching actors play at heroic life in such films as *Purple Heart* and *Midway* and *Back to Bataan*. As a boy in New York, I remember, I would wake to hear Hitler's voice fading in and out over the radio shortwave to the accompaniment of those chilling roars of the Nazi crowds. When my father became an air-raid warden, I'd slip up to his room and secretly strap on his gas mask and try to wear his white steel helmet. Later, when he went to the South Pacific as a war correspondent, I pored over every one of his stories trying to put myself in his place.

He wrote me an extraordinary letter on the eve of the invasion of Okinawa, on Easter Sunday, 1945. As he said, at risk of embarrassment to us both, he had some things he wanted to say before the landing at dawn the next morning. I was thirteen at the time—the same age he had been when his father died at the end of World War I.

"I firmly believe that when it comes to setting a standard of values in life—a code of ethics or whatever you want to call it—there are certain things each man must discover for himself," he wrote. "For myself, I believe I have made an important discovery. I believe that the most important thing in life, as far as I am personally concerned, is maintaining one's personal honor and integrity. As a nation that is what we are fighting for now: national honor and integrity. But it goes deeper than that. I am talking now about the individual. . . ." He apologized for preaching, and hoped he didn't sound sanctimonious.

When I graduated from college the Korean War was in its second year, and I was drafted as an Army rifleman. While I wasn't so foolish as to wish to go into combat, I felt it was better for me to serve than my young brother—and I entertained few doubts about the need for, or wisdom of, having America fight again in Asia. A decade or more later, when we began dispatching combat troops away from the coastal enclaves into the elephant grass of Vietnam, my initial reaction was one of support for the president's rationale and actions. I was still thinking like a young lieutenant shaped by all that had gone before. But as I studied at first hand in Washington and overseas what Senator Fulbright perfectly described as the arrogance of power in action, I began to change my mind. Not only did the war itself seem unacceptable but it was destroying American principles and values at home. Not the least of the damage, I came to believe, was to our own political process.

By 1968 we already had sown the seeds of what we came to know inadequately as Watergate: paranoia in the presidency, end-justifies-the-means mentality in government, preoccupation with secrecy and "national security," willingness to use state powers against the individual, often illegally, an amassing of greater power in the office of the presidency.

I had never supported Richard Nixon, nor did I in 1968, but I believed he had a chance to be an effective president. He had worked and waited too long not to profit from the mistakes of his predecessors, I believed, naïvely again. His goals, it seemed, were right: to limit the powers of the government in Washington, cut back on the bureaucracy, transfer authority to the states and municipalities and gradually withdraw from our self-appointed role as the world's policeman. But as we all know, despite what he promised, Nixon accelerated the process of consolidating power in Washington, particularly in the White House. This "conservative" president tried, in fact, to alter radically the balance of power within the government. Impoundment of congressionally authorized funds, expansion of executive staff and budgets, hiding from the courts behind "executive privilege" and "national security," conducting the business of the people in unparalleled secrecy—in effect, Nixon refused to recognize any power other than his own. When, belatedly, the nation reacted to this accumulation of unchecked power it may have appeared as if Nixon and Watergate and impeachment were an aberration. But Kennedy in Cuba, Johnson in Vietnam, Nixon at Watergate all sprang from the same historical forces. It's impossible to unravel one from the other. Now, when I look back on those events, I think of the way two people reacted.

One day in Robert Kennedy's Justice Department office, while he was still attorney general in 1964, we were talking about the Cubans and the Bay of Pigs. Kennedy became emotional. He swivelled around in his chair, gestured behind his desk, and pointed out what he said were two kinds of "trophies" he kept to remind him of the problems facing leaders in government. One trophy was a white U.S. marshal's helmet, dented from a thrown brick, that had been worn by a member of the federal force he had dispatched to Mississippi during the racial disturbances there. The other was a crude, handmade rifle mounted inside a glass case. It had been taken from a dead Vietcong guerrilla. The helmet represented our domestic problem, Kennedy said, the rifle our foreign. And the question in his mind was whether the U.S. government was strong and tough enough to act forcefully and effectively in handling either challenge—and whether the citizens had the courage and the stamina to support the actions of their government.

That kind of attitude, held widely among top government officials in the early 1960s, led us to the sponsorship of innumerable clandestine activities (including assassination plots), the creation of our form of guerrilla forces like the Green Berets, and the greater reliance on government power that came to typify much of the decade of Vietnam and Watergate.

The other memory is of Martin Luther King, Jr. After his glory days in the South, King's effort to deal with the reality of black urban life in Chicago in 1966 had failed; despite his passionate words, he had no discernible influence in stopping the escalation of the war in Vietnam. Worse, from his personal viewpoint, he knew he was beginning to lose his following. Although still only in his late thirties, King was regarded by many blacks as a figure from the past. In the process, he changed. When I last saw him, in 1968, after an absence of a year, I was struck, even shocked, by his tired look and diffident manner. He had aged and appeared less assured. It was not the buoyant King I had seen before.

In a political sense King, like Robert Kennedy, typified traditional liberal attitudes. With his exhortations and emotional appeals, his calls for a Marshall Plan for the cities and his belief in the efficacy of big government programs emanating from Washington, King was espousing the conventional ideas of two generations shaped by the experience and philosophies of the New Deal. Whether King came to doubt those premises by the end of his life I can't say. But his demeanor and actions hinted that he, too, like so many of us, was harboring new doubts.

For many of us, watching some of the Great Society's experiments left us with a deep distrust in the government's ability to solve certain national problems. In 1964 I had gone to the Catoctin Mountains, near the presidential Camp David retreat, to watch Lyndon Johnson and Sargent Shriver welcome with speeches and slogans the first of the Job Corps volunteers, a group of young blacks from the slums of Baltimore and young whites from the hollows of Appalachia. The president and his poverty warriors made ringing declarations about "total victory" and spoke of banishing poverty from the land. Professors left their campuses and consultants their businesses to lead the War on Poverty. They crowded into leased Washington offices to plan the strategy and dispense the tens of millions of dollars Congress quickly made available. Later I traveled into the byways of eastern Kentucky with the first VISTA members as they took up their posts. Then I made trips into cities and hamlets across the country to see the battle at first hand.

In less than three years those programs had disappeared so completely it was as though they had never happened. I'll not soon forget visiting one of the first permanent Job Corps installations on a brilliant winter day in the stark simplicity of the Acadia National Park, on Maine's Mount Desert Island, overlooking Bar Harbor. There, surrounded by deep snowbanks and commanding a magnificent vista of mountains, woods, and ocean, were the buildings the government had constructed a few years before to house the young school dropouts. The buildings were empty, all of them: the gymnasium and dormitories, the splendidly equipped kitchen where they had been taught meat-cutting and cooking, and the classrooms still decorated with posters imploring the young charges to "Start the Day Right on Time" and "It's Tough to Work with Needless Noise. Keep It Down." All had been abandoned. In a dormitory, standing against a wall, were fourteen pairs of brand-new skis with boots and poles. A tangle of new ice skates lay on the cement floor. Hockey sticks were neatly stacked in a corner, along with two complete scuba-diving tanks and outfits and six bicycles.

After the Job Corps abandoned its site there, when the War on Poverty quietly faded from national consciousness to be replaced by the war in Vietnam, the government leased the facilities to indigenous Indian tribes in Maine and the Maritime Provinces. One of the Indians told me, "When the Job Corps people went away they left all their records behind them. We found the written reports they made on the trainees. It was depressing to read what they said privately about those kids. We burned them."

After I returned to Washington, I called a friend who had been one of the first to join the Job Corps executive staff; we had talked about collaborating on a book examining the experiences of the first group of trainees. He had tried to get the government records of those young men, he said, after going back to his university position. But they no longer existed. No one knew what had happened to them. No one even knew their names.

□   □   □

Henry Adams, that querulous but provocative aesthete, thought of himself as having been educated to hold eighteenth-century values totally unsuited to dealing with twentieth-century problems. Nevertheless, Adams was more contemporary than he thought. "Modern politics is, at bottom," he said, "a struggle not of men but of forces. The men become every year more and more creatures of force, massed about central powerhouses. The conflict is no longer between the men, but between the motors that drive the men. . . ."

It's with those political forces, those motors that drive the men in power, that I'm concerned. I'm not attempting another narrative history of another presidency.

If I've learned anything these years in Washington, it's that the natural journalistic preoccupation with personality obscures or falsifies the most significant issues of government. I've come to distrust most accounts of what purportedly happens in the inner circles of government—those dramatic scenes that show how wisely or resolutely the leader addressed, and solved, the problems at hand. I can pull down from my shelves volume upon volume of supposedly informed works that fail even to mention many of the critical events we now know affected our lives and our politics. Besides, what did we *really* know about Franklin and Eleanor, or Jack and Jackie, or Dick and Pat? How much do we still fail to know about the critical decisions made during the Roosevelt, Kennedy, or Nixon administrations?

I have also learned all too well the limitations and temptations of journalism as practiced in Washington. With Robert Kennedy, I discovered how easy it was to cross the line that supposedly—and properly—separates journalists from public figures. I didn't know Jimmy Carter during his campaign, and my only personal session with him then left an impression of cold, even disturbing, self-assurance. For many reasons, I distrusted him; but I did vote for him in the hope his presidency would represent a welcome change in national directions. His promise was to move the United States into a new political era of realism after all the shocks and disappointments of the 1960s and 1970s. I believed, more out of instinct than anything else, that his presidency could establish a more mature style of leadership for a country approaching its most mature period.

The election of Carter seemed the most interesting since Truman's. Not only was he different from all the other presidents but the conditions he would inherit, nationally and in Washington, as the first leader in the post-Vietnam and post-Watergate era, were far more complicated than ever before. Given Carter's background, the events of the preceding decade that created his opportunity, and the forces that made possible his victory, the outcome of his experience at governance could be historic.

These were political reasons enough to watch his fortunes closely, but I also had personal ones. I had been born and raised in New York, but both my parents were natives of Georgia who moved north in the 1920s. Like many Southern whites of that time and place they long had been outraged and embarrassed by the acts of brutality and ignorance that stained their region. How much the Carter campaign meant to people like them was brought home to me forcefully by an incident that occurred not long before the Democrats convened in New York in the summer of 1976. Carter had run into some last-minute difficulties; there was fresh talk he might be denied the nomination after all. It had been nearly fifty years since my father left Georgia for New York, and now he was critically ill in the hospital, with terminal cancer, but he rose up in his bed to say, with a passion and bitterness that stunned me: "They'll never let a Southerner be president." That kind of regional thinking was entirely uncharacteristic of him, and I never had heard him speak that way about the South. I was struck by what deep historical currents the candidacy of the elusive Jimmy Carter obviously were stirring.

But by the time Jimmy Carter came to Washington, much of the old gratification that men and women had long enjoyed in government service had evaporated. The attitude toward public service among both the politicians and members of the press had grown notably critical. At mid-point of Carter's first term I was talking one night with one of the most respected figures in Washington, himself a presidential possibility. What he expressed in his congressional office was a view held privately by many other politicians:

> I don't know where the hell the country's going or where the hell the government's going or where you're going to get good people to man it. Government's becoming increasingly unattractive to people. A lot of guys I know are saying the hell with it.
>
> They're retiring for a mixture of motives: the times have gotten so complex and the issues are tougher and meaner. The public is dissatisfied and unhappy. It used to be you were The Honorable Congressman or The Honorable Senator, but there's no honor in being here anymore. People would look up to you when you went home, and they'd get excited about what was going on in Washington, about building a great society or ending discrimination. Now, who cares? A lot of the income here is psychic, and if you're not getting that and you're working your ass off and the people are angry at you at home, why knock your brains out for this "plush" salary they pay you? Frankly, if it weren't for my committee chairmanship I don't think I'd stay on. It's gotten to where the anguish and the pain and the drudgery and the constant demands of the workload far outweigh the gratifications I used to get from it.

That kind of negativism was certainly not uncommon in the press, albeit from a different perspective. The tenor of the press had become harsh, too, partly as a result of previously being too trusting of political leaders, especially presidents. But if we no longer exalt the president we still examine his doings in great detail, at the expense of studying other critically important parts of the government—in the Congress and in the bureaucracy. I intend to explore some of those areas, to try, if possible, to go behind the government's gray exterior and see how it really functions and what its real problems are. Despite our fascination with "politics," the race and the game and the scorecard, I don't believe many of us in the press understand the workings of government well. I now know I have not. Nor, despite its angry reactions and easy denunciations, does the general public—or, it appears, many of our political leaders, including our presidents.

Some of my colleagues despair of determining the "truth" either through daily journalism or longer nonfiction works. "I ceased to believe that facts could lead me to the truth," said Ward Just, in explaining why he left journalism to write novels. "And when that happens, when you lose a certain essential respect for fact, you are useless as a journalist." I haven't lost my respect for facts, but I concede holding serious doubts about fully ascertaining them. In fact, I know I cannot.

I'm certain, too, that at times I'll be guilty in these pages of the sin cited by Lippmann: "Let him cast a stone who never passed on as the real inside truth what he had heard someone say who knew no more than he did."

With such qualifications in mind, I intend to address these themes:

A basic conflict existed between the politically inexperienced outsiders who came to Washington in 1977 and the men and women already in the capital who held governmental power.

They all, new and old alike, were reflecting and reacting to deeper political problems that stemmed from the tortuous events of the last few decades. While many of us had watched and recorded and at times celebrated the public fortunes of the leaders who wielded authority in those years, we had failed to see that the very structure of government was changing, making it more difficult for anyone to exercise authority effectively.

While citizens at large wearied of the workings of Washington and grew more cynical about politics, Washington itself was becoming a preserve of wealth and privilege and power, a place apart from America.

Themes are one thing; the search for personal meaning is something else. I find, as I take up the narrative, that the "pictures in my head" have not prepared me for the personal and political changes we face in the 1980s and beyond. My mental pictures have been shaped by two decades of reporting; but now I see that my assumptions about power and its uses, politics and its practices, government and its techniques, have about as much relevance to the closing years of the century as the views of life held by Europeans on the eve of World War I did to the bloody era in which I was born. As Lippmann wrote of them in the summer of 1914: "All over the world as late as July 25th men were making goods that they would not be able to ship, buying goods that they would not be able to import, careers were being planned, enterprises contemplated, hopes and expectations entertained, all in the belief that the world as known was the world as it was. Men were writing books describing that world. They trusted the pictures in their heads." We sail for the Indies and find America, we diagnose evil and hang old women, we promise reforms and produce repression, we react to excesses of power and become powerless.

Governing remains the issue. "In framing a government," Madison wrote, "the great difficulty is this: you must first enable the government to control the governed, and in the next place, oblige it to control itself."

BOOK ONE

CHANGE

1

THE CHANGE

GAUNT AND gray, weakened by cancer surgery and radiation treatments, battling flu and a high fever, Hubert Humphrey had gone to Georgia anyway. His colleagues there were shocked when he turned up in Plains and tried not to show it, but he knew how they felt.

For days he'd looked in his mirror each morning and said to himself, My God, this is unbelievable. His prospects frightened him, despite what his doctors said, and he had refrained from telling his wife how ill he was: she'd never have let him out of the house, he was certain. It had been a nightmare, that trip—a blizzard in the morning in Minnesota, an entire hour to get to the airport, a mistake in misjudging the Georgia climate by bringing only a light coat. Under almost any other circumstances he wouldn't have made it.

But this was no ordinary occasion, nor was Humphrey an ordinary politician. It was December 1976, and the new president-elect had summoned the leaders of his party to confer about the return of the Democrats to power in Washington after eight long years.

Humphrey held a special place among the Democrats, and he knew the way Washington worked as well as anyone. Not only was he the best known of the liberals but he was the last of the political figures that had dominated American politics for a generation. Eisenhower, Stevenson, the Kennedy brothers, Johnson all were gone, and Nixon was finished as a political force. Yet Humphrey also knew political realities dictated that none of his previous ser-

vice, whether as mayor or congressman or senator, vice-president
or presidential nominee, would amount to much if he weren't in
on the beginnings of Jimmy Carter's administration. He was determined to play a decisive part.

"In politics," Humphrey told me later, "you can be alive and get
buried, and once you're buried you don't get out of the tomb. If I
hadn't turned up in Plains when they had those meetings down
there I knew that I would have been buried politically. So I was going to be there physically, even if I looked like I was about ready to
collapse. Whether I was there in spirit—I mean with vitality—was
unimportant."

That day in Plains left a strong impression on Humphrey. "Jimmy Carter had us in that damp pond house of his for five hours
and I nearly froze to death. He gave us Coca-Cola and a damned
old sandwich with stringy roast beef wrapped in cellophane. We
should have been treated better than that."

He wasn't the only Democrat to be bothered. Watching and listening and occasionally booming out a blunt response in his pronounced Boston accent was Thomas P. ("Tip") O'Neill, Jr. Florid
of face, with long white hair and a massive frame that held two
hundred sixty-five pounds of girth, a political pro whose service to
his Massachusetts constituents began in the statehouse in 1936
and continued in Congress starting in 1952, Tip O'Neill was a
Democrat to the core. O'Neill really believed in his party's platform; when he spoke about the Democratic record of providing
work and wages for Americans, he meant it. He was to be the new
Speaker of the House of Representatives and a power in Jimmy
Carter's Washington.

O'Neill held John Kennedy's old congressional seat. He liked to
recall a time when Jack Kennedy walked into his Boston office. It
was the day after the 1958 election, and Kennedy had just been reelected senator by an overwhelming margin. They fell, naturally,
to talking about politics. Kennedy turned to O'Neill's assistant, another Boston Irishman, and asked him to point out the various
precincts in his old district. As the assistant called out the numbers
on a map, Kennedy gave a brisk analysis of the demographics in
each: this one, so much percent Italians, so much Irish; that one,
so much black, so much Nova Scotians. Precinct by precinct he described the voting records and patterns, the ethnic and religious

compositions, the white- and blue-collar sections, the union leaders and opponents, the issues and areas of change. This guy's the smartest politician I've ever seen in my life, O'Neill thought.

At first he had been amused but later was nearly as impressed by the hard political savvy of the ex-governor of Georgia who was running for president. Carter, then a virtual unknown, had called on O'Neill in Washington in early 1975. With exasperating assurance he had proceeded to spell out precisely why he would have the Democratic nomination locked up before the party convened in New York a year and a half later. Methodically and coldly Carter explained why Edward Kennedy would not be a candidate, why Humphrey would not run, why Henry ("Scoop") Jackson would fail, and why the only person who possibly could beat him, Walter ("Fritz") Mondale, had dropped out of the race before the 1976 election year began. By the time he reached New York, he'd have no real opposition left and would be a certain first-ballot victor, Carter said.

This guy Carter's a good pol, O'Neill told his fellow Democratic leaders as they prepared to convene in New York; he was becoming the presidential nominee exactly the way he said he would.

Now in the house by the pond in Plains, O'Neill was listening as Carter told the leaders what his legislative priorities would be in the new administration. He wanted the new Democratic Congress to enact authority to reorganize the federal government, pass a strong ethics package, and an energy program.

The ethics we're going to have trouble with, O'Neill was thinking, the reorganization nobody likes, but he's a new president and we can give it to him. The energy is going to be one tough fight, because for twenty-five years nobody's been able to put that together. But O'Neill was disturbed by what he believed to be a glaring omission from Carter's agenda. He spoke up strongly. They couldn't leave without talking about an economic-stabilization program, he said. A recession was going on. What people were going to hit Carter with right away wasn't reorganization or ethics or energy: it was jobs, and what the new president was going to do about it. That was the basis of Democratic Party politics. They *had* to do something about that.

More than that was on O'Neill's mind. During a break in their meeting he found an opportunity to tell Carter privately what was troubling him. They walked toward the pond behind the house, and, while leaning against a tree, O'Neill said: Mr. President, I want you to understand something. Some of the brightest men in America are in this Congress of the United States. Don't make the mistake of underestimating them. They've been there for years, and on any specific piece of legislation they know why every comma, every semicolon, every period is there. We want to work together, but I have a feeling you are underestimating the feeling of Congress and you could have some trouble.

Carter instantly replied: I'll handle them just as I handled the Georgia legislature. Whenever I had problems with the Georgia legislature I took the problems to the people of Georgia.

O'Neill continued: The Congress doesn't operate like that, Mr. President. I want you to know something. Seventy-six percent of the people in that Congress ran ahead of you in their districts. While the image of Congress may be exceptionally low on the national basis, these congressmen have a very high image at home. I don't know what the image of Tip O'Neill would be nationally, but I know from a recent poll that I'm seventy-eight in my own district and I was seventy-five on election day. And, Mr. President, it just doesn't work the way you think.

□   □   □

After Carter's election his friend and counselor Charles Kirbo, the Georgia lawyer who was his closest political adviser, had predicted the new president would get along well with Congress, "better than anybody else you've seen lately." On the surface, it would have seemed so. For the first time in almost a decade one-party rule was being returned to Washington. The Democrats held huge majorities in both House and Senate. Their proportions were similar to the FDR and LBJ landslides that enabled the legislative packages of the New Deal and Great Society to be enacted. The ugly period of confrontation, stalemate, veto, and bitterness that had characterized White House and congressional relations during the Nixon-Ford administrations appeared to be over. A Brookings Institution scholar in Washington, James L. Sundquist, completing a lengthy study of previous presidents and Congresses, was euphoric in assessing what lay ahead for Carter and Congress: "The chances for a durable peace between [executive and legislative] branches will be better than at any time in this century."

Reality was something else. Seldom had a new president come to power amid such sourness and mutterings—and this among the key elements of his own party. Washington on the eve of Jimmy Carter's presidency was filled with bitter stories about the campaign disasters committed by Carter and his crew. These were not just the idle gossip that accompanies any political shift in power, or merely an outpouring of resentment because Carter had campaigned against Washington and the major elements of the Democratic Party. Yes, he had taken them on and beaten them all. This had left bruised egos and wounded vanities, but the complaints dealt with substantive charges.

The essence of the case was this: that Jimmy Carter, through a miserably managed, inept, and error-prone campaign, had almost succeeded in achieving the historically impossible—he had departed from the Democratic convention bearing impressive evidence that the party was finally united, holding an extraordinary 35 percent lead in the opinion polls, and running against the record of the discredited Nixon administration, now headed by an unelected successor whose pardon of the disgraced former president had driven his own popularity to perilous lows; and all this at a time of rising unemployment and a declining economy. Yet Carter had managed to eke out a victory by only the slimmest of margins. He had won 49.98 percent of all presidential ballots cast in an election notable for the negative spirit among the electorate. (His percentage of the votes in the two major parties was 51.05.)

The decline in voting was startling evidence of further political disaffection. There had been 150 million Americans of voting age in the bicentennial year of 1976, but only 54 percent of them chose to vote for president; a downward trend at the polls was continuing. Until the turbulent decade of the sixties began, American voter participation in presidential elections had been in the range of 60 to 65 percent of the electorate. But for five straight presidential elections starting in 1960 the percentage of nonvoters steadily increased. By comparison, as Arthur T. Hadley writes in *The Empty Polling Booth,* in 1940 when only 14 percent of the peo-

ple had high-school educations and poll taxes and other impedi-
ments to voting were standard in many areas, nearly 60 percent of
eligible voters cast presidential ballots. The better educated
Americans became, the less they voted; the more they knew of the
political process, the less they apparently believed in it. And when
the official 1976 count was completed, it showed that Carter had
received the support of less than three out of ten Americans who
might have voted for him. Indeed, with a switch of only a few
thousand votes in Hawaii and Ohio, Carter would have lost.

A closer look at the election results disclosed other problems.
That Carter had carried all the states of the Old Confederacy (except Virginia) was not surprising; regional pride and loyalty in
having the first Deep South candidate since the Civil War mandated those results. But Gerald Ford had swept the entire West, a
band of states across the Midwest, and most of New England. In
the end Carter's victory came down to his carrying such key industrial states as New York, Pennsylvania, and Ohio—the heart of the
old Democratic coalition that had elected presidents since Roosevelt. And there, the angry postmortem voices in Washington were
saying, was where Jimmy Carter would have blown the election
had it not been for them.

Carter set himself apart from the party professionals of other
campaigns. He didn't try to use the old party stalwarts like Humphrey. He ran the campaign itself from Atlanta, and this reinforced his separation from the political establishment in the
capital. That was all right with the regulars in Washington; they
wanted to win at least as much as Carter, and if they served as a
public foil during the campaign, they understood the politics of it.
What infuriated them was that they hadn't been consulted on campaign strategy. They came to feel that Carter wasn't just making a
symbolic gesture about the old ways of politics and the evils of
Washington—he was telling the Democratic pros that he didn't
want or need their political talents. Coordination with other politicians outside the Carter camp was fumbling or nonexistent. Consultation with congressional or state leaders was poor at best.
When advice was accepted, it was often ignored. Carter's liaison
with Congress was, as one top Democratic aide said, "dismal, a
joke." Meetings were scheduled and canceled, phone calls went
unreturned, offers of help spurned.

Carter's campaign emissary to Capitol Hill was forty-year-old Frank Moore, who had handled legislative lobbying in the statehouse during Carter's governorship in Georgia. Democratic leaders on Capitol Hill said they tried to tell him that senior members of the House delegations could be helpful in such vital states as Pennsylvania, Ohio, and Illinois. Nothing came of their efforts. "Moore's been totally unavailable, to the point where people are wondering whether the Carter camp has some kind of paranoia about doing business with anybody with any experience," an important Capitol Hill staff member said.

As Carter's lead eroded during the campaign, criticism increased. Stories about the incompetence of his campaign structure made the rounds, until even one of his strong supporters said wearily: "The great untold story of this campaign is that the campaign offices in Atlanta are abysmally organized. Here is a man running for president on a promise to reorganize the whole federal government, and he can't even organize his own headquarters." More unsettling was the conviction that many Washington politicians shared about Carter's own views on politics. "He really believes all this stuff about the corrupt Washington establishment," one Democratic veteran complained. "He really thinks we're all John Deans."

When the election was over, as Tip O'Neill pointed out to the new president, it wasn't Jimmy Carter who had carried in members of Congress, but they who had run ahead of him, and in that sense elected him. (Only in Tennessee, for instance, had Carter gotten more votes than the successful Democratic Senate candidate.) The political coattails were worn by congressmen, not Carter.

But the Carter people didn't seem to understand that. "There never was sufficient appreciation of the fact that Democratic congressional nominees have, in every year but 1964, run ahead of the presidential nominee," one congressional leader said afterward. "There was a great reservoir just waiting to be tapped, dying to be tapped, and they never tapped it."

The Democrats in Congress owed Carter nothing. "Carter's people had good intentions," a House aide told a *National Journal* reporter immediately after the election, "but they're ignorant. People now say, the hell with them."

The election experience left another Washington operative with a gloomy appraisal: "Ignorance is as bad as arrogance."

☐   ☐   ☐

During the Vietnam-Watergate years, concern centered on the "imperial presidency" and the accumulation of power in the hands of the chief executive. The Congress, so supine, so deferential, was becoming a rubber stamp for the White House. Historians expressed the fears that the ideas of the Founding Fathers were being perverted: the tripartite system of separate but equal branches of government which they had devised was failing.

But in those years of crisis an equally fateful struggle was taking place: the battle for Congress to regain its lost powers. In both foreign and domestic affairs Congress was fighting to limit the power of the president to act without its consent. It was a struggle that took many forms and was fought on many fronts.

In foreign affairs, congressional enactment of a War Powers Resolution in 1973 directly checked the president's power to act alone in involving the United States in armed conflicts anywhere. The resolution, passed over a Nixon veto warning that it would place "unconstitutional and dangerous" restrictions on a president's actions, was the result of congressional determination to avoid further Vietnams. In domestic affairs, the establishment in 1974 of Congress's own budget office gave the legislators greater power over the purse. Until then, Congress had been a hostage of the executive department's proposals that shaped the federal budget; now, through its own office, gathering its own information, Congress could regain much of its old authority over the dispensing of federal funds.

Stronger efforts were made to oversee executive departments and agencies, such as the CIA. In hearings and investigations congressional committees and subcommittees aggressively asserted their right to know what was going on. The habit of yielding to presidential requests to refrain from examining supposedly sensitive matters because of "national security" was broken. Through more vigorous staff inquiries and supervision, Congress was demanding—and getting—closer cooperation in obtaining information from the federal bureaucracy, information which in the past often had been denied by the president's doctrine of "executive privilege." Congress also exerted greater control over presidential appointments: highly placed aides to the president were now required to be judged and confirmed by the Congress before taking their jobs. Now each house of Congress had the power to neutralize a president's actions by what were called "legislative vetoes." Disapproval by *either* House or Senate was enough to kill a presidential order on the allocation of oil imports, for instance. And during the struggle with the White House during Vietnam and Watergate, Congress had devised another method of bypassing presidential acts and frustrating his will: the use of concurrent congressional resolutions. (The concurrent resolutions required only a majority vote of the two houses and did not need presidential approval to take force. Joint congressional resolutions, the technique favored in the past, needed a presidential signature to become effective and a two-thirds vote of Congress was required to override a White House veto.)

All these developments occurred in a rather brief period—and nearly all were obscured by the more visible and dramatic public debates leading to Nixon's final fall. But more important than the new statutes aimed at redressing the balance of power was the new sense of will on Capitol Hill, reinforced by new kinds of people coming to Congress, people who expressed the national reaction against the abuse of presidential power exemplified by Vietnam and Watergate. They were younger, less wedded to party structure and political ideology, and more independent in action. They initiated, and won, reforms in the old seniority system that had permitted political barons with long years of service to control what went on in Congress. They tended to take a more critical approach to the executive departments toward which they had legislative responsibilities, thus tying those agencies closer to the Congress and lessening presidential influence. They did not bring to Washington the long political experience in local and state levels that had been the accepted path to power. Many of them shunned the old traditions that had encrusted the workings of the Congress. They viewed themselves as a new breed, and acted accordingly.

No agreement existed among scholars about how lasting or significant these changes were, but few on Capitol Hill doubted what had happened: the Congress had changed, and its members knew it. Several years after, Tip O'Neill looked back on the formation of the Carter administration and the new political conditions in Washington and declared passionately, pounding his fist on his desk: "The change in Congress had come. We had recaptured our powers to the extent that we were almost an equal voice. The press didn't read it. Jimmy Carter didn't read it. They didn't appreciate the power and the strength of the Congress of the United States. Jimmy Carter thought he was going to be another president with the powers of a Nixon or a Kennedy or a Johnson, and he didn't have 'em when he arrived here."

In preparing for his presidency, Carter had been briefed by many experts and read voluminous papers drafted for him. But perhaps none of these was as helpful as a shrewd piece of advice from Dean Rusk, whose career of counseling presidents and gauging political currents and realities spanned the postwar era. Rusk was a fellow Georgian who had become a Rhodes Scholar and then a veteran diplomat. It was the strong backing of such Democratic and foreign-policy luminaries as Dean Acheson and Robert Lovett, the New York financier and secretary of defense under Truman, that had sufficiently impressed John Kennedy to name Rusk as his secretary of state. During the difficult Kennedy-Johnson years Rusk's pattern of presidential counseling never varied: he rarely stated his own conviction in forums such as the cabinet sessions, preferring instead to tell the president what he really thought alone, and orally.

Whenever we had a problem in the old days, Rusk told Carter, we would take it to the whales, the political Big Fish. We'd go up to Capitol Hill and sit down with old Sam Rayburn or Lyndon Johnson or Ev Dirksen or Dick Russell or Bob Taft, and tell them what our problem was. And if they agreed to help us, we knew our problem would be solved. But there were no more whales in Washington. The way a president dealt with congressional or other groups and personalities would require greater skill and understanding. The era of the big power broker would never return.

Sam Rayburn had personified that period. The Speaker of the House in all but two terms from 1940 to 1961, serving longer than anyone in American history, tough, forceful, versed in every aspect of politics, he understood power and how to use it. There was nothing fancy about it: you rewarded your friends, chastised your enemies, relied on your word, and maintained iron control. A call from old Sam could send a shudder through a member of the House. Everyone had a story about the way he operated. Rayburn would call up the chairmen of committees and order bills introduced, with certain items included in them; he would let it be known that a certain member needed a harbor dug in his district; he'd call the Corps of Engineers and order work started immediately on a canal project, because another campaign was beginning and the Democrats there needed jobs in their area. What he wanted he got; no questions asked.

One congressman had a problem with the Internal Revenue Service. The case had been hanging for three years. Finally, he went to Rayburn. It was like the Chinese water torture, he explained to the Speaker; the uncertainty and pressures were destroying him and his family. Could the Speaker do something? Either have the case pressed or dropped? Anything to get it over.

Rayburn went to work. A call to an IRS official, then a call to the U.S. attorney handling the case: they had had the case for three years, and that was time enough; Rayburn wanted it cleared by five o'clock *that day*—and he wanted it presented as a civil case, not a criminal one. It was settled that day. Civil.

The grateful congressman promised Rayburn would have his vote whenever needed. Good, said the Speaker. He wanted him in the front row for a controversial vote scheduled the next day. "If I don't need you I'll tell you and you vote the other way," the Speaker said, "but you gave me your word and if I need you I'll expect your vote." Old Sam had twenty people lined up in the front row that day. He won, of course.

Rayburn himself was removed from contact with most members of the House. He held court, along with the other political whales, in a room off the Speaker's lobby. There, behind closed doors, with a Capitol Hill guard posted outside, he and Lyndon Johnson and a few others would convene regularly in what they called their "Board of Education" sessions. Bourbon and branch water and ice were set up for them and their guests. Admission was highly sought and by invitation only for even the most important committee chairman, and then you could come only once every several weeks. "You'd walk by the room and they'd say 'That's where the Speaker is. He's in the Board of Education,' " Tip O'Neill remembered. "Then you'd have a guest of your own, and you'd walk by and show him where the Speaker was. Behind closed doors. I thought it was an honor to have old John McCormack bring me into the Board of Education the first time."

By the advent of Jimmy Carter, that kind of individual power on Capitol Hill was a thing of the past. At both ends of Pennsylvania Avenue governing in Washington was going to be more difficult.

□   □   □

In sixteen years Washington witnessed the passing of presidential power five times. Some were sudden and shocking—John Kennedy's assassination, Nixon's resignation. Some were orderly, but the order masked depths of private bitterness—Eisenhower to Kennedy, Johnson to Nixon. Three vice-presidents, two of them unelected, served in the three years before Carter's election; and for the first time in American history the nation had been governed by a man who hadn't received a single vote as either president or vice-president.

Despite the accelerating pace at which presidents and vice-presidents had been brought in and replaced, the transition from Gerald Ford to Jimmy Carter marked only the third time since World War II that the transfer of political power had been so total. That is, complete control of the government was moving from the hands of one political party into another. And not since Herbert Hoover had a sitting president seeking reelection been turned out of office.

Every defeat brings a period of bitterness and recrimination, of postmortems and second-guessing—*if we had only done this, or that, then we would have won.* In the Ford White House after the 1976 election, the feelings were the same. The personal adjustments on giving up power are always difficult, and so they were for the Ford assistants who had exercised it. They found the pace of their lives slowing as they moved from politically active to passive roles, their phones ringing less often, their appointment calendars less full, their opinions less sought, their futures suddenly less certain.

Outside, where cranes lifted stacks of lumber onto the sidewalk in front of the wrought-iron White House fence, where carpenters busily constructed parade platforms along either side of Pennsylvania Avenue, and where police sank concrete stanchions and strung cables from them to hold back the inaugural throngs in Lafayette Park, noise and activity dominated the scene. Inside, the White House had a different look: the normally bustling press room was nearly deserted; a secretary watching Jimmy Carter holding another television session from Plains announcing more appointments, sighed and said, "More names to learn to spell, the same old garbage"; a White House policeman at a corridor desk near the Rose Garden idly thumbed the pages of an old newsmagazine and yawned; and down the hallways, past the empty but still guarded Oval Office, the outgoing president's senior aides talked quietly in their offices about working in the White House, and about Washington and the passing of power.

"I've lived through and seen some very unusual events in the nation's history," Lieutenant General Brent Scowcroft was saying, with wry understatement. Scowcroft was President Ford's national-security affairs adviser, Henry Kissinger's old post, and he sat behind the same desk that Kissinger had occupied in the bright and airy West Wing corner office. Before the Nixon administration the entire permanent White House press corps had been housed in that office, but the reach of the presidency was fast lengthening. In 1973 Scowcroft, who had been brought into the executive mansion as Nixon's military assistant, was named Kissinger's chief deputy in the National Security Office. Now, as he prepared to relinquish command of the intelligence secrets that he monitored and passed on personally to the president each day, Scowcroft worked behind a desk covered with stack upon stack of papers. He kept a scratch pad beside him, and from time to time jotted down another thought. "There are a thousand things in my head that I want to pass on," he said to me one day. "I want to make sure that we leave behind as complete a body of knowledge as possible."

In Scowcroft's view, the Ford people were passing on a world "not that bad in comparison with the past." Jimmy Carter would not have to face the crises that other presidents had faced—Roosevelt and the depression, Truman and the cold war, Eisenhower and Korea, Kennedy and the Bay of Pigs, Johnson and Vietnam, Nixon and a bitterly divided citizenry, Ford and a shattered presidency. This view was shared by virtually every one of Ford's major counselors, and by Gerald Ford himself. In the last days of his abbreviated presidency, Ford told me he thought Carter had "unique opportunities" to fashion "great success." Conditions in the Middle East and southern Africa were then at what he believed to be "a very crucial breakthrough situation. Both of those areas are on the brink of either success or potential catastrophe," he said. "It's almost a situation that hasn't occurred in the past and may not occur in the future. They are just at the right point." Specifically, the prospects for a Middle East settlement appeared better than at any moment in the past, and achieving an agreement with the Soviet Union over a second strategic arms limitation agreement was highly likely.

The same was true on the domestic front. Ford saw Carter coming to power "at a very crucial point, where great skill and good judgment" could make the difference in restraining inflation and restoring confidence in the economy.

Many of his own aides were even more sanguine about Carter's prospects. Over in the Old Executive Office Building, that grand mass of gray stone and turrets adjoining the White House, one of the president's men reflected on what he had witnessed during the Nixon-Ford years. One memory stood out—of the 1971 weekend of May Day demonstrations against Vietnam and a period of great tension within the White House. He was in the Treasury Department Building that day, across the street from the East Wing of the White House. "They had two thousand soldiers inside that building. They were armed and posted behind every window," he recalled. "I remember thinking to myself, My God, we're becoming a banana republic." What had happened since, he said, made him think "in many ways Mr. Carter has a very great opportunity, one of the greatest in history." Carter was coming to power at the end of an era of national government that began with FDR. He had a chance to start fresh, to lead the people into a new relationship with their government at all levels. Citizens were ready for it. The process needed only the right kind of leadership.

It was a time, said John Marsh, another presidential counselor, for reality. And the realists who were to inherit the White House would have a signal opportunity to make substantial changes in the way government functioned.

This sense of something different approaching, of new political possibilities, went along with something else, an uncharacteristically introspective attitude about the nature of power and lessons of trying to exercise it in Washington. Back in his large corner office overlooking the White House grounds and offering a view of the sweep from the Washington Monument to the Jefferson Memorial and the Potomac beyond, Richard Cheney reflected on his years in Washington. They had changed him, he knew. He was the White House chief of staff, H. R. Haldeman's old job, and he worked in the room where Haldeman presided so long with so much strength.

Cheney was only thirty-six, quiet and studious, but he already had long experience in government. He had worked on Capitol Hill as a congressional aide to William Steiger, a Republican from Wisconsin, had served in the bureaucracy at the Office of Economic Opportunity, and twice had been in Nixon's White House before becoming Ford's chief of staff. When he had left the White House the first time in 1971, he thought he knew how it worked. The more he was around, though, the greater he understood how limited his knowledge was.

"I come away from my eight years in government in Washington considerably more conservative than when I came here," he said to me. "I'm less optimistic or confident about the ability of government to do so many things for people. Policy tends to get made by advocates, and it's increasingly difficult to manage the government. Overall, my skepticism has increased since I came here as a graduate student from the University of Wisconsin. Today, sometimes I think the best solution for government is to do nothing. Maybe you have to measure success in terms of what didn't happen."

Like so many of the survivors of the Nixon White House, Cheney was keenly aware of the potential for abusing power, not only political power but personal power. "I have a strong sense of this town," he said. "This city is full of people who sit around waiting to be called to serve again. They're like ghosts waiting for life to be infused. You've got to remember you don't get all these phone calls, all these invitations to parties, and all that attention from the press because of yourself personally. It goes with the turf, and it ends when you leave. To some extent the value of the experience in Washington depends on being able to know when it's over."

His was a common theme. "This is a hard, cruel town," said Frank Zarb, the head of the Federal Energy Administration and a veteran Washington bureaucrat. "My view has always been that I'm just here temporarily, that I'm just passing through. I think that's healthier."

Upstairs, in John Ehrlichman's old office, where much of the secret bugging of supposedly confidential conversations had taken place, James Cannon was winding up his affairs in government service. He had come to the Ford White House by way of Nelson Rockefeller, for whom he had worked, and by long service as a political journalist. When he took over Ehrlichman's job as head of the White House Domestic Council, Cannon found a legacy from his predecessor. Now, as he talked, he got up from his chair, walked across the room to a magnificent wooden liquor cabinet, unlocked it, reached inside, and drew out a bottle of Old Fitzgerald bourbon. Across the top was a silver label. It read: "Bottled Expressly for John Ehrlichman." He was going to leave that bottle behind as a symbol for his successor in the Carter administration. It was a reminder not to get trapped in the importance of the job or be corrupted by the power of the office. "It's a reminder," Cannon said, "to do right."

Whatever their background or experience, these men were disturbed about the problems of governance, about the difficulties of effectively laying hands upon the federal establishment, and about implementing policies and inspiring action. Each had a particular story of frustration, or defeat. James Lynn, Ford's bespectacled senior budget director, who previously had been secretary of the Housing and Urban Development Department, had been briefing his successor, a bluff, portly Georgia banker named Bert Lance. Lynn remembered an image that an old Washington hand had used to describe things and he passed it on to Lance: The United States government is like a peat bog. When you stand in one place you can make an impression, and the longer you stand there, the deeper the mark. But when you leave, the impression will disappear completely unless someone immediately steps in your place. Even then, it is hard to find any footprints on the permanent peat bog of government.

You hope, Lynn was saying, that your service in government is not like that. You hope it's not like building a road through the jungle where three years later a stranger can't even tell a road was there.

□   □   □

Immediately after his election, Carter's staff gave him a blueprint for taking over the federal government on inaugural day. A key recommendation was that he personally come to Washington for three or four days a week to deal with the transfer of power, to oversee the formation of his administration.

At first Carter agreed. He recognized, some aides said, the difficulty in trying to do the job from Georgia. But in the end he chose to stay at home. In Plains, he concluded, he could be more reflective—removed by almost a thousand miles from the inevitable new political demands on his time in the capital.

Planning for the presidential transition was the most elaborate in American history. That in itself wasn't saying much. Most transfers of power had been casual—and sometimes personally bitter—affairs: the Adamses, John and John Quincy, refusing to attend the inauguration of their successors, Jefferson and Jackson; Hoover and Franklin Roosevelt, after disagreeing over national policies, riding together in tight-lipped silence from the White House to the swearing-in on Capitol Hill. But by the 1960s the presidential transitions had been institutionalized. In 1968 Nixon became the first president to receive a federal outlay to assist in the work, thanks to a law passed four years earlier. His transition team was authorized $900,000, and the amount had risen to $2 million by the time Carter was elected.

Carter's initial preparation had begun months before he won his party's nomination. By the summer of 1976, his transition operation was in full swing in a suite of offices in Atlanta. Throughout the full campaign the transition-planning group, with many consultants, produced flow charts, option papers, briefing books, and other studies characteristic of the computer-technology techniques of corporate America.

All this was in sharp contrast to the last time a Democratic president succeeded a Republican. Instead of all the people and all the studies and all the apparatus, one old Washington hand had quietly organized the change in presidential power. Several days after his nomination, John Kennedy had called Clark Clifford, a lawyer who had been counsel to Truman and was regarded as the quintessence of the Washington political operative, the true insider's insider. He asked Clifford to prepare a plan on how to take over the reins of power "in case I am elected president." As Kennedy told Clifford, "I don't want to wake up on the morning of November ninth and say, 'What do I do now?' " Instead, on November 9 Clifford gave Kennedy a twenty-two page memorandum, outlining how to get working control of the government. A top layer of Kennedy appointees would fill the highest posts—in the cabinet and at the head of the federal agencies. A second, larger group would penetrate deeper into the permanent bureaucracy and assure control over the regulatory agencies. Finally, an additional three thousand appointments, including all those appointments exempt by law from civil service, would fill the remaining important policy-making and executive positions in the federal government. That same day, Kennedy appointed Clifford as his liaison to the Eisenhower administration. The transition proceeded directly from within Washington. It was successful.

The Carter plan was more complex and certainly more ambitious. After his election, a transition team of 132 people, many of whom had been operating in Atlanta, moved into their Washington headquarters at the foot of Capitol Hill. They were young (only fourteen of them were forty or older), eager, and anxious—fresh faces, many of them, typifying the promise of the Carter campaign. Through the issues "clusters" to which they were assigned—in such areas as justice, agriculture, government reorganization, general economic or foreign policy—they were supposed to see that the Carter administration was well staffed and instantly ready to govern. No Washington insider like Clark Clifford headed their effort. The ranking "coordinator," Jack Watson, Jr., was a slim young curly-haired lawyer who had worked in Charles Kirbo's firm and headed the Atlanta transition office.

An air of bustle, confusion—and self-importance—permeated the corridors and offices of the Carter transition team. Transition headquarters was seen as the temporary seat of the government-to-be, the great prize of the campaign, the springboard for the future. Indeed, nothing could have been more appropriate than the building itself: the Carter people were occupying the command center of one of the great Washington bureaucratic nests—the Department of Health, Education and Welfare.

When you walked into those gray corridors you were greeted with a blizzard of signs. Arrows in green colors pointed to incomprehensible letters signifying incomprehensible government offices: OE—arrow that way; SSA—arrow there; PHS—arrow; SRS—arrow. Large color portraits informed you that "The Honorable David Mathews" and "The Honorable Marjorie Lynn" (HEW's secretary and under secretary) were in residence. Underneath their faces was a government-issue cartoon warning against crime in the office: a thief was being thwarted in the act by a diligent secretary who had secured an office typewriter to a desk. Other walls contained further warnings about crime: "CRIMES against your government concern YOU!" they proclaimed in red letters. Next to these signals were the postings of the HEW directorate, with the agencies and overlapping titles listed: Commissioner Food and Drug Administration; Administrator Health Resources Administration; Director National Institutes of Health; Special Assistant to the Secretary for Health Policy; Administrator ADAMHA; Commission on Aging; Assistant Secretary for Education; Director National Institutes of Education; Commissioner of Education; Administration of Social and Rehabilitation Service. . . .

It wasn't long before the atmosphere in the HEW Building began to exert its own influence. "You know what I've decided is the matter with the government?" a senior transition official said. "It's these buildings. They're too damned big. You don't have a sense of being connected to anyone or anything else."

Physically, though, the Carter office was cramped and cluttered. Equipment—desks, chairs, phones—was short. But the work proceeded, and the trash overflowed the cartons placed outside the doors, and the phones rang constantly (and often went unanswered), and the doors swung open and shut, and the Carter planners strode briskly down the corridors to attend one conference after another. Mail and messages and gifts from around the world poured in with such volume that it was hard to find space to hold them, much less sort, process, and route them. In one corner office, automatic machines keyed to a computer clattered endlessly, typing out form letters giving supposedly personal replies from the new president and first lady, while autopens soundlessly signed letter after letter "Jimmy Carter" and "Rosalynn Carter." Watching the autopens move, unattended, all on their own, scratching out signature after signature, was transfixing: you couldn't tell the real signature from the model. Neither could the people who received them. That was the idea.

All the while the résumés from office seekers and potential Carter appointees continued to pile up. There were stacks everywhere: two thousand of them arrived each day. These were added to the already staggering numbers previously collected and computerized. Out of these, it was said, would come the key jobs for the new administration; this was the heart of the highly publicized and much-touted "Talent Inventory Program" (TIP for short). Thus, anyway, the plan. Supposedly, all these lists had been assessed, quantified, and categorized—and were moving on from Washington to Plains for the final decision.

The reality of Carter's "transition," like the reality of his political campaign, taught some hard lessons. It was quickly apparent to Carter's inner circle in Georgia that the transition effort in Washington had serious flaws. One couldn't really choose a cabinet by computer. Nor were many of the memos and briefing papers prepared by the transition group well suited to political judgments and decisions. A nasty struggle ensued, pitting the transition group against the political operatives who had directed the campaign. There was no contest; the political group won.

Other factors compounded the difficulties between the Washington transition workers and the political operatives in Georgia. Jimmy Carter, prompted partly by his study of the Nixon White House, had decided to deemphasize the role of his staff. That was going to be a key to his style of governing: he would have no

strong chief of staff, like an H. R. Haldeman, nor a secondary major power center in the White House like that headed by a John
Ehrlichman. Instead, Carter was determined to put primary emphasis on the authority of his cabinet, which, he hoped, would for-
mulate and implement executive policy. His White House staff
would be smaller, less rigidly structured, and subservient to the
cabinet secretaries. All its members would be equal in rank, all
spokes of the wheel whose hub was the Oval Office. As a consequence, Carter put off naming his own staff until his cabinet was
chosen, and the cabinet selections were slow in coming.

Drift and disarray began to be felt, particularly in the Washington headquarters. You would hear complaints that the president-
elect didn't know what was happening in Washington—or, if he
did, that it didn't seem to matter. People already in the government became impatient: as someone in the Justice Department remarked, "What's the sense of talking to a bunch of thirty-year-old
kids when an attorney general has not been named and they don't
know any better than we do the way things are going to go?"

As the weeks after the election passed and the inauguration approached, the strains and tensions within Carter's Washington
headquarters surfaced publicly. Some were bitter. They felt betrayed, that their work had gone for naught, unappreciated,
unrewarded. They had labored hard in the campaign and had followed through loyally after the election, but without any assurance
of a role in the government they thought they were trying to form.
Others voiced more general criticism: they feared that Carter was
not fulfilling his promise of attracting the best independent figures to government, truly new faces for a new political era. They
wondered aloud if they were not part of some public charade,
caught in a place of managerial "overkill," of posturing, of naked
ambitions. They came to see that all but a few were working in
limbo, without any discernible influence in the new administration.

A well-educated young transition volunteer I spoke to one day,
an early member of the Carter "Peanut Brigade," was typical of
many you'd meet. She left the transition operation dismayed and
disillusioned. "I tell my friends that you can just see it in the corridors here," she said, "you can just see it in the way people walk
down the halls. I mean, it's cold, impersonal, ego-tripping, power-

tripping. People stay together in their little clusters. And you can see the way power is flowing. One week they'll all circle around someone who seems 'in.' The next week it's someone else. Maybe I'm naïve, but I think this group is supposed to start out caring for each other. If they don't care about each other, how can they care about the country?"

And indeed, the prospect of power swiftly affected some people: a young man of obvious ability and favored background, who had been introspective and politically astute during the campaign, suddenly exuded pomposity and self-importance when it was over. Another literally swaggered as he walked. Yet many approached their tasks with becoming modesty. Jack Watson, for instance. He was sitting at his desk late in the afternoon of a hectic day as the inauguration neared when I saw him. He said of Carter:

> He must resist the seduction of his office, and its power, and its trappings—and yet he must lead. It's an office full of paradoxes, and he must understand those paradoxes. He must understand that what the public wants of him is contradictory: he must be an eloquent spokesman, a charismatic leader, a public teacher; at the same time, he must be just one of us. We don't want him to be surrounded by a palace guard, or to act or look like a king. And in fact he's not a king. There's something else that everyone expects from their leader—they want him to be tender and compassionate and sensitive, and at the same time be tough, and, even when necessary, be ruthless.
>
> I want us to do well here. I would hope that we can do well here on one's own terms. To prevail on terms that are not acceptable is not to win. James Madison and all of his cohorts had a great sense of history, a deep sense of their obligations to the Americans who would come after them. In today's world we don't fully have that sense of posterity. It's something we seem to have been losing. We have a hard time pulling back, and asking ourselves how we will be judged when it's all settled and past. But if we don't keep that long view, we're not likely to do well here.

Watson himself had experienced frustrations and setbacks. The grand scheme of his transition plan, he knew, had turned out to be something other than intended. Naïveté and misunderstandings had contributed to designing a faulty transition structure that had

to be discarded. But part of the difficulty lay in the attitudes about
Washington held by those who would govern with Carter. None
was more certain, in conversation at least, about what they would
face in Washington than Hamilton Jordan, the young campaign director who had drafted much of the political strategy that successfully pointed Jimmy Carter toward the White House. Jordan, a
Georgian, came to Washington several weeks after the election,
and assumed the leading role in selecting top Carter appointees. It
was Jordan who had prevailed over Watson, Jordan who had
passed on Watson's memos to Carter with the judgment that many
were irrelevant and useless, Jordan who convinced Carter that the
transition had to be constructed to "mesh the political people with
the experts."

During the campaign Jordan had been in charge of some sixteen
hundred people, and he felt responsible for their interests. Suddenly, in the flush of victory, he discovered that another group—
the Watson team—was putting together the new administration.
With Carter's approval, he moved swiftly to put himself at the center of the political selection process.

Jordan stayed in a transition headquarters office only briefly before he moved out. It was too noisy, too distracting. He set up
shop quietly in an office at Democratic National Committee headquarters. Jordan was almost studiedly casual in the way he
shunned ties and business suits, and seemingly incapable of pretense. Solidly built, dark-haired, boyish, and courteous, he gave
the impression of a thoughtfulness and maturity that belied his
years and experience. Those who worked with him found him to
be decent and gracious, although he was by common account disorganized and a poor administrator. He and Jody Powell, Carter's
press secretary, were among the people closest to Carter; they
knew Carter best, their words counted most.

Despite his shrewdness in judging the national political climate
for Carter, Jordan had a certain naïveté. Washington had sneered
when it read his prescription for staffing the new administration.
"If after the inauguration you find a Cy Vance as secretary of state
and Zbigniew Brzezinski as head of national security, then I would
say we failed," he had told *Playboy* magazine during the campaign.
"And I'd quit. But that's not going to happen. You're going to see
new faces, new ideas. The government is going to be run by peo-

ple you never heard of." When Cyrus Vance and Zbigniew Brzezinski were named to precisely those specific jobs, and when the
rest of the Carter cast turned out to be highly conventional, and
when Jordan himself did not quit, the Washington cynics—or realists—felt their judgment confirmed.

But Jordan was better than that. In talking about Washington
and the government and what was to come, as we did at length
one night shortly after his arrival, Jordan conveyed unassuming
and impressive attitudes.

They knew they didn't know much about Washington, he said,
and they knew they didn't know as much about the bureaucracy as
they should, or about those personalities in the capital who knew
best about the exercise of power. Nor had they come to town with
a grand concept of placing a special Jimmy Carter stamp on the
government and nation—no New Deal, no New Frontier.

What they did hope, and were determined to achieve, was something less grandiose, but probably more important: they would
like to have it said of them, when their time in power was over,
that people believed they had made the government work better.
If people began to feel that *their* personal contact with the government was better, that *their* dealings with a specific agency like the
Post Office were improved, then they would have made an important contribution. It would have been worth it.

Jordan was echoing the advice given Carter by Robert Ball, then
Senior Scholar at the National Academy of Sciences. Since the
New Deal days Ball had played a dominant role in establishing and
administering the Social Security system, and was regarded in
Washington as a wise man. In the summer after the Democratic
convention Ball had written a memo for Carter's consideration to
Stuart Eizenstat, the campaign "issues" coordinator. It read, in
part:

> People will certainly judge the next Administration in terms of
> how effectively it deals with the big issues—foreign affairs, unem-
> ployment, inflation, national health insurance, welfare, and the res-
> toration of financial integrity of the Social Security program—but
> the *efficiency* of government will, in my opinion, be judged primarily
> by the effectiveness, the helpfulness, and the overall impression
> that people have of three huge agencies of government: the Post
> Office, Internal Revenue, and the Social Security Administration.

These are the only direct-line operations of the Federal Government that huge numbers of people come in contact with every day. They are Uncle Sam in every town, village, and city in America. If the employees of those organizations are friendly and considerate and the organizations give good service, that will mean to most people that government can make things work. If these three organizations are unresponsive, bureaucratic, and make mistakes, then that is the impression that the ordinary citizen will have of his government.

My point is simply that although the Federal Government does hundreds of important things, not many are visible on a daily basis to every family. These three give people their impression of how well or how badly the whole Federal Government is working. I don't know how to do it, but, in my opinion, it is worth a great deal in investment of manpower and brains to make these three organizations models of both efficiency and warm human relations so that at the end of four years, if not earlier, people will say: "I know how the Federal Government works because of what Social Security did for my mother and father and because of the pleasant young man in Internal Revenue who was so understanding of the mistake I made on my income tax."

As for himself, Jordan knew one thing: he was going to stay away from the Washington social scene. He would not get caught up in the frivolous parties and froth that constituted so much of the after-hours atmosphere of the capital.

When asked about the Congress, and whether he didn't think Carter might have trouble there, Jordan's reply was quick and almost word-for-word what Jimmy Carter had told Tip O'Neill: We'll have no more problems handling Congress than we did with the Georgia legislature.

☐ ☐ ☐

In a cynical city, where ceremonial courtesy so often cloaks harsher emotions, true feelings are seldom expressed. Behind the surface camaraderie, the polite smiles, and pompous public words about the "distinguished" senator or "the honorable" representative, lies a different reality.

Few genuinely close friendships exist among politicians. Personal ambition and political pressure dictate otherwise. They don't know each other well, and don't choose to; but they understand the pressures exerted on them all and work to contain them; and they all appreciate the difficulties they continually face. "Underneath, everybody tries to make certain that whatever you do to each other on issues, votes, legislation, it's not going to get personal," as one senator with long experience puts it. "There's a very fine line that everyone's careful to observe, and that's why you hear all this 'My distinguished colleague' business. Everybody's sensitive, because everybody knows that everybody's vulnerable. We try to separate the issues from the personalities, the spirit from the flesh. We're very courteous to each other because of our own potential vulnerability. It's that constant delicacy of finding out how to deal with each other."

In the days when power was passing in Washington from Ford to Carter, two personal incidents said much about the political climate on the eve of the nation's forty-eighth inauguration. The first involved Hubert Humphrey, who returned from his trip to Plains still hoping to play an important part in the new Congress that was to deal with the Democrat in the White House. The previous years had not been easy for him. His return to the Senate in 1971, after two years as a visiting professor of political science in Minnesota, had been the beginning of one of the most difficult periods in a career that had seen heartbreak and humiliation. Being a defeated presidential candidate didn't do much for him on Capitol Hill. Individually his colleagues were cordial and respectful, but as for his work, he was going to have to start all over again, as if it were 1948. "I started out at the bottom of the rung in everything. I was ninety-seventh in seniority. I had the smallest staff, the smallest rooms," he told me. "I was put on nothing. I wasn't on the policy committee. I didn't get on my old committees where I had served before. Nothing. For two years I bit my fingernails and took that. Because I didn't complain, I think the leadership finally figured, 'Well, by gosh, he isn't gonna make any fuss so we'll start to help him.' "

Eventually, Humphrey returned to the prestigious Foreign Relations Committee and was appointed to the Joint Economic Committee, where he moved up rapidly in seniority until he became its chairman. After all, Humphrey was regarded in the Congress as a superb legislator, one of the best the Senate had seen. He knew how to get things done. As Richard Nixon's fortunes fell, Humphrey's rose. He was speaking out again on issues and building a national constituency. In the election of 1976, as Carter was winning the presidency, the voters of Minnesota reelected Humphrey by the greatest margin in the state's history. Then Hubert Horatio Humphrey suffered one more blow—cancer, and removal of a malignant bladder. His illness only strengthened his determination. He decided to challenge Robert Byrd for the majority leadership position in the Senate, the post from which Lyndon Johnson had wielded such power.

Byrd, whose rise from a background of hardship and prejudice (he had been an early member of the Ku Klux Klan) in West Virginia had been one of the more intriguing in recent years, was a senator to whom courtesy and respect were important personally. A painstaking legislative technician, as his influence increased his dress had become more fastidious, his demeanor more solemn. Humphrey had gone to Byrd privately and informed him of his plans. There was nothing personal in his challenge, Humphrey explained, but he had some specific ideas about how to run the Senate. He spelled them out—the organization of the Senate itself, the committee structures, the scheduling and meetings, the numbers of roll calls, the conferences. Byrd, in turn, was polite and deferential.

On January 4, 1977, the Ninety-fifth Congress convened. It was the day for customary rituals, as dictated by tradition, and for the serious business of selecting leaders. Humphrey had been extremely ill the night before, and was aware he didn't have the votes to defeat Byrd. At eight o'clock, shaken and weak, he picked up the phone in his home. He told Byrd he was withdrawing from the leadership contest; he didn't want to leave any wounds or bitterness, and hoped they would have a harmonious relationship. It was all very polite. Humphrey knew he would lose anyway, and didn't want to force any of his colleagues to have to vote against the man who would have some power over them. And he knew something else: "They were all happy that Hubert withdrew, and I was happy that I withdrew."

As the Democratic senators filed into their marbled caucus room off the ornate lobby to choose their new leaders that day,

they passed beneath oil portraits of earlier great figures. Daniel
Webster, the dour, baggy-eyed orator and brandy drinker, peered
somberly toward the patrician Charles Sumner, equally unsmiling
but apparently well-fed; Sumner in turn gazed stolidly at a satur-
nine John C. Calhoun, a study in black with a shock of unruly gray
hair, and a prim Henry Clay, hands folded neatly in his lap. Humphrey strode into view. He was dressed in brown, his step was
jaunty, and he was smiling widely—but his appearance came as a
shock to the crowd of reporters, camera crews, and citizens gathered to watch the drama, for he looked frail, ravaged, cadaverous.

The senators met behind closed doors for three hours. When
they emerged the new leaders went out of their way to salute
Humphrey. Byrd said he had appointed a committee to study the
possibilities for giving a special post to Humphrey. Not that Hubert Humphrey needed a new office or new assignment, the Senate's leader quickly added: "He is, has been, and always will be a
national leader." Later, there were more tributes in the Senate itself. Members of both parties stood in the aisles and gave Humphrey an ovation as he assumed his seat. It was Humphrey who
was greeted most warmly and attracted the most attention from
old and new members. He chatted at the back of the chamber with
Fritz Mondale, a protégé from Minnesota who was about to take
his old job and preside over the Senate as vice-president. He
greeted many others who, like himself, had sought the presidency
unsuccessfully over the years—Edmund Muskie of Maine, Henry
Jackson of Washington, Frank Church of Idaho.

Looking down on the scene from the galleries above you could
see men who had served in the Senate when it was the center of
national political power. Now power was shifting away from the
Washington congressional insiders to a one-term Southern governor and a group of Georgians who never had worked in Washington. What relationship they would forge with the new Senate and
House leadership was unclear, but on that day the spotlight was
fixed clearly on the Senate and Humphrey.

After taking his bow in the Senate, Humphrey talked to me
about himself and his future. He was asked about Jimmy Carter
and the promise of change. "The dream," he said, "is sometimes
larger than the reality." In saying that, he was speaking as much
about his own career as the next president's.

Another rare moment of genuine sentiment occurred a week later. This time Washington paid tribute to Gerald Ford, who, like Humphrey, was reaching the end of a long political career in the capital. Ford traveled to Capitol Hill to deliver his final state of the union message. What he had to say was not memorable; state of the union messages almost never are. They are usually optimistic and usually dull; they rarely touch off a spark of interest and are rarely remembered. But Ford's appearance went beyond the sterile hail-and-farewell ritual. It was hard to recall a time when Congress and president felt so comfortable with each other, so warm was the greeting given him and so spontaneous the spirit of goodwill displayed in the applause that swept over him repeatedly. It was Jerry Ford the Congress was saluting, one of its own, and everyone present that night understood what he—and they—had been through.

Those members of Congress knew Jerry Ford. He had served among them for a quarter of a century and, like his three immediate predecessors, had gone on to the White House from the Congress. They understood, too, how difficult Ford's particular task had been. With little preparation, he had served well. He had dishonored neither them nor the country.

Now he was going out with tears in his eyes, his voice cracking from emotion, and the cheers of his colleagues ringing in his ears. He was, as the new Speaker of the House reminded the assembled Congress, "an old friend." "He was the right man at the right time," said Tip O'Neill, the leader of Ford's political opposition, expressing the prevailing congressional opinion. "The country couldn't have been better served."

No such applause awaited Jimmy Carter. Unlike the Humphreys and the Fords, to Congress and to Washington Carter was unfamiliar and untested. Given all the political changes since the last inauguration, and the temper of the political operatives, this president would have to prove himself to them.

□ □ □

Jimmy Carter's inauguration, an event that would be remembered more for his symbolic act of walking his way into the White

House than for what he said to his fellow citizens in an inaugural address, was followed by the traditional round of parties throughout Washington. It was supposed to be a "People's Inaugural." No bleachers had been constructed along the mile-and-a-half route from the Capitol to the White House; no one had to purchase tickets to watch the president and parade pass by. Free bus service from city and suburbs was provided. Two hours of free rides on Washington's new subway system were offered.

But "People's Inaugural" notwithstanding, some people were more equal than others. As at all inaugurals, a political-social pecking order determined which of the seven parties you could attend. The most sought after were tickets for the party and show at the Kennedy Center, overlooking the Potomac. There, the leaders of Washington's political establishment gathered to salute the new president and change of power.

Tip O'Neill, having paid $300 for his tickets, was enraged and humiliated to discover his seats were in the last two rows of the gallery. When the Speaker of the House of Representatives gets tickets like that, he thought, it has to be intentional. The next day, still fuming, he called Hamilton Jordan, whom he knew had been in charge of the main political arrangements. "Hey, you had to give me the worst tickets in the house by design," he said in his most outraged Boston tones. "I just want you to know something. Some damned day your boss is going to be looking for something, and he'll be asking you where the hell it is. And then I'll teach you the lesson of your life, because what he wants will be in the Speaker's pocket, and it will be all locked up."

A trivial episode, perhaps. But it reflected the tensions that already existed between those who would exercise power in Washington in the White House and on Capitol Hill.

2
THE GOVERNMENT

IN THE flowering of the New Deal, Congress passed a law. Truckers were prohibited from driving more than ten hours a day. The purpose was admirable: to promote public safety on the nation's highways. And the reasoning made sense: tired drivers are more likely to make mistakes that increase the risks for all citizens using the highways. Solution: regulate the hours they operate. Authority for the new law had its roots deep in the history of the national government—all the way back to 1887, when Congress created the Interstate Commerce Commission, giving the federal government the power to regulate business crossing state lines.

As always with new legislation, the immediate question about regulating truck drivers was how to enforce the law. Thus the truckers' daily log was created. Every fifteen minutes, every working day, truckers were required to jot down their activities, how much time spent driving, how much resting. In due course, a federal form was prepared to help them fill out their logs. In triplicate, naturally: one copy for the driver so he could prove compliance with the federal regulations, one copy for his company, one to be filed with the government in Washington. Records were required to be kept for six months.

The logs were useless unless the government checked to see whether they were in order, and whether the records in Washington matched those of the company or driver. So a team of federal inspectors was created, charged with keeping watch over the truckers' daily logs. For years and years, starting in 1939, those logs were filled out daily, and the field inspectors were supposedly overseeing how the system was working. Everyone knew the truckers' log was a fruitless exercise, that an infinitesimal number of prosecutions for violations was being obtained (some three hundred a year), that no way existed to prevent fraudulent record-keeping. But it was the law, and the law must be obeyed.

By the time Jimmy Carter came to Washington, 1 billion 200 million pieces of paper were being filled out each year for the truckers' daily logs.

☐   ☐   ☐

The cost of federal paperwork to Americans, by the government's own reckoning, was running well over $100 billion a year in 1976. At least a third of that amount was deemed to be wasteful or unnecessary. Yet it continued, ever growing in volume and complexity. The forms and the federal requirements had a life of their own; to millions of citizens, they *were* the government. Everyone, it seemed, could recite an example of government red tape and stupidity.

Everyone could tell how the demands of government were intruding on private lives; but the burden fell most heavily on those least able to fight back. If you were poor you might have to fill out sixty separate forms to get help. Federal welfare applications alone exceeded 100 million forms a year, and within that statistical mass individual horror stories abounded. In Boston, a woman spent more than three hundred hours in one year completing assistance forms. In New York City, a single case file drawn at random by federal investigators contained more than seven hundred application documents. In another city, an Army veteran made a 130-mile round trip to complete paperwork at a Veterans Administration office—only to be told a few months later he would have to revisit the office personally to provide the same information for a different program. Elderly persons applying for Social Security benefits were required to submit information that had been in the agency's files for years, sometimes decades. In one case, a disabled woman was denied federal Medicaid payments for more than six months while welfare workers insisted she provide a bank statement even though she had no bank account. It was, by universal agreement, a system needlessly complex, inefficient, inequitable, and costly. Still, it grew.

And something else: the forms themselves were faulty. "The forms, questionnaires, and surveys used to collect information are inconsistent, incompatible, redundant and, at the extreme, unusable," a government study concluded. Still, they multiplied. Not only were the paperwork requirements burdensome, the results of the data collected bred more misfortune. If you wanted to know how much oil the United States was importing, for instance, the oil-import data collected and disseminated by three major federal agencies were invariably in conflict: in one month the Census Bureau reported 9.1 million barrels of oil imported daily, while at the same time the Federal Energy Administration showed 6.8 million barrels daily, and the Bureau of Mines 6.6 million.

Such examples were commonplace public symbols of a sprawling, wasteful federal Leviathan centered in Washington. Virtually every politician with presidential ambitions inveighed against the Washington bureaucracy. Red tape and red ink were repeatedly cited as evidence of government gone awry. Pollsters found government service ranking last among all professions in the national esteem.

Certainly, the role of the federal government in American society had yearly become more complex and pervasive. Federal programs and agencies proliferated so rapidly that it was hard to keep track of what the government was doing in any one field. Even for federal employees, the helter-skelter nature of new programs was confounding: by the bicentennial year, fifty-one different federal retirement plans were in operation, for example. No overall retirement policy existed; these separate plans, covering everyone from civil service and military workers to Supreme Court widows, resulted in duplicate or inconsistent benefit payments and serious gaps in personal protection. And rising inflation rates notwithstanding, the cost of government clearly was increasing with inexorable, geometric progression. Jimmy Carter's first budget of $500 billion was five times greater than John Kennedy's, fifty times that of Franklin Roosevelt, five hundred that of Woodrow Wilson.

Nor could anyone deny the range of bureaucratic blunders and abuses that kept making national headlines. In one brief period, citizens could read about these examples: the Housing and Urban Development Department spent $83 apiece on thirty-two new ashtrays for its training centers; the Agriculture Department spent $113,000 to find out that mothers didn't like to iron their children's clothes; and, it was reported, one government unit had purchased enough bulbs to replace burned-out streetlights for the next five hundred years. Where was that government unit? Washington, D.C.

What was being overlooked in the political rhetoric about the federal bureaucracy were more significant figures. For example, it wasn't true that the "bloated bureaucracy" of the political candidates' scorn was mushrooming in size. In fact, the size of the federal work force had remained fairly stable for more than a quarter of a century while the demands on government increased dramatically. In 1950 the number of civilian federal government employees was 2,117,000. In 1976 it was 2,874,000 federal employees. That is, the proportion of federal workers among every thousand persons employed in the United States had risen from thirteen to only fourteen in a twenty-six–year period, and that later figure had remained *exactly* the same for twenty years. Size of the federal work force wasn't the problem.

The startling growth in American government came elsewhere. Again beginning with 1950 and ending with 1976, the number of *state* and *local* employees had tripled, from 4,285,000 to 11,755,000 a generation later. Bureaucratic growth was occurring not in far-off Washington but in the governments closest to the people at home, people who were demanding more and more services. The representatives they sent to Washington provided these through new legislation establishing new programs and agencies, and new bureaucracies at home arose to handle the federal largesse.

While the politicians fanned the flames of citizen ire against Washington's bureaucracy, they themselves profited from the results of the new Washington spending. George Wallace drew great cheers when he railed against "the pointy-heads" in Washington, but he didn't mention that the state bureaucracy in Alabama had doubled during his term in office while the federal establishment there had shrunk.

Jimmy Carter was even more successful in "running against

Washington." "I have personally seen the almost total impossibility of administering the uncoordinated, conflicting, and wasteful hodge-podge of programs and laws that result from the present disorganized condition of our federal government," he said during his campaign.

Candidate Carter's prescription for cure was also familiar. He pledged "a thorough and massive reorganization of the federal bureaucracy," something which nearly all presidents sought and which in fact was often done. "If Carter tries to reorganize this outfit," a government manager said in exasperation just as Carter was coming to office, "well, we've had it with these illogical reorganizations. We don't understand them ourselves; yet we're supposed to explain them to our people and make them understand and accept. We've been through that time after time. It always happens when a new group comes in and wants to make it look as if they're really doing something. Christ, we've had it with reorganization."

Blaming the bureaucracy might be effective politics, but much of it came down to classic scapegoating—blaming "it" for most of society's ills, for the fact that there were poor people, sick people, disabled people, uneducated people, a recession, a depression, a failing industry, an ailing one; demanding from "it" better public health and safety and stronger national defense; and asking "it" to do something about all of them. Something was wrong with Washington, all right. But how and why it got that way, and what was the symptom and what the cause—and what, if any, the cure—were factors not well understood. In fact, they were hardly ever seriously discussed.

☐ ☐ ☐

When Andrew Jackson came to Washington, he was determined to change things. One of his targets was the entrenched, unresponsive Washington bureaucracy. "The trained officials in Washington," Old Hickory proclaimed, "constitute a dangerous bureaucracy, and continuance in an office will lead to . . . proprietary right to that office." Jackson was a president who not only meant what he said but actually did what he said he was going to do. The bureaucrats were axed, and he put his own people in place. Andy Jackson and his presidential successors were firm believers in that old adage about victors being entitled to spoils. And spoils they did dispense—year after year, administration after administration.

By the time Mark Twain chronicled what he called "The Gilded Age," that cynical, bawdy, corrupt period of American industrial growth and national expansion after the Civil War, the spoils system was a fixture in Washington. Political job seekers boldly advertised in the daily papers. Typical was one from a gentleman, self-styled, from Philadelphia. His ad said:

> WANTED—A RELIABLE GENTLEMAN will furnish the best political papers and will pay $150 to anyone who will help him secure a position of any kind in Washington. Address in confidence, Capt. A. Y. R. Devere, Philadelphia, Pa.

Office seekers were not restricted to men in those days: women were equally eager to provide a payoff for obtaining work. Another ad of that time:

> WANTED—A young lady will give $150 to $200 to anyone securing her a position in any of the departments, paying from $60 to $65 per month. Capable in every respect. Address Discretion, Star Office.

It took a presidential assassination—Garfield's in 1881—by a disgruntled office seeker to awaken the nation to the corruption of the spoils system.

Civil-service reform became the great issue of that time. A modest, red-haired young correspondent for a Cleveland paper who signed his Washington dispatches "Carp," and whose irreverence was scarcely equaled by any journalist who came after him, perfectly captured the flavor of that day for his Ohio readers:

> The Washington hotels are crowded, and office seekers are as thick as shells on the beach. They make a motley crowd and long hair, red noses, and shiny clothes are seen in all public places. At Willard's Hotel the gang appears especially seedy and desperate; and among them guarded denunciations of President Cleveland's

civil-service ideas are not infrequent. The city will be overrun with these office seekers until Cleveland has firmly established that civil-service reform is to prevail, not only in spirit but *in fact.*

...The clerks in the various departments are not feeling secure. They do not sleep well of night, and they fear to go to their offices in the morning lest they find the sentence of official decapitation on their desks.

Out of that turmoil came the creation of the U.S. government's civil service, a system designed to guarantee that all federal workers would be selected only because of what they knew, not whom. And their jobs would be protected from the vicissitudes of political interference and reprisals, from favoritism and cronyism. Farewell the spoils system, enter the merit era of progressive American government. At least that was the hope. Presidents and cabinet officers, congressmen and senators would come and go but the career civil service would remain as the constant ingredient of the American government. In a real sense, the bureaucrats *were* the federal government.

Creating a career service didn't end complaints about government performance, of course. Nearly every president complained about his difficulties in controlling the bureaucracy. They included, with fitting irony, those same chief executives whose policies and leadership led to the creation of more Washington bureaucracy. Franklin Roosevelt, whose New Deal spawned so many "alphabet agencies," once said to a top aide: "When I woke up this morning, the first thing I saw was a headline in *The New York Times* to the effect that our Navy was going to spend two billion dollars on a shipbuilding program. Here I am, the Commander-in-Chief of the Navy having to read about that for the first time in the press. Do you know what I said to that?"

"No, Mr. President."

"I said: 'Jesus *Chr*—ist!' "

Roosevelt went on to say, in words that would be echoed by every president who came after him: "The Treasury . . . is so large and far-flung and ingrained in its practices that I find it is almost impossible to get the action and results I want—even with Henry Morgenthau there. But the Treasury is not to be compared with the State Department. You should go through the experience of trying to get any changes in the thinking, policy, and action of the career diplomats and then you'd know what a real problem was. But the Treasury and the State Department put together are nothing as compared with the N-a-a-vy."

Harry Truman, another strong president whose actions greatly expanded the federal government, was bemused at the thought of Dwight Eisenhower taking his White House job. "He'll sit here . . . and he'll say, 'Do this! Do that!' *And nothing will happen.* Poor Ike— it won't be a bit like the Army. He'll find it very frustrating."

When things went wrong, leaders were quick to blame the bureaucracy instead of themselves, and sometimes they were right. High bureaucrats in the Pentagon assured one president that the Chinese would not enter the Korean War, assured another president that Brigade 2506 could land at the Bay of Pigs and "liberate" Cuba by simply heading straight forward and turning left into Havana, and advised another president that American troops could start home from Vietnam by December 1965. Occasionally presidents would vent their frustrations, though mainly they expressed their outrage privately. In his anger at the Bay of Pigs disaster, John Kennedy said he wanted to smash the CIA into a thousand pieces and scatter it to the winds, something he never said publicly.

And there were enough other examples of serious bureaucratic mistakes to concern any citizen. In 1960 the Census Bureau failed to count 3 million blacks—which reduced federal spending for their benefits, affected the building of schools and countless other U.S. programs. In 1966 the President's Council of Economic Advisers incorrectly concluded that the Vietnam war could be fought without raising taxes, without affecting domestic prosperity, and without instigating a rapacious inflation which in fact began afflicting the nation from that point. In 1967 the Budget Bureau underestimated federal spending by $12 billion. In 1974 a bureaucrat at the Bureau of Labor Statistics made an error in computing used-car prices nationally, which pushed up the Consumer Price Index from one-tenth to three-tenths of one percent; for the next seven months that single error helped increase benefits for millions of Americans receiving weekly or monthly checks based on the fluctuations of that index. In 1975 Social Security analysts failed to anticipate the true long-term costs of their system, and eventually it was concluded that unless huge payroll tax increases were made in the future, possibly as high as 50 to 75 percent, Social Security wouldn't be able to pay promised benefits.

Yet ridiculed though the bureaucrat was, the government could not function without him. It was the federal civil servant who wrote the checks, delivered the mails, collected the taxes, inspected the meat, checked the drinking water, safeguarded banking practices, kept the books, and administered the multiplicity of programs that touched the lives of every American from birth to death. It was the federal servant who was handed the tasks of sending men to the moon and spaceships to the distant planets, of cleansing the nation's air and streams of pollution, of waging war simultaneously on poverty at home and in the rice paddies of Southeast Asia abroad, of policing the very world itself and guiding the economic development and destinies of dozens of nations. Surely never in human history had a society asked so much of itself—and seldom had a society become so critical of the people it assigned to carry out the things it demanded to be done.

A distinction between the individual, hard-working bureaucrat and the insensitive bureaucracy was not often drawn. That the bureaucracy was in effect created by all of us—by special-interest groups representing farmers, veterans, laborers, manufacturers, teachers, doctors, retirees—and that all of us were demanding special legislation to create programs and regulations: these problems were ignored. The bureaucrat was depicted as the "headless nail"—once in, you couldn't get him out—living comfortably off the public trough and doing as little as possible to get by.

In reality, the bureaucrat was as much a victim of the bureaucratic system as any other citizen—and, as we shall see, his frustration and anger were at least as great, if not more so. Within the government, the corrosive effect which this public attitude had on public servants was profound. But that was only part of the problem. Presidents were even more important.

Presidents dominate the news. What they say or do, how they look or move receive greater attention from the press and public than all the rest of the government put together. They come to office having promised great deeds and pledging to make specific changes. Inevitably, they cannot accomplish them. They feel stymied and come to believe they are besieged by opponents all around them. Particularly they single out the federal bureaucracy, that "ten-ton marshmallow" as one presidential aide called it. In their darker moments, they doubt the bureaucracy's loyalty to them. They begin to take steps to circumvent the laws, regulations, programs, and departments established through proper democratic procedures long before their presidential tenure.

Every president since World War II has gone through this phase, and every one has sanctioned actions—often covert, and often with dubious legality or outright illegality—to get around the system they've inherited. That isn't to suggest all their problems are imaginary, or that the bureaucracy isn't chaotic and almost unmanageable—as we shall also see. But the fault lies at least equally with the presidents' own failures of leadership and public persuasion, their own misconceptions and misreadings about the nature of the bureaucracy and the government, their own lack of realism about what can be accomplished.

Most recent presidents have believed the bureaucracy was an enemy rather than an institution composed of people willing to serve and be led. But no president came to office more determined to change it, by whatever means necessary, than Richard Nixon—and none led a more determined assault with more ominous intent. What happened to the federal government during the Nixon years had a devastating effect on the career public service that Jimmy Carter inherited.

Nixon's attempt to control the bureaucracy by placing loyalists in key positions was more than an ideological effort to change government policies and programs. It was a blueprint for political subversion and executive tyranny. By seeking to compel loyalty not to the people of the United States but only to those in political power at the moment, the Nixon White House threatened the integrity of the career civil service and the ability of government officials to administer impartially the programs mandated by law.

A lessening of standards, a yielding to political pressures from both the White House and Capitol Hill, a winking at rules and regulations had been growing for years, even decades, in Washington. As the complexities of government and demands on it had multiplied and as the power of the presidents had increased, civil-service officials had become more subservient to the wishes of the executive. "Responsiveness" and "flexibility" in applying hiring and firing standards—these became the operative bywords. Internal enforcement procedures atrophied. The civil service stagnated. A desire to please rather than police was a hallmark. Too often, managers of the federal service became comfortable and complacent. Too often, their hands were tied by regulations designed to protect one group or another. Too often, they went along.

Employees found the political pressures difficult, if not impossible, to resist. They felt they had to go along, too. Ironically, it took one of those faceless career bureaucrats in one of the government's gray office ant hills in Washington to blow the whistle. The actions that followed offered a case study of what was wrong with government.

□　□　□

In the spring of 1973 an internal inspection team was visiting one of its personnel offices in the General Services Administration (GSA), the government's housekeeping agency that oversees all federal buildings and office supplies, everything from pencils and paper to motor vehicles and computers. It was routine, a standard evaluation of personnel management procedures—specifically, how the folders were being maintained in one of Washington's largest personnel offices.

While they were going through the records, an employee, Arthur G. Palman, approached the inspection leader and asked him to come into his office. Palman closed and locked his door; then he proceeded to lay out a startling story, complete with specific charges and documentation.

Palman was a veteran bureaucrat who had entered government service in 1940 with a master's degree and work toward a doctorate in American history from New York University. His first job was in the Census Bureau, in personnel. In the decades since, he had worked in personnel, in the Air Force at home and abroad and then back in the civil service in Washington. A graying, mild-mannered sort of man, Palman was not a maverick. He had been at GSA as a regional personnel director for six years.

What had been going on, he told the inspection leader in the privacy of his office, was a subversion of the civil-service merit system. He and other personnel officers were being forced to take on unqualified people and remove qualified ones solely on political grounds. He had evidence, and so did his senior staff, of political abuses going back four years, to the time when the Nixon administration first began. *That* was what they should be investigating. Palman and his staff were prepared to testify and give evidence.

Palman was speaking out of desperation and anger. For several years he had been trying to bring these conditions to the attention of his superiors. No one would listen. No one wanted to rock the boat. He had met with a high executive of the Civil Service Commission, whom he had known for years, to no avail. Nothing could be done; it wasn't like the old days when the civil service meant something, he was told. He had shown the chief of his inspection unit a box containing five-by-eight-inch cards listing names and dates of political job referrals. Palman had compiled seven hundred such cards. His chief inspector didn't want to see them. Too hot, too sensitive.

Palman was not a naïve man or some rigid moral purist. He told me later:

My biggest objection to what was being done wasn't that they were bringing in people who were unqualified, but that they were making a mockery of the civil-service structure. In other administrations, political liberties were taken, all right, but they were never systematized. There was never a formal procedure about how to go about it. And never on such a scale. The Nixon administration was going out of its way to force out good career people so they could bring in people they wanted. What they were doing was dastardly, and unprecedented so far as I knew from previous administrations. I saw the tragic consequences: people being forced out of their jobs, being forced to retire, or being forced into situations where they would break down in my office in tears from the pressure. I saw people getting high blood pressure and heart attacks, and one of them died. It's one thing just to read about that kind of subversion, but it's quite another to have a man, a high-level man, come into your office and see him break down and later that night get a call from his wife saying he has died. These things were causing tragedies, and they were facts.

If the Civil Service Commission wasn't going to make an honest investigation, Palman told the inspector, he and his associates would make public their case through the press. He demanded an immediate reply. The inspection team leader left, shaken. Later that same day, Palman was told to put his charges in writing, and they would be considered.

On June 11, 1973, Palman wrote a formal letter, signed by five members of his staff, that set in motion, albeit slowly, and most of all reluctantly, a government investigation. In time, unprecedented abuses of the civil-service system were documented. They proved that the Nixon administration had made a concerted effort to politicize the entire federal bureaucracy. Not just the huge GSA was involved; the effort extended to the massive Departments of Health, Education and Welfare, and Housing and Urban Development, the Office of Economic Opportunity, ACTION, and the Small Business Administration. "Special referral units" to oversee the placement of political hacks had been established. Political hiring quotas had been set forth. A system of singling out the political favorites for key jobs by marking their files with pink slips was operating. "Must" political hirees were designated. And a specific written plan instructed personnel officers on how to get around the legal requirements of the civil-service system.

This plan—the infamous "Malek Manual"—had been drafted in 1971 when Frederic Malek headed the White House Personnel Office. Each government department was ordered to create a special political personnel office headed by a special assistant to the cabinet secretary, to be chosen in conjunction with the White House. The political officer would have an office near the cabinet secretary's, as a symbol of his power. "Both the physical location and the majesty and decor of the offices of the political personnel office," the manual stated, "will communicate to both the bureaucracy and the public apparent power and authority." Those hired had to be "philosophically compatible with and loyal to the president." They were to be placed "in leadership positions," and "personnel decisions should be made and announced to maximize political benefit and minimize political costs." Government personnel officials from the various departments and agencies were summoned to the White House for regular meetings on how to hire and fire people outside authorized merit-system procedures.

In questioning one personnel officer about those meetings, civil-service investigators were told that what the White House was doing had the backing of the Civil Service Commission. This confirmed what the investigators already had begun to suspect as soon as they began looking into Palman's charges: that officials of their own Civil Service Commission, the heart of the system created to guarantee integrity in the federal work force, were partners in the corruption. Less than a month after the investigation started, one high-ranking CSC employee had told them: "We don't trust you guys. Why are you looking at us? You've known for a long time what has been going on, since you are a part of it." But it wasn't for another year, as the investigation wound its way upward in the bureaucracy, that they began to harbor far more disquieting suspicions. The higher they went, the more their authority was challenged. Finally they were told the acts they were investigating were being committed by the highest officials of all, the overall authority for their inquiry. Personal files of the three Civil Service commissioners were searched. They disclosed some thirty-five political job referrals—including at least ten in the files of the commission chairman himself, the person given ultimate responsibility for protecting the integrity of government employees from political interference.

Two cases drawn from the files of Commission Chairman Robert Hampton were particularly illuminating. I give them in some detail here because they show so vividly how perverted the merit system had become.

The first occurred in the early months of the Nixon administration. Robert Kunzig, administrator of the GSA, received a letter from Robert McCune, who had been executive director of Nixon's Inaugural Committee. McCune was recommending "a good Republican friend," an L. Emory Hutchison, Jr., for a civil-service job. He enclosed a résumé, and a handwritten postscript informed the GSA chief that "I advised Harry Flemming that I was forwarding this letter to you." (Flemming was then head of the White House Personnel Office.)

Two days later another L. Emory Hutchison, Jr., résumé was sent to GSA, this one from Civil Service Chairman Robert Hampton. "Is there any chance that GSA can use his services?" Hampton wrote. Hampton had also written Hutchison that day, telling him his résumé had been sent to GSA and asking him to fill out enclosed civil service job-application forms. "Complete them," Hampton told the job seeker, "and return them to me and I will see that they are promptly rated."

At that moment there existed a waiting list of some twenty thousand civil-service job applicants. Months would elapse before any one of them was informed of his job prospects. Often more than a year went by before someone received civil-service job ratings. But here, in one stroke, the Civil Service chairman had cut all the red tape and given the political friend preferential treatment. Two weeks later Hampton personally gave Hutchison a high government job rating. A secretary was instructed to send the rating with his recommendation to another top GSA official. Mark it "personal," the chairman ordered.

The favored treatment—and the pressure—continued. Within a week, Harry Flemming wrote on White House letterhead to the GSA administrator: "Mr. L. Emory Hutchison, a staunch Republican, has had long and varied experience in business as indicated by the enclosed resume. . . . I'm sure he would be a valuable addition to your office." By hand, Flemming wrote: "I am interested in this one."

Down through the bureaucracy went the job seeker's application, with accompanying glowing GSA recommendations ("appears particularly well qualified"), but at a lower level, the bureaucracy balked. Only one possible position existed for which he might be qualified, the word came back, and that would require years of training. The manager of another bureau said he wasn't qualified at all. "Is this a must case or not???" asked an administrator in a note to his superior. "No," the answer came back. There was no need to go further.

But there was. More White House pressure was applied. The Civil Service Commission obliged by rewriting his job-specification description to fit one tailored for him. An internal memo from the GSA assistant administrator to the agency's administrator gave the Hutchison denouement:

"He was a must case sponsored by Harry Flemming, Bob Hampton, and Bob McCune," the memo said. That is, by the head of the White House Personnel Office, the U.S. Civil Service Commission, and the Nixon Inaugural Committee. "Fine," read the penciled reply of the administrator. With the help of such friends, L. Emory Hutchison, Jr., got his $27,400-a-year job in the government as a "Specifications Writer in the Federal Supply Service."

The second case from Chairman Hampton's files had nothing to do with party favoritism; it showed that the old style of political influence was still at work in Washington.

In the fall of 1970 Chairman Hampton had gone on a hunting trip with a congressman from Texas, Robert Price. When they returned, the congressman wrote the chairman a "Dear Bob" letter: "This in regard to my friend I discussed with you on our recent hunting trip. His name is Mr. Dwight W. Jones, 307 Scott Street, Livermore, California 94550."

Actually, as the chairman knew, Mr. Jones was more than a friend of the congressman. He was his cousin, and he wanted a government job. The chairman's personal secretary was instructed to turn the case over to a special assistant who handled such matters: Tell me where you stand by the close of business three days later, the chairman ordered. The next day his special assistant suggested the chairman contact GSA about Mr. Jones.

Instantly, a letter went out from Hampton to GSA: "If at all possible, I would like to help Congressman Price and would appreciate your letting me know what his cousin's chances are for employment." The GSA official passed on Hampton's request to an aide with these instructions: "Urgent, put in mill and see me." Five weeks later, Mr. Jones had *his* $27,400-a-year government job.

Everyone involved knew precisely what they were doing and why. An internal memo in GSA's files contained this advisory to the top of the agency: "Bob Hampton has referred an applicant, Dwight W. Jones of Livermore, California, to us for a GS-13 or 14 position in the Federal Supply Service. Jones is . . . a cousin of the congressman from Texas, and Bob Hampton would like to help the congressman. I told Bob Hampton that I knew you would want to do everything possible to help. I gave the papers to Jack LeMay and asked that he give this matter urgent priority." To which the GSA top official, in a handwritten note of his own, said: "Let's do all we can—I agree. Thanks."

The Dwight Jones case ended several days later when Congressman Price wrote to Hampton: "Just a note to thank you for your consideration of my recent request. I look forward to another hunt with you soon. Best wishes in your work and if I can ever be of service to you, please don't hesitate to call me."

That you-help-me-I'll-help-you pattern was as old as politics itself, but that wasn't the way it was supposed to work. The investigation touched off by Arthur Palman's charges uncovered the most serious attempt to subvert the merit principles in the ninety-three years of the Civil Service Commission's existence. Top commission officials, as well as the commissioners themselves, had in the judgment of a congressional report "severely compromised their roles . . . by engaging in improper activities not unlike the activities for which agency officials were charged."

Inside the agencies, knowledge of the way the system was being compromised during the Nixon years was commonplace, for there was little subtlety in the political pressure cases, and few attempts to hide the sponsors. One personnel officer was ordered to hire a driver for Attorney General John Mitchell, even though a hiring freeze was on; to hire Jeb Magruder a driver; to hire Presidential counselor George Schultz's son ("We established a job we did not need and at a location of his choosing"); to hire Deputy Attorney General Richard Kleindienst's son. When the job application of Chief Justice Warren Burger's son arrived at the Civil Service Commission, it was immediately tagged as special and five top officials met to consider it. He got a $35,000-a-year job as "Special Assistant to the Assistant Commissioner for Space Management" at GSA.

Government employees learned to understand other realities about the merit system. "Cleaning up the files" before a government audit or inspection meant destroying incriminating evidence. Raising the salary of a non–civil-service congressional aide before his job expired, often for only one day, allowed him to receive a higher permanent salary grade with a subsequent civil-service appointment. "Inquiring about job availability" and "referencing the Commissioner's" name was a polite way of saying that the top official of an agency wanted the Park or Forest Service, say, to hire certain people for summer jobs. Understanding "political acceptability factors" in approving career government jobs meant recognizing delicate and unwritten factors: "For instance, in OEO [Office of Economic Opportunity], blackness was considered to be a necessary qualification for sound performance," one examiner testified.

The entire story of the civil-service-system abuses never will be known. Wholesale destruction of masses of incriminating documents occurred during the investigation. (After learning that a senator was making inquiries, one group of employees worked all one night and for several days putting files in boxes and permanently removing them. A member of one staff under investigation testified before a congressional subcommittee in 1976 that he drove into a Washington department-store parking lot on upper Wisconsin Avenue and threw personnel files into a trash can. The material was never recovered.) Although the civil-service investigators agreed that numerous illegal acts had occurred, they also agreed that too much documentary evidence was missing to permit effective prosecution.

The civil-service scandals never attracted the public attention they should have had. Watergate, impeachment, and Nixon's resignation overshadowed everything else. And while there was outstanding reporting on the abuses (notably in *The Federal Times* and *The St. Louis Post-Dispatch*), the full energies of the big newspapers and television networks were not engaged. To the press, the civil-service workings of government are dull at best, and besides, the press perpetuates and reinforces the popular view that the bureaucrat is the legendary bumbler, unworthy of much respect to start with. Like the fight in Congress to recover lost legislative powers, the battle for the bureaucracy to maintain its integrity was obscured by Watergate. Yet they were parts of the same struggle.

The experience in both cases led to a new determination to fight executive-department abuses. Leading and motivating the disheartened federal employees would be more difficult. Morale had fallen to an all-time low. No one knew better than the workers themselves what life inside the federal government had become. They knew how the public regarded them, and they knew even more intimately how great the government's problems were.

□   □   □

In the late summer of 1976, as the presidential campaign was beginning, a small group of bureaucrats in the Department of Health, Education and Welfare began preparing for the change in administrations. Whoever won, they would be affected. Ford, elected in his own right, would want to set his own agenda. As for Carter, well, Carter was promising greater changes and reforms than any president since Franklin Roosevelt.

The bureaucrats were particularly sensitive to the oft-repeated charge that their department was unmanageable. They set out, privately, to study the workings of HEW and draft recommendations about it for the next group of government leaders. By mid-December, after Carter's victory and a month before his inauguration, their study had been completed. The central finding, as drafted in their internal paper, was refreshingly candid. "Any attempt to refute the long continued and widespread charges that the Department is unmanageable and out of effective control through organizational restructuring, in and by itself, is unrealistic," they wrote. "No matter how the Department is structured, the problems will continue in more or less intensified form until there is basic reform of the Department's programs."

The sprawling Department of Health, Education and Welfare reached into every corner of every American's life. How it got that way, and what it had become, was the story of government in America itself. As a bureaucrat who had watched HEW change from within since the 1950s told me, as Carter was about to become president: "No enterprise that I know of, government or otherwise, has ever grown as fast and reached out into so many areas. The dynamics of change are very rapid, perhaps even overwhelming. HEW is now self-propelling. It has a motion and thrust all its own. You can change the leadership, and the tempo will pick up or decline depending on the quality of its people, but there's a certain amount of activity that's inevitable now. That's true of the whole government, though. Look at the uncontrollability of the federal budget. Look at the Congress—continually looking for new space. Its appetite for new offices is insatiable."

Even that pessimistic appraisal didn't begin to give the dimensions of HEW or express the nature of its problems. In the twenty-three years of its existence, HEW had been led by eleven cabinet secretaries, their average length of service a scant 2.1 years. Any experienced Washington hand knew it took almost that long simply to learn the names of all the offices and bureaus in the department. And every change of a secretary brought a change in the entire upper management—the under secretary and assistant secretaries and all the other presidentially appointed executives who oversaw the department's manifold functions. Nor was HEW some aberration in the government hierarchy. (The same managerial impermanence—always leading to internal instability if not turmoil—existed elsewhere. From Kennedy to Carter, for example, there had been seven secretaries of labor and nine secretaries of commerce—a turnover almost every two years.) Top management teams were leaving after barely becoming acquainted with their organizations and responsibilities. Understanding the programs they were charged with administering, to say nothing of establishing their own policies and procedures, was difficult at best. Necessity forced them to depend on the management directives of their predecessors, to walk on the barnacles of the government past.

HEW was created in 1953 out of a governmental reorganization of its precursor, the Federal Security Agency, which in turn had been born during the New Deal. As the far grander bureaucracy, HEW began with what even then were impressive numbers. Its 35,000 employees administered some eighty programs and spent $7 billion a year. By the end of the Ford administration, HEW's budget had soared to $128.5 billion annually; it was expending more money than most nations in the world. The number of its employees had increased to 145,000—more than fourfold. They were responsible for some four hundred government programs.

Each program had a special constituency. Each was related to a congressional committee or subcommittee. Each extended into different state and local government components.

The programs were so intertwined that to change one, or create another, meant affecting a host of others. Two hundred separate health programs were being administered. For example, HEW was operating: the Alcohol Community Service Program, Alcohol Demonstration Programs, Alcohol Formula Grants, Alcohol Fellowships, Alcohol Research Development Awards, Alcohol National Research Awards, the Alcohol Research Program, Alcohol

Training Programs, Special Alcoholism Projects to Implement the Uniform Act, and Alcoholism and Alcohol Addiction Research.

Closely related though such programs obviously were, they were scattered all over HEW. HEW's Office of Human Development and the Social Security Administration were both managing drug-abuse programs, and several others serving state and local communities were lodged in the Alcohol, Drug and Mental Health Administration. The education part of HEW oversaw one hundred programs. Separate ones dealt with deprived children, handicapped children, children of migrants and migratory fishermen, children in state schools, children in state institutions serving neglected or delinquent children. Other programs sent money to assist states in expanding educational programs for disadvantaged children. Welfare policies and legislation wound their way through subcommittee after subcommittee on Capitol Hill before being deposited in the hands of HEW. Ten congressional committees had jurisdiction over welfare; the action of one committee often affected a program under the jurisdiction of another.

Directly linked to the congressional committees were the special-interest and lobbying groups. Every program had a sponsor. Every sponsor had long-established ties with the congressional committee that passed on every program.

Relationships with the state and local governments were, if possible, even more confusing. Each level resisted efforts to rationalize the conflicting programs. Neither was willing to relinquish control or power to the other. And no matter how loudly the states or localities inveighed against Washington, they wanted more, not less, from it.

Grants from the federal government to the states had reached nearly $83 billion a year by 1976, more than one-third of *all* federal spending—and an enormous increase from the modest under $2.5 billion spent in 1950. Government regulations had become unbelievably complex and voluminous. Reading the regulations that came out of HEW in only *one week* was equivalent to wading through twice as many words as *War and Peace*—words, it barely needs saying, that lacked the clarity of Tolstoy's. They were in fact often incomprehensible to any but the expert in the esoteric. The bureaucracy was dispirited and distrustful. And it was much more difficult for any cabinet officer to exercise authority. In HEW alone, Congress had specified literally thousands of things a new secretary couldn't change. One education program, for instance, required HEW to write ninety regulations in two hundred forty days—and the law set the exact date on which each regulation had to be issued. There were 381 programs set up by statute that could not be changed except by new legislation. No matter which way a new secretary wanted to move, he was a hostage to specifications in the law and the power of the special-interest groups. That, assuming he knew how the programs were operating to begin with, and what should—or could—be done about them.

A new president and new HEW secretary were authorized to fill only 144 jobs out of the department's 145,000-member work force. Inevitably the old cycle of trying to get around the regulations began anew, along with the old pattern of blaming the bureaucracy for not being responsive enough to the wishes of the new leaders, who wouldn't last long anyhow. But for many HEW bureaucrats, it didn't matter all that much who was president. "Except for their pet projects, I don't think they have that much impact at my level," said the head of one big bureau. "Almost none. The president himself has virtually no impact on me."

He wasn't expressing disloyalty. His distinction—and it was critical—was between the independence he enjoyed in day-to-day matters of getting the job done, and the tone of a new administration and new president. What tone a president set, whether supportive or abusive, can make a great difference. But Congress, in passing laws, leaves much of the responsibility for implementing them to the executive departments and agencies. In promulgating regulations for such things as the truckers' daily logs, the agencies assume law-making responsibilities. As the scholar Peter Woll points out, when the Agriculture Department issues regulations on food-stamp eligibility, it makes law, and when the Environmental Protection Agency sets standards for auto emissions or permissible levels of air and water pollution, it makes law. By being familiar with the programs and administering them and by dealing closely with the congressional committees and subcommittees that create them, the bureaucrat possesses expert knowledge. It's knowledge that gives him power over his superiors at the head of his department.

But the bureaucrat serves many political and congressional masters, who in turn respond to many demands from many national
constituencies. The cumulative strain on the government and its
officers is well-nigh intolerable.

A federal welfare program for the aged, blind, and disabled, administered in HEW, is a case in point. A federal bureaucrat, operating out of an office thousands of miles from Washington, is
required personally to inspect a welfare recipient's living arrangements each month. If the cooking arrangements have changed,
that may determine whether Aunt Mary remains on the rolls or
whether her benefits go up—or down.

The deeper you delve into the permanent federal bureaucracy,
the greater the evidence of fatigue and resentment. To a striking
degree, the government workers and officials stress the same
themes. They speak of reaching—and exceeding—the saturation
point in programs, services, benefits; of programs eventually turning inward and becoming self-destructive; of the uselessness of
struggling to simplify legislative dictates affecting those programs.
"I don't think Congress is interested in simplification," one official told me wearily, "because the law is filled with provisions that
protect everybody. I really don't think anybody is interested."

This kind of situation led one veteran HEW bureaucrat to say to
me, bitterly, in the privacy of his office, "The system is corrupting
itself." He didn't mean corruption in the simple sense of theft,
bribery, fraud, greed. He meant that the government was growing
out of control and the federal system was in danger of breaking
down because everyone, everywhere, was placing more demands
on it. "The whole society is involved in a rip-off, if you want to put
it that way," he said. Fraud and scandal were facts of life in Washington, sometimes of stunning proportions, as we'll see. But what
almost never receives as much attention was perhaps the greater
corruption—the attempt to do more than is prudent or possible
and the failure to realize the real danger in placing greater burdens on government: the threat that government will collapse of
its own weight. Persuasive evidence could be found that such a
danger point was approaching. Perhaps most telling of all the
cases I've examined was the experience of the one government
agency that directly affects the lives of more Americans than any
other and that until recent years stood as the brightest ornament

in the ever-expanding federal establishment, the Social Security
Administration.

□   □   □

For decades, the Social Security Administration ran the largest
retirement program in the world. It delivered with great efficiency
and élan billions of dollars each month to tens of millions of
Americans. To work for Social Security was to be part of an elite, a
model of what government could do for the citizens it serves. Social Security's proudest boast was that it was thought of as the
people's friend, the agency closest to them.

Figures in the mass are almost meaningless, but not in what they
represent to individual human beings: as Jimmy Carter took office,
one out of every seven Americans was getting a monthly Social Security check. Thirty-six million people, young and old, sick and
disabled, retired and alone, were receiving billions of dollars
month after month after month. What's remarkable is that Social
Security carried out its mission so well for so long. Its very success
led to its problems; that and the demands placed on it by everyone—politicians, presidents, and people in general.

In the early days, the mission was simple. Deliver the right check
in the right amount to the right person at the right address—and
on time. Social Security did everything asked of it, and did it su-
perbly. The rewards of success were more benefit programs to administer, more complicated personnel records to process and
maintain. By early 1977 Social Security payments were being
made to half a million sufferers of black lung disease, at a rate of
$79 million a month . . . to 835,000 young people drawing survi-
vor's benefits, a billion dollars a year, much of which was financing
higher education . . . to millions of Medicare claimants, the largest
single government health-insurance program, at a cost of $22 bil-
lion a year.

Placing these differing programs inside Social Security wasn't
part of a logical overall government plan. Social Security got the
assignments mainly because it had a reputation for getting things
done. As new responsibilities were added, Social Security kept
growing. Again, typical of the federal government, growth oc-

curred not so much in the number of employees but on the money spent and the physical space occupied.

In the beginning, back in the New Deal, Social Security leaders had studied the way the English civil service maintained its records. The British advice to the Americans was not to count on keeping more than 3.5 million individual records. The British believed the American effort would fail because it was too large. But the Americans had confounded them. With diligence and efficiency, the Social Security bureaucrats kept pace with their ever-growing volume of record keeping. For years all of the agency's records were written on paper and kept on bamboo strips. Huge tubs filled with bamboo strips were stored everywhere.

When the paperwork finally began to engulf Social Security, technology came to the rescue. The age of the computer began. With typical confidence in technology, government officials believed the computer held the key to the future. The computer system created for Social Security was one of the marvels of Western society. It represented a world unto itself, in some ways the center of the world of government.

To enter it, down a long corridor behind locked doors marked "Secured," is to witness the technological umbilical cord of our society. There is the government link that reaches out and touches everyone, for everyone is linked to that system. It's a quiet, clean, uncluttered world, certainly not the common picture of the computerized bureaucracy impressed on the public mind. Nor one reminiscent of Orwell's omnipresent government structure where Big Brother always watches. Not many people there, in fact: the greatest sense of activity comes from the faint humming that emanates from banks of machines in gray casings. The machines are always humming. They never stop. The volume of work grows and changes no matter who sits in the White House or in a cabinet officer's chair or in a seat in Congress.

"Every night we pass through the system every personal record we have in our master file," explains the government official cleared to admit you to that sealed-off chamber. "It's constantly changing. All the records are kept current and active." In other words, the records of *all* 330 million Americans who have received Social Security numbers since the birth of the agency in 1936 pass through that computer system *every* night. Death does not stop the citizen's continuing life story here. Long after death, his records keep whirring through the Social Security computers, night after night after night.

With a Social Security number, the government bureaucrats can determine your name, your father's name, your mother's name, and her maiden name. They can tell your date and place of birth, your race and sex, where and when your Social Security card was issued, and what your address and phone number were at that time.

If you're employed, they know when and for whom you've worked. They know when you changed jobs, and the address of your employer, and your employers' corporate officers and stockholders. They know how much money you make. All your earnings records are on magnetic tape. They know if you're married, divorced, or have children under eighteen. If you go on Medicare, they know what drugs you're taking and your medical bills and the name and address of your doctor. When you die, the computer incorporates data about when and how your life ended and where you are buried. The records are more complete than those of the Internal Revenue Service.

"Where you're standing now comprises the largest computer operation in the free world," the government guide says. "That excludes our intelligence agencies, and the Russians. Now you can see why we don't let people in here. It needs to be kept confidential."

At the time of the Carter inauguration, when I visited the site, construction of a twentieth huge building was under way at the Social Security headquarters. It would be the biggest of them all, containing 350,000 square feet of space—the first building ever designed and constructed solely to house computers.

But by then much of the early glow about the wonders of computer technology had dissipated, for Social Security had been through a traumatic experience.

The computers had gone catastrophically awry. They had spewed out erroneous information resulting in massive over- and under-payments. Social Security had been extended to the breaking point. It had been assigned to administer one more massive program too many.

In 1974, for the first time, Social Security entered the federally subsidized welfare business. The new program, called Supplemental Security Income (SSI), gave the agency responsibility for another 4 million people—the aged, the blind, and the disabled on the state welfare rolls. In Congress, the program was claimed to be simple to administer. It wasn't. States added their own complicated requirements. For example, in California a person eligible for the federal welfare payment could get additional money—if he was living alone, taking meals twice a day in a restaurant. When he stopped having meals in a restaurant and started cooking at home, however, the financial grant would have to be adjusted, up or down. As a top agency administrator said, "From the standpoint of the federal government administering it, that's just a monstrous thing to attempt to do."

If Social Security was confident about anything, it was its ability to deliver checks. Not this time. Almost everything went wrong. Many of the state and local welfare rolls turned out to be in error; case after case had to be reconstructed from scratch. The process of gathering information, checking its accuracy, and then entering it all correctly into the computers was much more time-consuming and complicated than anticipated. And for once, Social Security failed to get its payments out.

At local offices around the country mob scenes occurred. Some thirty thousand Social Security personnel began working around the clock to try and bring order out of the chaos. After intensive efforts for more than a year, and great internal strains and pressures on the system and its workers, Social Security officials thought they were winning their battle.

Then came the greatest shock. People were getting a great deal more money than they were entitled to. And money was going to people who weren't eligible in the first place. In the first two years of administering the welfare program, *Social Security overpayments totaled about $1 billion.* Error rates were running between 10 and 25 percent. The program was a disaster.

When I visited agency offices in the aftermath of that debacle, I'd hear expressions of one frustration after another: The job was getting harder all the time. . . . No time to keep up with the new government manuals issued to explain the new government programs. . . . A public increasingly hostile. . . . Instances of abusive behavior common. . . . High personnel turnover, good replacements harder to find. . . . No sense of being appreciated or respected.

□ □ □

Office managers all over the federal government often exploded in anger—not so much at the public but at the government itself. The farther away from Washington, the more irrelevant the sounds and actions of the president and cabinet officers seemed to the government's own workers and managers. On the lowest level, where the repetitive, grinding work was performed, those far-off decisions in Washington weren't the immediate concern to the employees dealing directly with the public. Their problems were more mundane—and difficult. They involved such seemingly simple things as obtaining file cabinets and qualified clerk-typists. Neither was easy. Harassed office managers wound up fighting within the bureaucracy, and often losing. "If you want to ask me what are the largest barriers you have to overcome to do an efficient job," one told me, "you know what my answer would be? The Civil Service Commission and the General Services Administration. These agencies do not serve us. They're there but they're there to block us. Their sole preoccupation is to keep themselves in power without rendering service." Strong words, but not exaggerated. The civil-service system had become corrupted, and the GSA, the government's central housekeeper and purchaser of all supplies, was the center of even greater corruption. For years, probably decades, the federal government had been defrauded by schemes stemming from within the GSA. (It was estimated that the government was being cheated out of as much as $100 million a year. GSA employees systematically and boldly had been charging the government for repairs never done, supplies never delivered, maintenance never completed and other sundry old-style corruption—bribery, kickbacks, padded equipment costs.)

The low quality of employees approved by the civil service was another common complaint in Social Security. Mistakes on claims made by incompetent or careless clerk-typists were incorporated into the computer and from the computer into incorrect payments. "Here's an agency that needs to get the best possible employee," said a Social Security office manager, "and here's a system that dooms you to the worst."

Why such employees were approved in the first place is something else. Pressure to hire minorities, particularly in the urban areas, properly had been great during the 1960s and the subsequent creation of government equal-opportunity mandates. But standards *had* been relaxed. Supervisors *had* learned to fear being accused of discrimination, real or imaginary. It gave them one more thing to worry about. Often they concluded the pain wasn't worth the effort.

More than that, managers complained about a decline in the quality of work among employees generally. One official, a black man, told me angrily about getting the kind of run-around from a clerk in his own office that many citizens had learned to expect at some government installations. "By God, here I am a deputy bureau director getting this kind of treatment," he said. "If that's the kind of service we're giving out here now to our own employees—how in hell is Jimmy Carter going to change that?"

Missing file cabinets and incompetent clerk-typists and disgruntled employees (like the one who says he reaches the point where he throws an occasional citizen's claims file in the trash basket—"that's one you don't have to worry about") may not seem matters of great moment in the world of government. Or, to be lofty, in the world of democracy and the rights and responsibilities of citizens and society. But of course they are. No one realizes it better than the people who have experienced what it's like to be in the midst of the system. If they've been in government service long, they'll usually tell you that working for the government now bears little resemblance to the government they once knew.

□   □   □

Jefferson may have been correct in believing that government governs best which governs least. But American appetites have dictated otherwise. They have wanted more. "Liberals" who vote for the big new social programs are tagged as big spenders by "conservatives" who vote for the far greater and more wasteful spending programs in the sacrosanct Pentagon budgets—together they add more layers of bureaucracy that impose greater burdens on the bureaucrats forced to deal with them. Hubert Humphrey expressed the need for some system of federal governance as effectively as anyone when he said: "I have no apologies for the federal government doing things. Who's going to take care of the environment, establish the standards? You? Me? I have no apologies for the government being interested in people, in nutrition, in education, in health, in transportation. Who's gonna work out a national food policy? The mayor of New York? Who's gonna work out our transportation problems? The B and O Railroad? We've got to have federal government activity. The only question is not the size of the government, but does it work?"

The answer to his last question is that government isn't working well—and no one knows that better than the bureaucrats. The view of many is that Americans literally and figuratively were getting what they paid for: that for years they had gotten a government perhaps better than they deserved, given the nature of their support, but that was no longer the case. "We're working as hard as we know how in this bureau," said a middle-management official, "and yet the quality in this outfit is terrible and we can't seem to get it any better. People have reached the point where they don't feel like the job is something they want to do."

Government workers know that public confidence in them has eroded, just as they know they have lost confidence in their own abilities to do their jobs well. None of the descriptive terms—defensive, disenchanted, weary, angry, cynical—fully captures their emotions. For many, working for the government has become an embarrassment. "The public has begun to think of us as animals instead of public servants," a bureaucrat said to me, recalling the attitudes he'd encountered on trips around the country. "That's a terrible thing for people who, rightly or wrongly, perceive themselves doing something positive for the public."

To many inside, government has become an endless struggle to survive. Few outside seem to recognize this. "What it comes out to," an agency director said, "is this: everybody's got to hold on to that ledge just a little longer. It's twenty stories below and you're dead if you fall. So you just hang on as long as you can."

An obvious point about the state of the government and its workers is easily forgotten. Government workers are only a reflection of American society. They have experienced the same doubts, fears, and shocks as the rest of us over the assassinations, riots, wars, civil-rights struggles, and presidential misdeeds of the past. Their attitudes about work and their belief in institutions have changed, too. Their cynicism, like ours, is greater. Their faith in the ability of government also has lessened. They feel all these acutely and more, for they are at the center of the government's efforts to deal with every crisis and solve every problem.

Bureaucrats seldom get credit for candor, courage, selflessness, or hard work. Yet after spending weeks and weeks interviewing dozens of them, my strongest impression is of how frankly they concede their mistakes and how thoughtfully they suggest the need for improvement. They are concerned about the future, and believe government has reached a critical juncture. As one official said to me, "For whatever reasons, we're no longer performing in the manner to which the public became accustomed and which they have a right to expect. It may be simply that we've grown too fat and complacent. We'd be deluding ourselves if we simply adopted a 'this-too-shall-pass' attitude. The United States of the 1970s is not the United States of the thirties or even fifties, and we must be sufficiently flexible to attune ourselves to new times and new needs. Institutions that fail to bend must surely break."

No less candid was the head of Social Security. "Most of our decline occurred in the three years I've been here," said Bruce Cardwell ruefully during the week of Jimmy Carter's inauguration. "In the last three years the agency has been beaten down. It's had some outright failures, failures for which it has no alibi."

Cardwell had been in federal government service for thirty-five years, and the changes he'd seen were discouraging:

I think we've fallen into a state if disrepair. We've lost a lot of ground in the government, we've gone into a deep slide. I think this department has changed in the way it feels about itself, its basic capacities and competencies. Ten years ago HEW was populated by people who were essentially optimistic. It's too early to tell what the new people at the top will be like, but the group who just left were very doubtful. No matter what they said publicly, they really had become very doubtful about the capacity of government in social problem-solving to be as effective as they wanted it to be, or thought it could or should be.

Today I'm convinced the pendulum has started to swing toward the legislative branch. If I were to try to draw public attention to government—what's good about it, what's bad about it, what's uncertain about it—I would spend more time on the legislative than the executive branch. The Congress is now beginning to behave the way the White House did back in the forties, fifties, and sixties. The executive branch saw itself as the ultimate problem-solver, and armed itself with the tools and devices it needed. Now the legislative branch is saying, The problems weren't solved. They're arming themselves.

The system will suffer as a result of these two camps building up. I'm not at all sure whether they can be calmed down through the force of the new personalities coming into this administration.

The Nixon administration, in its behavioral problems and its attitudes vis-à-vis the Congress, produced a lot of these developments. There was something there even before Watergate occurred. I found what happened very shocking. My training had been to make the system work by following the leadership of the political appointee. And I prided myself on doing it with integrity. I was shocked to see people in the Nixon period of power so often express a natural We-They attitude toward the Congress and the bureaucracy. If you characterized the administration as a person, it was a person inherently suspicious, inherently defensive, with inherently misguided ideas about how the government works. It's possible this group with Carter can do something to repair that. I certainly hope so. I certainly hope they have a different attitude about how the system runs.

Cardwell's deputy, Robert Bynum, in charge of Social Security program operations, had a more specific wish for the next era of governance in Washington when we talked. The new president and new Congress should be extremely cautious about enacting new programs and not proceed without thoroughly examining everything else on the books; they must also insist on undoing some existing programs. "If this president and this Congress don't somehow get a grasp on how to do that over the next four years," he said, "then we are truly going to reach a very chaotic kind of situation in this country."

□ □ □

Jimmy Carter campaigned against Washington and its bureaucrats, but most government workers supported him. Their backing was not paradoxical; it was practical. Their relationship with the White House couldn't have been worse in recent years, and Gerald Ford had sometimes exceeded Carter's rhetoric about the evils of Washington bureaucracy. Federal workers didn't know Carter, nor had they formed distinct impressions about him as had many congressmen on Capitol Hill. But they believed Carter was a Truman-Kennedy progressive who appreciated the role of government.

There were two ways the government could go, as one veteran bureaucrat with a "passion for anonymity" observed to me. It could be heading into a renaissance or sinking back into more cynicism and hopelessness. "The whole question is motivation and direction—leadership," he said, in January 1977. That would be Carter's test.

Jimmy Carter was watched with some wariness, but at least he was starting with the basic goodwill of the bureaucrats. They too wanted a change.

3

THE CITY

ON THE morning of January 20, 1977, an arctic wind swept the clouds from the skies, and the capital glistened with ice under a brilliant sun. Along Pennsylvania Avenue, red-white-and-blue bunting hung from government buildings. Flags set every few feet along the curbs snapped in the breeze. Mounted police patrolled the route.

I was making a last-minute inspection of the presidential inaugural setting. The farther I went down Pennsylvania Avenue toward the Capitol, the more surprising the scene. By that hour, in previous inaugurals, no matter what the weather, crowds would have been forming, with people already standing two or three deep. Now the streets were almost deserted.

As I moved closer to the Capitol, a mass of people appeared off to the right. They were outside the National Gallery, in lines extending around the building. An exhibition of King Tutankhamen's treasures, on display for a month, hadn't yet opened, and they were waiting to buy tickets. "Many more Tut than Jimmy," I scribbled in my notebook as I walked on toward the Hill and the inaugural platform.

□　□　□

In *Decline and Fall of the Roman Empire,* Gibbon recalls Juvenal's lament about the hardships of the poorer citizens of Rome: they should depart at once from the smoke of the city and purchase in the small towns of Italy cheerful, spacious homes "at the same price which they annually paid for a dark and miserable lodging." From that, Gibbon concludes about the state of Imperial Rome before the fall:

"House-rent was therefore immoderately dear; the rich acquired, at an enormous expense, the ground, which they covered with palaces and gardens; but the body of the Roman people were crowded into a narrow space; and the different floors and apartments of the same house were divided, as it is still the custom of Paris and other cities, among several families of plebeians."

Washington wasn't a case of patricians vs. plebeians, riches for the few, poverty for the many. It was not only the most powerful world capital but the wealthiest—and it was the wealth of the many that was so striking. A mandarin class unlike any ever seen had been created in America's capital. Probably never had so many people in a capital city been so much better off than the citizens of their country. Washington's economy has always been special. It has been virtually recession-free, propped up by the stability of the federal government work force, and the population has been composed solidly of professional people, with many couples earning two high incomes. But Washington never experienced anything like its boom toward the end of the 1970s.

Signs of affluence were everywhere. Specialty shops, restaurants, shopping centers sprang up all around. The housing market soared dizzyingly. Washington had always regarded itself seriously, in a leaden self-important sort of way, but now the city was brisker and assumed a new style. Suddenly it was fashionable, even glamorous. Its peculiarly intertwined social and professional relationships—all knit around government, politics, and power— were more complex and dynamic. Its absorption and preoccupation with power grew.

As more and more professional people—lawyers, doctors, consultants—came to the city to do business with the federal government, the wealth increased. By Carter's inauguration day, Washington's metropolitan area had far outstripped all other urban centers in America in income, education, sales, and per-capita consumption of luxury goods. The demographics were stunning. Average household income was $27,722 and rising. More than a quarter of Washington's adults had college degrees, and 15 percent had done postgraduate work. Two of its suburban counties, Montgomery in Maryland and Fairfax in Virginia, had the highest proportion of households in the nation earning over $25,000. It had the largest percentage of white-collar workingwomen—two out of every five—earning more than twice as much as women nationally, and the highest percentage of overall white-collar employment. Its work force was also the most stable. Some 80 percent of its adults owned one car, nearly half the households had two. Nearly half a million people in the Washington area owned imported cars—Mercedes and Volvos and Audis were seen everywhere. In 1977, seventy thousand people bought new automatic dishwashers, and nearly a quarter of a million purchased new electric crockpots. Its net buying income per household outranked New York, Chicago, and Los Angeles. Its proportion of scientists and engineers per household was double that of any other major city. It had more lawyers and psychiatrists per capita by far, consumed proportionally more alcohol, and used more telephones.

Both the 1960 and 1970 censuses showed Washington with the highest growth rate of any major metropolitan area. Its growth mirrored that of the federal government: from 1940 to 1960, the area's population had doubled from one to two million. Close to another million were added during the 1960s. Then, in the early 1970s, Washington's population growth slowed (as did the nation's). But while the country struggled through the worst economic slump since the depression, the capital's economy in the mid-1970s expanded robustly. Across the nation federal employment was decreasing; in Washington it was rising. Family income continued to climb well in excess of national averages. The unemployment rate, although higher than before, still remained well below the nation's.

One indicator best showed the nature of the changes. By 1970 metropolitan Washington had become the number one retail market in the United States. Despite the economic slowdown elsewhere, Washington witnessed tremendous increases in the number and size of its retail facilities. In the first four years of the 1970s, eleven new shopping centers opened—more than 5 million square feet of new floor space, equal to 70 percent of the retail space built during the growth years of the 1960s! And there was more to come. In 1977, two massive new shopping centers containing such luxury department stores as Bloomingdale's, Neiman-Marcus, and Lord & Taylor opened in the area, and still the boom continued. To go out to those stores, on any weekend, was to step into a laboratory for the sociologists. Nothing in dress, manner, or demeanor marked the throngs of shoppers as a special class: no trappings of nobility, no airs of the old carriage trade. Just hordes of people, many of them young, intently buying diamonds at Black, Starr & Frost, copper espresso machines at Bloomingdale's, furs at Neiman-Marcus.

But the greatest sense of such widespread affluence came when one traveled through any neighborhood, on any day, wherever houses were advertised for sale. In twenty-eight of the District of Columbia's fifty-three residential neighborhoods, half of the houses on the market were selling for over $100,000. Several neighborhoods had median sales of well over $200,000, one over $300,000. Across the Potomac, in Arlington, a year-old townhouse was advertised one Saturday morning. So many potential buyers showed up within hours that even the veteran agent found the situation "unreal." A contract was placed on the house that day. The purchasers put down $100,000 in cash. In northwest Washington, where many top government officials and bureaucrats live, the lowest price range for a house considered barely habitable was between $75,000 and $100,000. In the central city, where flames from the riots in 1968 had left piles of bricks and people afraid to walk the streets at night, neighborhoods were being "renewed," but not by the government. There, people were paying $65,000 and up for what an agent candidly called "just a bombed-out shell." In the Cleveland Park section of Washington, west of Connecticut Avenue and away from Rock Creek Park, a house was advertised at $450,000. It was snapped up that same day—for cash. A realtor reported another property for sale in the same section, a house needing complete repairs and renovation. The asking price: $200,000. It sold immediately. And Georgetown, Spring Valley, Wesley Heights, Forest Hills, Embassy Row boasted even greater overall property values.

"Nobody ever thought we'd see the prices we're seeing today," said a longtime Washington realtor whose listed properties began at $112,000 and went up to an embassy structure at $750,000. "The market's going crazy. And this pressure is building. We have more real-estate agents than houses. Everybody's coming to Washington, everybody wants to be in the city."

□   □   □

Since the 1960s, the lawyers, lobbyists, trade-association representatives, and members of private consulting and research firms in Washington had been multiplying. As they became a greater force in the economy, the proportion of federal employees in the area's total work force declined from about 40 to about 25 percent.

Corporations greatly expanded their Washington operations. Some began moving their headquarters there. By the end of the 1970s, Washington had surpassed New York as the leading trade-association city. More than a fourth of the nation's 4700 major trade groups were based in the city. Their growing involvement with Congress and the regulatory agencies created demands for more lawyers, lobbyists, public-relations consultants. The number of lobbyists alone was said to have doubled in five years' time. In less than a decade, so had the number of lawyers. Trade-association groups were employing some fifty thousand people and pouring nearly a billion dollars a year into the Washington economy. With their high salaries and expense accounts, they set off intense pressures for more office space and homes—and for restaurants and watering places.

Washington was transformed. Along K Street, in the center of the city, a cosmopolitan strip of expensive restaurants sprang up alongside new airline ticket offices to China and Czechoslovakia. Those restaurants exemplified the expense-account economy in America as it specially applied in Washington. The scene was the same in each one, night after night after night: glowing candles softly illuminating the paintings on the wall, French waiters bringing tray after tray of drinks (at $4 a glass) to tables filled almost all by men, the sounds of Southern drawls and Western twangs mix-

ing with the tones of Boston and the Midwest. Dinner for two—
$80.

Interspersed with the restaurants were the offices: the arms consultants (retired admirals and generals among them); consulting
firms dealing with the Middle East; lobbying headquarters, like the
American Association of Retired Persons representing 10 million
people. (From the multitudinous associations listed in column
after column in the telephone directory you could chart the nature
and growth of national power groups.) Everyone, and everything,
it seemed, was now represented by a special-interest group. None
of these talents came cheap. The lawyers and lobbyists often commanded extraordinary salaries.

The relationship between the government and the law firms was
rife with potential conflicts of interest. Bar association committees
on ethics debated about the so-called "revolving door" syn-
drome—the practice by which lawyers left a government agency,
joined a private Washington firm, and began working on cases
they had been substantially involved in within the government. It
was an old question, and there were not many good new answers.
Corporations naturally wanted to hire lawyers and firms with the
most expertise—and personal contacts—in areas directly affecting
their interests.

Two weeks after Carter took office, the Senate Government Operations Committee issued findings of a year-and-a-half-long investigation. The results underlined what everyone already knew: a
flow of officials in both directions was occurring between federal
regulatory agencies and the industries they were supposed to regulate. "There should be an arm's length distance between the reg-
ulators and the regulated industry," said the chairman, Senator
Abraham Ribicoff of Connecticut. "Instead, all too often the regu-
lators either have been—or soon become—the regulated." Responsible regulatory agencies had done "very little," the report
said, to ensure enforcement and policing of conflict-of-interest
laws.

Washington offices were filled with people who had held high
government posts—cabinet officers, agency heads, senators, members of the House, governors, White House officials. Joseph Califano, who was to be Carter's first secretary of Health, Education

and Welfare, was a classic example. Califano had worked in the
Pentagon for Robert McNamara during the Kennedy years and
then in the White House under Lyndon Johnson. During the eight
years of Nixon's presidency, Califano was in private practice with a
Washington law firm. He earned $500,000 the year before he went
back into the federal government at the age of forty-five.

People like Califano were all over Washington. Autographed
pictures, framed copies of Herblock cartoons, and other political
mementos of their government careers adorned their offices.
They'd show you pictures taken at two in the morning of some
fateful presidential phone call or of a tense group gathered to deal
with a now-forgotten national crisis. Like Califano, who was also
general counsel to the Democratic National Committee after leaving the White House, they kept up their political contacts, lunched
at the same clubs, went to the same dinner parties, and waited to
go back into government.

Some formed a senior old guard, whose experience made them
invaluable to the government and to those who paid for their private counsel. Many of the most noted names registered with the
Justice Department as agents of foreign governments or businesses. Clark Clifford's Washington law firm, for instance, had been
paid $1,725,000 on an annual retainer from 1971 until 1977 by
the government of Algeria. The Algerians also retained the Washington law firm of which J. William Fulbright, former chairman of
the Senate Foreign Relations Committee, had become a member;
and they paid Nixon's attorney general during Watergate, Richard
Kleindienst, nearly $10,000 a month after he left the government.

These kinds of figures were not the average Washington lawyer,
or firm, but they were standards against which others measured
themselves. Knowledge of such fees and annual incomes tended to
force increases in legal bills all down the line.

Competition for talent was stiff, and demands for a strong
Washington presence were rising. An internal memo from one
Washington trade-association representative to his individual cor-
porate clients three months after Carter took office was revealing:

> Every aspect of Government affects the carpet industry. There is
> no agency of government, whether the Federal Trade Commission,
> the Consumer Protection Agency, the Justice Department, the

White House Office of Consumer Affairs or the Federal Housing
Authority, that does not have an impact on our business. At least
five of the President's new energy proposals will directly alter how
we are currently doing business. And, finally, there is virtually no
committee of Congress that does not directly or indirectly pass legislation which affects us.

The message to that billion-dollar industry was typical: its trade
association, the Carpet & Rug Institute, "must continue to be vigi-
lant in Washington. The Government Affairs Committee has in
the past, and will in the future, play a major role in our Association."

Lewis Engman, former Federal Trade Commission chairman,
was typical of many officials who left government. In Carter's first
year he opened a Washington office for a Grand Rapids, Michi-
gan, law firm. "Government regulations used to affect only the
General Motors' of the country, but now they affect medium-sized
businesses in Kalamazoo," he said. Just how dramatically those
regulations had grown could be seen in the pages of *The Federal
Register,* the official publication listing each new U.S. regulation. In
1970 *The Register* published 20,036 pages. Five years later the
number was 60,221—a 201 percent increase. Either more regulations were being passed with greater rapidity or they were more
complicated. Whichever way, it meant that more lawyers were
needed to interpret them, and more lawyers and Washington
"reps" meant more business and higher costs for the Washington
area.

It wasn't just the regulatory agencies and the law firms who had
revolving doors; the defense establishment had long supplied personnel and money to firms in Washington doing business with the
government. Nearly 150,000 people worked for the Defense Department in the Washington area, some 60,000 of them in uniform. Those billions of dollars in defense contracts let each year
by the Defense Department supported a vast number of private
businesses.

This explosion of private money and talent came on top of a
hugely increased payroll for federal workers in Washington,
whose financial fortunes, while nowhere near the level reached by
private firms, had improved notably over the years. In the Wash-

ington area, the average federal worker was earning $18,862 when Carter assumed power. The civil-service scales went up from a grade one messenger low of $6219 a year through eighteen other grade levels to a top of $58,245. Mandated pay increases provided for annual raises over a ten-year period in all but the top categories. At the top were the cabinet jobs, paying $66,000, the deputy secretaries at $57,500, the under secretaries at $52,500, the assistant secretaries at $50,000, and the unit administrators at $47,500—all those serving at the pleasure of the president, without civil-service protection.

In the years when federal pay rates had lagged behind private business, the oft-expressed danger was that poor pay would drive the best people out of government. But public-opinion polls showed that government workers then were esteemed and esprit was higher. As Herbert Hoover said at the time he headed his monumental commission on government in 1946, "Our biggest problem is to get the kind of men and women the government needs and to keep them in government." A key to that objective was better pay. After long struggle and debate that battle was won. By 1970 the federal government had adopted the principle of paying its employees the same rate as comparable private jobs. But while the pay and pensions were equal if not better—and some studies strongly indicated that government now led industry in wages and benefits—morale had plummeted and public disapproval soared.

Still, the money was good and government service could be an apprenticeship to more affluent service as a business consultant, research-foundation adviser, lobbyist, or lawyer.

□   □   □

When I came to Washington in the summer of 1957, the city was segregated and smug. It was still largely the Southern outpost of the past, and its leisurely pace and insular ways bred a stultifying atmosphere. Everything revolved around politics and government, and these moved with a motion of their own: they affected all relationships and defined all styles. The simple clean lines of the White House and stately grace of the Capitol remained as testaments to the best instincts of America's early Federal period, but already the monumental cast of mind that enveloped the city and its inhabitants was at work, with ill effects. I saw government, in its wisdom, try to destroy some of Washington's grandest structures—the graceful old State and War Department building next to the White House; the Court of Claims across the street; the Post Office, with its turrets and elegant stonemasonry, standing watch on Pennsylvania Avenue midway between the Capitol and White House; the rows of splendid Federal homes surrounding Lafayette Square. (Thanks to sufficiently vigorous public protests, these were saved.) At the same time I saw government, in its wisdom, put up some of the most atrocious buildings in America—great cold buff-colored blocks of cement, neo–Third Reich style, like the J. Edgar Hoover FBI headquarters, which resembles a gigantic pillbox set on stilts, an ultimate bunker; the massively pompous Rayburn House Office Building, the most expensive of all government buildings until it was succeeded in price and ugliness by the FBI headquarters; and the forbiddingly unattractive Housing and Urban Development Building—a fitting expression of the government's sense of urban renewal.

I have also seen Washington's special way of life at work in other ways—in the dispensing of privilege, in the growth of congressional power, in the formation of new and deeper relationships among the politicians, journalists, lobbyists, and professional staff officers—but nowhere was it more visible than on Capitol Hill.

When Jimmy Carter raised his right hand on that frosty high noon of his inaugural day, a half a billion dollars' worth of federal construction was under way in the Washington area. Of that, half was for the needs of Congress alone. On Capitol Hill, the sound of jackhammers rang out daily. Along Constitution Avenue cranes rose from a huge hole in the ground: the site of Senate Office Building Number Three, a $123 million job that would add another private gymnasium with indoor tennis court and private dining room offering a rooftop view of the city, among other amenities. On the other side of the Hill, workmen were laboring on another marbled governmental home: the third building to house the ever-growing needs of the Library of Congress, a project that, when completed, would be the most expensive federal building ever constructed ($130 million would top by a million or so the FBI headquarters). Farther away, along the railroad tracks, more work proceeded: a major extension to the United States Capitol Power Plant, which provided all the steam and water for all the buildings on the Hill. If Parkinson's Law dictates that work expands so as to fill the time allotted to it, Washington's law ordains that space expands to house the people to perform the work that Congress creates.

In 1965 a management-consultant firm studied Congress and concluded: "In the twenty-five years between 1940 and 1965 the context of congressional performance has been altered dramatically: population has increased forty-seven percent; gross national product, six hundred sixty percent; the federal budget, one thousand percent; defense spending, thirty-five hundred percent; and federally sponsored research and development, five thousand percent." For another decade, up to the presidential election year of 1976, Congress's appetite for new staff and new space remained voracious. The number of House and Senate employees doubled, while the number of House committee staff members increased nearly fourfold. Accompanying this was an exponential rise in subcommittees: *their* chairmen and ranking members were given authority to hire more staff members to take on more tasks. Congress was not only more assertive in exercising its powers but aggressively expansive through the committee and subcommittee structures. The House Ways and Means Committee, for example, which deals with vital tax and health insurance legislation, had only fifteen members in 1960; by 1976 its staff had increased to seventy-six—lawyers, economists, speechwriters, analysts—and its subcommittees numbered six.

In 1976 nearly twenty thousand employees were on the congressional payroll. Its special police force of some eleven hundred uniformed officers ranked perhaps as the largest in the world in relation to the number of people protected. Special operations such as the Congressional Research Service produced reports and data on any subject an individual member or an entire committee wished. Nor does this take into account the thousands and thousands of people working directly for senators and representatives in their Washington offices. Congressmen employed some seven thousand people on their personal staffs.

Space—lots of it—was needed to accommodate these and many

other workings of the legislative branch, and space—cost notwith-standing—was provided. Numbers of employees and square foot-age of office space and dollar figures aren't the most significant measure of Congress's imprint on life in Washington, but they of-fer a clear symbol of political privilege.

In 1933 Raymond Clapper, a superb reporter, described a Washington that has essentially remained constant, no matter how many other changes swept the city and country in the years to come:

> When Senators and Congressmen arrive in Washington for the first time, they quickly fall under the influence of a very congenial, comfortable and comparatively luxurious atmosphere.
>
> "There is nothing that will sap the backbone of a man like life in Washington," said Senator William Borah once in discussing the seductive influences which numb the conscience of the unwary pub-lic servant.
>
> These new arrivals in the Congress find free barbershop service, free use of the mails, mileage which they vote themselves some-times without even leaving Washington, and comfortable jobs into which they may slip wives, children, in-laws and other relatives, many of whom do not even live in Washington.
>
> The Senator soon realizes that he is a privileged figure, rather than a public servant. He steps up to a private elevator, gives three sharp rings and the elevator hurries to carry him. He enters a pri-vate dining room in which only he and his personal guests may eat food that is served by waiters who are paid out of the Senate appro-priation. The taxpayer who supports these comforts eats in a less sumptuous restaurant outside of the sacred portals. Should he be so hapless as to be riding on an elevator when a Senator wishes to use it, he continues to ride up and down until the Senator is taken aboard and disposed of.

Two generations later masseurs still toil over pink forms in the steam baths of the Senate, waiters still serve the fine cut-rate meals subsidized by public funds in the private Capitol Hill restau-rants, congressional employees still operate the private elevators, barbers still snip away at the locks of senators and congressmen at reduced charges, chauffeurs still maneuver fleets of gleaming gov-ernment limousines, carpenters and craftsmen still frame the pho-tographs and cartoons for congressional members to display for their visiting constituents, and clerks still sell everything from stationery to typewriters at discount rates in the basement shops under the House and Senate Office buildings.

Each new marbled palace that opens on the Hill becomes another monument to a way of Washington life. When the Rayburn Office Building opened in the spring of 1965 its marble and granite walls enclosed five handsomely paneled handball courts, tiled steam baths, a $500,000 swimming pool, His and Her gymnasiums—all carefully screened from public view—as well as thirty elevators, twenty-three escalators, soaring committee rooms with mahogany paneling, two-storied rooms with ceilings in which American eagles were carved, heroic statuary, courtyards, fountains, and 169 congressional suites (each consisting of three rooms, two baths, wall-to-wall carpeting and appropriate furnishings), assorted restaurants, underground garages, and a subway.

Privilege took other forms: five well-equipped medical clinics, attended by Navy doctors and corpsmen, care for members of Congress and their staffs. Free medicine, free annual physicals, and complete laboratory and X-ray services are provided to the elected members as well as free immunization and allergy programs for them, their families, and their staffs. In a city of automobiles, with parking at a premium, Congress has more than taken care of itself. Special lots and underground garages can be found all over Capitol Hill.* To ease the strains of travel, a VIP parking lot for members of Congress, Supreme Court justices, and diplomats nestles at the doors of National Airport's main terminal, one of the busiest areas and most difficult in which to park. The VIP lot is, of course, maintained by the taxpayers at, naturally, increasing cost each year. (The government takes care of its own: out of 4500 so-called public parking spaces in Washington built at government expense, U.S. workers and airline employees are allowed to park in 3500 of them for $15 a *year*. The public pays al-

---

*The underground parking lot is a Washington fixture. During the depths of the depression, in the Hoover period, senators found enough money to spend $817,000 for a new underground garage that included illuminated fountains and ornamental terraces covering it. That early garage covered two city blocks and came equipped with automatic doors that opened as a senator's car approached— then a rarity in the country. Interior Department employees were detached to care for the senators' cars.

most that much in a *day*—when it can find the space, which often it cannot.)

Rank is enshrined in Washington. Political "perks," depending on position, range from a government car and driver to a chopper leaving from a Pentagon or White House heliport. Cabinet officers, no matter how little time they serve, are captured on canvas by prominent artists in works commissioned at government expense. Upon leaving office, their life-size oil portraits become part of the permanent exhibit on the corridor walls.

Size of offices, grandness of appointments (a built-in bar enclosed in mahogany rates high), and luxury of furnishings establish an inviolate pecking order—an order that in time becomes fixed in formal government regulations. Amendment D-47, Subsection 101-17, 304-1, June 1974, of the Federal Property Management Regulations specifies "work station space" for each category of government civil-service workers. The lowest grades, one through six, are allowed sixty square feet per person. In the next four grades nonsupervisory workers are permitted seventy-five square feet each, supervisors one hundred square feet. These space allocations go up according to rank until the top three grades—they're permitted 300 square feet per person!

Cabinet officers are not governed by these strictures. Their suites are grandest of all, and often include private dining and conference rooms and private projection booths for the showing of films.

□ □ □

John Kennedy was our first television president, and Washington the world's first television capital. Through television, and the Kennedy administration's skillful use of it, Americans shared more intimately in the lives of their leaders than ever before. They saw the First Family at home inside the White House. They watched the president conduct live-television press conferences. They observed *Air Force One* lifting off at dawn, carrying the president and his party on a critical foreign mission. They witnessed the Cuban missile crisis through the eyes of the president. They participated in the death, funeral, and national mourning of a president through the television camera. Television personalized the presidency and by its ceaseless attention glorified it. In the age of television, all national events revolved around the White House and the Oval Office. Politicians seeking greater national exposure courted television. Would-be presidents aimed their strategies at projecting themselves most favorably—and most often—on it. Groups protesting national policies, from war and peace to abortion and civil rights, clamored to be presented over the camera. In my years there I've seen Washington become the demonstration capital, as well as the political capital. Indians, blacks, farmers, women, poor people all come to be shown back to the country via television. And television accommodates them.

The city abounds with electronic-media correspondents of local, national, and foreign affiliation. They are part of a larger, growing communications industry that embraces ninety-five separate establishments and employs twenty-five thousand people. Twenty-two hundred reporters are accredited to cover the White House and Congress.

Washington journalists too have become members of a privileged economic group. On *The Washington Post,* the city's largest paper, the average salary of reporters and photographers stands at $29,100, with the top at $50,000. Within four years of work after college a reporter is guaranteed at least $26,000. Throughout the city journalistic salaries in the $50,000–$60,000 category are common. Syndicated columnists, commentators, editors, and specialists earn much more, their incomes often handsomely augmented by fat lecture fees—as high as $3500 a speech. Some columnists make forty and more speeches in a year.

Thanks to extensive public exposure and attention focused on the press during the Watergate years, some journalists have become celebrities. When Jimmy Carter was first introduced to Bob Woodward, the president told the reporter how honored he was to meet him. And for some, a tour of government duty enhances their professional standing. John Chancellor became a network anchorman after serving as director of the Voice of America under Lyndon Johnson. Carl Rowan became a syndicated columnist after work in the State Department, then ambassador to Finland and director of the U.S. Information Agency. Bill Moyers and George Will came to the press after working in the government—Moyers in the Peace Corps and White House as press secretary, Will as aide to a Republican senator. Other journalists go from the press into government. Capitol Hill offices hold many former Washington newsmen.

Ideological bias isn't the problem with the Washington press. If anything, the press is biased toward the system, suspicious of the new, distrustful of the maverick, comfortable with the conventional. The Eugene McCarthys and George Romneys are written off as hopeless because they don't know the game, and if there is anything the press knows it's the game. The press knows the players, travels with the politicians and presidents, makes the campaign swings, recites the political lore. Presidential elections are seen as horse races and so written. The press is the handicapper, it picks the winners, and it expects the winners to perform in customary political ways.

Sometimes, of course, close relationships develop between individual members of the press and politicians. They aren't in the best traditions of an independent press, nor in the proper adversary role of the press toward the government.* And sometimes the press is too protective of politicians, particularly presidents. In the summer of 1967 Senator Fulbright described *The Washington Post* as "a newspaper which has obsequiously supported the administration's policy in Vietnam," and President Lyndon Johnson told the editor of the *Post* that his editorials were worth a division to him. (LBJ later appointed J. Russell Wiggins, the editor, as America's ambassador to the United Nations.)

Watergate and the saga of Woodward and Bernstein gives a false impression of the Washington press corps. Its reputation for tenacious independence and unremitting criticism of government officials is, at best, a recent phenomenon and generally unde-

---

*In 1968 I had such an experience. Over the years Robert Kennedy and I had developed a close, if sometimes stormy, friendship. On the night before he announced his presidential candidacy, he asked me to work for him. I declined. Several months later, just before his campaign moved to the West Coast, a mutual friend brought another request from Kennedy: he didn't feel he was getting through to the public and asked if I'd write a speech draft for him. I did. When I got to Oregon, where I saw him for the first time during the campaign, I listened to my words coming from his lips. The next day, I joined his campaign, as he left for California—where he was killed one week later. I had crossed a line a reporter never should.

served. For years the relationship developed between the working press and Washington officials had been comfortable. The press cooperated—indeed, it often helped draft the rules—in mutually advantageous private meetings, during which public officials advanced positions—many dubious, many purely political—under a cloak of anonymity. These "background" meetings, as they were called, became grist for the Washington press mill and indispensable for Washington officials. The press was their willing accomplice in government secrecy, trial balloons, and justifications for policy failures.

Back in the 1930s background sessions were usually reserved for a privileged few newspapermen, an elite who spoke with authority and influence from their long status as national commentators. What Arthur Krock or Walter Lippmann or James Reston said was believed to come from the very top—and usually it did. All journalists willingly adhered to rules first promulgated by Ernest Lindley, then a *Newsweek* magazine correspondent and later a State Department consultant, according to which the journalists did not attribute to a named person the information they were told in "backgrounders." "It was a system of compulsory plagiarism and it served us well," Lindley recalled.

Over the years the background briefings became institutionalized. Diplomats, generals, admirals, cabinet officers, White House officials, and the president himself conducted such sessions for an ever-larger group of Washington correspondents. As the practice spread and the sessions proliferated, the backgrounder changed. It ceased to be an academic seminar for philosophers of the press and became instead a form of news conference conducted in private. Officials could promote pet projects and policies anonymously and pass on tidbits of gossip for which they would not be held accountable. Journalists liked the informality and the close association with the cream of the Washington crop. They could glory in the social friendships they developed. It was heady to be able to call the eminent cabinet member or famous ambassador by his first name, and even more gratifying and seductive to be referred to in turn on a first-name basis. This familiar practice reached its apogee while Henry Kissinger was secretary of state. Prominent journalists would refer, with casual pride, to "Henry," but when they traveled with Kissinger on his "shuttle diplomacy" flights they played by the rules and never identified him as the "senior official" who was so fulsomely quoted in their reports.

Social contacts revolved around the Washington political apparat. The press had its own associations—the White House Correspondents Association, the State Department Correspondents Association, the Radio-TV Correspondents Associations—and gave black-tie dinners which political notables attended. At the annual Gridiron Club banquet, a white-tie-and-tails affair with four courses, three wines, champagne, and entertainment by the Marine Band, everything anyone said, including the president, was off-the-record—and this in a room filled with the owners of America's press empires, leading columnists, commentators, and just plain reporters.

Private breakfast and luncheon groups were formed by heads of newspaper bureaus, columnists, and those writing about foreign affairs. At the private clubs—the Metropolitan, the Cosmos, the Federal City—officials and leaders of the Washington legal and lobbying establishment dined regularly with members of the press. The same was true of what passed for Washington society. In the Georgetown salons or Capitol Hill town houses, ranking members of the press were essential guests at parties congressmen and senators, ambassadors, and occasionally the vice-president attended. Politics was the purpose of these parties: power and position, who was in and who out, what policies were succeeding and what failing, whose fortunes were rising and whose declining were the topics that dominated the conversations.

From such gatherings, and from the daily "background" breakfasts and luncheons, emerged the great Washington cliché: the "conventional wisdom" of the city. The press dispensed this conventional wisdom to the nation—ingrown and smug, assured of its place, and content to remain a central part of the club.

But despite this smug fraternal air, attitudes within the journalistic community had altered by Carter's presidency. The legacy of Vietnam and Watergate was destructive: a near venomous state of relations between the press and the foreign-policy and executive establishment, with ill will growing out of mutual charges of deception, irresponsibility, lying, inaccuracy, sensationalism, news management, lack of credibility and trust. Much of the comfortable atmosphere that characterized press-government relations at the presidential level had dissipated. In the Vietnam-Watergate years the press learned it had allowed itself to be used by presidents. And the embarrassing example of two young unknown reporters' proving what many senior journalists dismissed as impossible or unlikely taught another lesson—not to be so trusting again. Probably no president would enjoy the kind of cheering-squad support granted by much of the Washington press corps before Nixon.

Jimmy Carter's personal relations with the press complicated what would have been at best difficulties for any new chief executive. By the time of his election, much of the acclaim dating from his initial primary victories had evaporated. The long campaign brought out mutual anger, strains, and suspicions between Carter, his young aides, and the press. "The more I see Carter, the more I wonder about his kind of behavior," James Perry wrote in *The National Observer*. "He is a very tough fellow, he seems to nurse grudges and he tends to lash out at people who criticize him, even when their intentions are purely honorable." That was a fairly typical press view. As Carter's campaign lead had dwindled and almost vanished, the Washington press corps had come to express the doubts and criticisms voiced by Washington political operatives, and it highlighted stories about Carter's ineptness, his enigmatic nature, his sweeping promises. And underneath everything was this reality: Carter and his people really *were* outsiders. They did not know Washington's political press as most of the other politicians did. Or Washington, the political city, either.

□   □   □

For decades organized labor was the predominant lobbying power in Washington. No other sector of the American people brought its collective weight to bear on so many aspects of government. It was labor that provided the base for most of the progressive social and economic legislation starting with the New Deal and, in some respects, labor could lay claim to being the heart of the Democratic Party; it had long mounted the single most effective political operation in the nation.

Labor was not enamored of Carter, and labor's leader, the

crusty octogenarian George Meany, didn't speak the same language or hold the same values as the Georgian. Their first meeting, during the primaries, had been icy, leaving ill will and obvious anger. "We noted that captivating smile that stopped at the eyes," an important labor operative said of Carter. But labor worked aggressively for Carter in the hope he would be a Democratic president in the Truman-Kennedy tradition—or could be taught to be so. In fact, Carter couldn't have been elected without labor's political efforts in New York, Pennsylvania, and Ohio. "You people do good work," Carter told Meany in a telephone call late in the night of his election. Meany, in his gruff manner, said he was delighted. Go on and be a great president, he said.

If labor feared that it was not going to have as much influence as it had in the past in a Democratic White House, its power on Capitol Hill was also waning. Big business, which had once been leery of public lobbying for fear of inspiring antitrust actions, had become much more aggressive. For the first time business political-action committees came close to matching the money spent by labor in the national campaign. Special-interest lobbies proliferated in Washington—well organized, often around single issues, and heavily funded, they were part of a fundamental change in the nature of power in Washington. Their influence would make presidential leadership all the more difficult.

□   □   □

In novels and television melodramas about Washington, the city is awash with fixers and influence-peddlers and bagmen dispensing bribes. In life, payoffs do occur, without doubt, although they are far removed from the Washington most people experience. For years one oil lobbyist in Washington passed out millions in cash. (When the wife of a newly arrived oil-company executive gave her first dinner party she told me she was shocked to find that some people there expected to receive envelopes containing cash.) The South Korean Tongsun Park, a prodigal Georgetown party giver, was his country's agent in attempting to influence Washington in the old-fashioned way—with cash. (A scene, testified to at a congressional hearing, of the Korean ambassador dis-

covered behind his desk counting huge stacks of one hundred
dollar bills could have come right off the evening television dra-
mas.) And you can talk to a former top aide to a congressional
committee and hear him say: "I could have made a great deal of
money when I was working on the Hill. I could have become rich.
When I say rich, I mean a couple of million dollars." Delegations
representing organized crime had sought him out, wanting him to
help introduce an immigration bill to bring a certain family to the
United States—or to keep another from being deported. The payoff for such services would be in cash, or in stock options, or in the
opportunity to lease a luxurious home at a pittance over a long-
term rental agreement. Gambling money also found its way to the
Hill, he said. "It's also true the amount of cash contributions by
lobbyists in this town is very substantial."

Other Hill aides tell of their problems with the seamier side of
politics, for their bosses' races. "Cash was always desirable," one
said, "because by the time election day came around there was always money to spend—hiring poll watchers, renting cars, getting
additional office help. I have made many, many trips back to my
state with a briefcase full of money—in twenty or hundred dollar
bills, as much as twenty-three thousand dollars at a time."

But these were not the most insidious aspects of corruption in
Washington. The city bred its own special form: a sometimes poisonous intoxication from close association with power. An assistant to a congressman (later indicted) would pick up his office
phone and announce, "This is the Speaker calling." Those who
received such calls recall his voice even took on the timbre and
pitch of his boss, Speaker John McCormack, whom he had served
long and anonymously. The aide was typical of some who came to
feel they were the real power behind the office, and in time began
acting as if they *were* the senator or congressman.

In the press the poison sometimes meant accepting gifts or en-
treatments—at the expense of later candid criticism in print. Each
New Year's Eve special messengers delivered the finest Iranian
caviar to selected Washington journalists: gifts from the shah of
Iran courtesy of the shah's ambassador, Ardeshir Zahedi, one of
the lions of the Washington social scene. Zahedi delivered more
than caviar; it seems he, too, was dispensing cash from a $25,000

monthly slush fund. But the daily reality for congressional staffs, the bureaucracy, and most of the press was more mundane.

The work of the congressional staffs involved more drudgery than drama. They answered and signed the senators' mail, wrote the speeches, arranged for interviews, became involved in patronage, helped to select witnesses and prepare for hearings, advised and briefed the House members on technical issues that affected every American, dealt with important constituents, lobbyists, the press, ordinary citizens, and contacted government agencies on a multitude of problems that were the essence of government work. Like the bureaucrats—and the reporters and lobbyists and lawyers—they worked long and hard hours. They were subjected to pressures, personality conflicts, and occasional temptations. Nearly all could make more money outside government. But despite their personal frustrations ("There's more intrigue in one congressional office than anywhere outside the Kremlin," one said), many chose to stay for a lifetime on the Hill, sublimating their own personalities and careers to those of their elected superiors. The headlines must go to the senator, not the staff person; to the congressman, not the committee. As one influential member of a prestigious Senate committee put it, "When the system works best, it works best unknown."

These people, along with all the other groups in political Washington, studied the "system" and eventually mastered it. They knew whom to call, whom to trust, what levers to push, what red tape to cut. On the Hill as in the press, they tended to travel in the same circles, attend the same private clubs, form their own social associations, and meet for theater and cocktail parties. One of the earliest groups, the Association for Administrative Assistants and Secretaries, was started in the 1930s as a means to get congressional aides a pay raise. "The first time I went to one of those functions, there were Lyndon Johnson and old Ev Dirksen," one person remembered. LBJ had served as a congressman's assistant.

Familiarity, anonymity, contacts, sources, influence—these are the hallmarks of Washington's political networks. To understand how the networks function requires experience, and also an appreciation of a common fact about the people who make up the various political components: they are in Washington, they'll tell you, because they are at the center of action; in their own right, they are people of power and influence.

"After a while you learn that there aren't any new issues, only the numbers on the bills," a legislative assistant said. "And while you want good public policy, you also know what's good politics for your man." They were in a position to affect the bills and the issues, just as the press affected the public's knowledge of them. They believed what they were doing was important, and for many it was; for others it was just a job.

□   □   □

Washington isn't America, it's often said. An addiction to politics, a preoccupation with power, a certain staleness, an incestuous society, and an enjoyment of widespread affluence certainly set the city apart. "Washington taste is much like Washington ambition: calculated," the British journalist Jan Morris wrote, adding: "Nowhere in the world, I think, do people take themselves more seriously than they do in Washington, or seem so indifferent to other perceptions than their own. Whether they are granite reactionaries or raging revolutionaries, they find it hard to see beyond."

True, all. Yes, Washington lacks the pulsating humanity of New York; the solid dignity and grace of London; the charm and vivacity of Paris. But the city I've seen evolve over the years possesses other attributes that distinguish it. I've witnessed another city besides the political one rising along the Potomac, and it's the more interesting.

Monumental stolidity notwithstanding, Washington always had been blessed by physical beauty. Its thick woods and streams, running throughout the leisurely length of Rock Creek Park, are filled with wildlife, with muskrat and foxes and rabbits; hawks still circle the city's patches of glens and forest. Streets are lined with splendid old shade and flowering trees; parks dotting the central city are tended with patient care and planted with an array of tulip and rose beds and annuals, with marigolds, scarlet sages, dahlias, snapdragons, begonias, geraniums. Washington, as one of its bureaucrats wrote in the year the atomic age was born, "makes room for nature in its midst and seems to welcome it." Louis Halle went on to draw a distinction between the physical look of Washington and the political reality:

> The government has no department that takes cognizance of life itself; it posts no watchers out of doors to sniff the wind and inform those within of eternity. That is volunteer work, good occupation for a man. It is not for government personnel, who are preoccupied with official transactions on paper. These are workers in the hive of our civilization, and the hive is their universe. They trouble themselves about the real universe, as Henry Adams puts it, "much as a hive of honey-bees troubles about the ocean, only as a region to be avoided."

For years Washington's character was defined by the government beehive. Though the political issues and topics seem to change, in reality they remain depressingly the same. To reread the newspapers about, say, a stifling week in August twenty-two years ago as I arrived in the city, is to find an eerie similarity in the news: the House is delaying for one year a bill on natural-gas regulation, senators are looking into a bribery story, Congress is debating "small" and "relatively clean" nuclear weapons, the president is worrying about spending pressures on his budget, a congressional committee is voting higher postal rates, the Post Office is promising a scheme to speed the mails, scientists are testing a cancer-detection machine, Bob Hope is opening a five-day engagement, the news organizations are talking about the prospects of opening bureaus in Mainland China. And Walter Lippmann, everyone's wise man, is pontificating thus: "What we are now saying to the Russians and they are saying to us about . . . China, the Middle East and disarmament is said without any expectation that it might lead to an agreement."

These immutable workings of political Washington served as something of an official screen, a Potemkin Village façade that hid the city as it was. The lines of agate type in the classifieds, not the news columns, gave best evidence of what Washington was really like then: COLORED—WIS. AV. and COLORED—KALORAMA.

For all intents, Washington was a place of prejudice and bigotry. The subject of race dominated conversations—and life. To be white was to hear fearsome tales of "colored" or "Negro" depredations, tales that fueled the notion of Washington as Crime Capital, USA. Washington was the nation's first city to have a black majority; the largest black city outside of Africa, it was said disparagingly. Whites were in open flight from the city. The suburbs were the sanctuary. Debate, among liberals, at least, was on how best to cut that suburban "white noose" around the city and permit "Negroes" to live out there, too. Professional clubs, without exception, were segregated.

Social life was in any case stagnant. No good restaurants existed. The city was a cultural backwash. (A great debate ensued about opening a sidewalk café on Pennsylvania Avenue. There was none in the city; it was against the law. Long articles quoted officials and prominent citizens as warning that the sidewalk café would pose problems to public health and safety. Finally the café was approved, and reluctantly the social experiment of outdoor dining began.)

While the country even then deprecated Washington boondoggles and its wasteful bureaucracy, and ideologues passionately denounced the government as having a liberal, New Deal cast of mind, the workers themselves couldn't have been more solidly safe. They were stable and cautious, middle-class and middle-think. Each dawn government workers in droves moved into the government hive, each dusk they returned to the safe and sanitary suburbs. They participated in PTA's, joined the country club, and voted Republican nearly as often as Democratic.

In the first five years of social legislative pioneering under Kennedy and Johnson, the Civil Service Commission carefully eliminated from its list of job applicants twelve Communists, several thousand homosexuals, excessive drinkers, and otherwise immoral persons. Its tests assured the country would be protected from politically aberrant thinking or other forms of deviant behavior:

Has any blood relation or husband or wife had syphilis, cancer, asthma, hives, epilepsy?

Have you ever had or have you now frequent trouble sleeping, bed wetting, nervous trouble of any sort, homosexual tendencies?

Have you ever been pregnant, attempted suicide, stuttered or stammered?

Answer yes, no or uncertain: (a) I think the spread of birth control is essential to solving the world's economic and peace problems. (b) I think it is wiser to keep the nation's military forces strong than just to depend on international goodwill.

Answer true, false or uncertain: (a) I am considered a liberal "dreamer" of new ways rather than a practical follower of well-tried ways. (b) When telling a person a deliberate lie I have to look away, being ashamed to look him in the eye. (c) I am very seldom troubled by constipation.

Within a decade, during the turmoil of events in Vietnam and Watergate (and, once again, overshadowed by them), a dramatic change had occurred. Whites were flocking back into the city. Sections in the center of the city openly restricted to "colored" not so long before, were the latest in the line from Georgetown to Capitol Hill to become newly fashionable—and expensive—residences. Even the nature of the government buildings happily was beginning to change. From the massive structures designed in the fifties and sixties and completed in the early seventies, an effort was under way to soften the next generation of public buildings. At the foot of Capitol Hill, on the last major undeveloped site on Pennsylvania Avenue, the I. M. Pei-designed East Wing of the National Gallery was taking form, an inviting combination of stone and glass and light and space. Those who oversaw federal government construction struck a welcome change in tone and perspective. To them, the FBI Building marked the end of an era. "At that time the whole scheme of things was to design a building unto itself," said James Stewart, in charge of federal construction in the Washington region. "We've learned to humanize things a lot more. How does it fit with its neighbors in the community? Does it invite you in and make you feel you're a part of what's going on in this town?" And on the Hill, the new Capitol architect, George White, was arguing for a different style of work. "Our way of life has been destructive," he said, "in the sense that we've been a frontier nation. You know, tear it down and build another one and move on. We're reaching a different stage now. We want to preserve our past so we can tell where we came from, so that maybe that will put us in the direction of where we want to go. We need something human, something with human qualities, with a texture, with a color." The British writer Henry Fairlie had been away from the city for several years before coming back in 1976. "Washington seems to me, on my return, to be almost exuberant," he wrote. "I have always loved the city, but have never before thought of calling it exciting. Much of its life has always engaged me, but I have not previously regarded that life as one of unusual complexity. Its new energy seems to me as various as it is abundant."

What struck Fairlie most was the sense of blacks in the city, and how different that was from the recent past. "In no other city in America are the blacks so evidently and so vividly a part of its whole life: the public life of what I have called the public city. They are one of the creators of its appearance and its mood." Compared to other cities, blacks had prospered most in Washington. Like whites in Washington, black families led the nation in income. A black professional class unequaled anywhere had taken root. Government hiring policies, spreading to private firms, had given blacks a better share of, and greater opportunities in, Washington's booming economic marketplace.

These were by no means the whole story of race in Washington. Blacks, in whatever profession, still lagged behind whites in income and position. As in every American city, an almost unassimilable bloc formed a core of black despair, with all the attendant problems of poverty. And the government's efforts to change those lives had failed as completely in Washington as anywhere. Washington's public schools were deplorable. Its attempts at public housing were disgraceful. Huge numbers of low-income blacks had been "relocated" through urban renewal from vast areas around the Capitol and White House—and removed across the river into Anacostia, a festering section of crime and violence centering around public-housing projects. They were a part of the city, but hidden from it.

Although all the old problems of race and prejudice had not been eliminated, tensions had significantly lessened. The more malignant expressions of hatred and fear were gone, and a newer feeling of tolerance could be found. In other ways an unheard-of openness existed. The public greens became what they should always have been—places for people to sit during lunch hours, to enjoy the seasons, the city, and the sights of joggers and sidewalk vendors selling everything from plants to egg rolls.

Fairlie believed Washington was on the threshold of a new era in which it would transcend its provincial past. As Washington increased in wealth, power, culture, dynamism, and national consciousness, New York had declined. As Fairlie put it, in the past while Washington *ruled,* New York *reigned,* but that was changing now, raising the prospect of a truly national capital city.

Looking at the city on that sparkling inaugural day in 1977 I shared Fairlie's conviction, and believed Washington was ready to shake off the depressions and shocks of the last decade, and head toward something better.

4

THE COUNTRY

FRED DOXSEE had some friends over to watch the last Carter-Ford debate in his home on Carroll Street in Boone, Iowa. It was Friday night, the last week in October 1976, and the forty-eighth presidential election in America's two hundred years was little more than a week away. Like Doxsee, nearly everyone who gathered in front of his television set in the small living room was uncertain about which candidate they would support. They listened and watched intently, absorbed in the figures and words coming over the screen.

The challenger was younger, slighter, paler, with cold blue eyes, glistening teeth, and a shock of sandy hair. He spoke softly, often musically, but with too much lilt and slur to follow easily, or to allow his words to stir his audience. But he was poised and confident, and he came over well. His opponent was older, heartier, taller and stockier, balding, earnest. He spoke methodically, often ploddingly, but his pace and timing and delivery had improved from previous months. He seemed brisker, more assertive, more like a president, less like a befuddled Everyman in the White House.

When it was over, Doxsee turned off his set and he and his friends tried to express what they felt, while my tape recorder on the coffee table picked up what they said. Their words had a searching, distrusting, halting quality, but they all agreed on the critical point—Jimmy Carter of Georgia had impressed them the most, even those who still remained undecided or leaned toward Gerald Ford. Gary Clark, a salesman who travels throughout Iowa, summed up: "Ford is a stable kind of person, but I'd rather gamble and see if we couldn't improve a little bit. What the hell, I'd rather throw the dice and let Carter try."

For weeks people in Boone, like people all over the country, had been waiting for their opinions to crystallize, and feeling more and more frustrated and disenchanted as they became more and more confused about the candidates. This last television debate was crucial for them, but it hadn't answered all their questions. Doxsee was typical. Pleasant, bespectacled, his easygoing manner matching a ready smile, he was in his early fifties and working in the real-estate business. Doxsee was a World War II veteran who survived the Battle of the Bulge. When he came home to civilian life he became a Republican as a matter of course, and continued so for twenty-seven years. By the election of 1976, though, he considered himself an independent. Fred Doxsee took his citizenship seriously. He watched television news faithfully and read the newspaper every day. He even bought Jimmy Carter's autobiography, *Why Not the Best?*, to try and understand him.

But no matter how much he read or heard, Carter troubled him. "What turns me off now is this goody-goody thing that he's trying to put over on us. He really gets kind of gushy on religion, and he's trying to be something to everybody." After the debate, Doxsee viewed Carter more favorably. "He came across to me tonight much better than I had originally expected. I don't know, maybe this guy's got what somebody's looking for. And he's sharper than I gave him credit for. I had this thought several times: Maybe I'm looking for this. And then, going back to Ford, I get the same impression of Ford I've had for two years. It hasn't gone up and it hasn't gone down."

The people who had gathered in his living room were a good cross-section of Boone. Republican or Democrat, politically committed or not, they were earnest and serious as they gave their views on what they'd just seen.

Ed Smith, a young school psychologist who had been leaning to Ford: "I'm still not any closer to a decision than I was before. I tend to want to vote for Ford mainly because of his character. He's honest, no matter what other qualities he has. But Ford did not look as good to me. He gave rather shallow reasons on several issues. On the other hand, Carter seems to stand for most of the things I personally believe in. Yet can he really accomplish that as president? I still have a lot of distrust about him. I really don't know what the guy's like. He looks good, but I'm awful distrustful at this point in politics."

Richard Furman, who operated a ceramics store: "I've always felt the incumbent president had the advantage because he's got a record to stand on—and this one has not a bad record. But Ford should come across better than he does. Carter has more charisma or something. When he says something, I listen. Yet he's never really said what he's going to do if he gets the job. I don't know yet."

Mary Clark: "I don't feel uncommitted anymore. Now don't anybody hit me, but Carter can do more for our family than Ford could. And I get scared when I see the president because he seems so mean. I don't get the feeling that he cares about people. I will vote for Carter."

Lucy Smith: "Carter really has that charisma, yet you feel very suspicious of it. You know, here's this guy you never heard of before. He seems very sincere, but I'm suspicious. Ford is very sincere, too. I trust him, and I have all along leaned toward him. But Carter was kind of impressive tonight. I'm not going to let the debates swing me."

Arlene Furman: "Well, like everyone else, I've been on the fence, and this debate tonight has made up my mind. I've got more respect for Mr. Carter than I had before. I liked a lot of the things he said. I don't know that I can pinpoint them, but the statistics he gave, if true, I liked. But how do you know?"

Maureen Walter, who had been a Ronald Reagan supporter and came to the Doxsees' wanting to support Ford: "It was a little bit of a plus for Carter tonight. I like his answers to the environment question, the energy question, the constitutional amendment question. I hadn't made up my mind before this, and I still don't know how I'm going to vote."

Kenny Walter, superintendent of the United Community Schools, and a Republican: "I don't have my mind made up yet, either, but I think Carter is tugging on the right heartstrings—unemployment and that sort of thing—for a great many people. And I would have to say this: it is time for a change."

Only one person had a completely negative response. Doxsee's daughter, Cheryl, spoke up after everyone else. "I don't think I'm going to vote. I'm registered to vote and I've been thinking about [the candidates] for weeks, but especially after tonight, I don't care who wins. I don't think Carter can do more than Ford. It's just one man against a lot of people."

What was being said in Fred Doxsee's living room that night was similar to what I'd heard elsewhere. The political demographers had told me Boone was about as representative of Midwestern attitudes as I'd find, and what I found in Boone was not much different from anywhere else: There was no regional political point of view in the 1976 election.

Boone was a cliquish town. It was settled by Swedes, Norwegians, Germans, and Irish after the Civil War, and took its name from a Colonel Nathan Boone, the son of Daniel. Although Boone's population of about 13,000 had remained stable for years, the city was not isolated. The state university at Ames lay fifteen miles due east across the prairie, and many people in Boone worked in Des Moines, an hour's drive to the south. Over the years Boone had seen the coalfields around its rich, flat farmland diminish, while the railroads built to serve the mines, which strongly supported Boone, gradually faded away. People in Boone still had a strong sense of that past.

Pauline Uthe, for instance. Her grandfather, a Civil War veteran who marched in Lincoln's funeral procession, joined railroad construction crews going West from New York. When the first railroad work crews came through Boone in 1865, they temporarily ran out of spikes. Her grandfather stayed. Pauline Uthe's life, like that of her father and grandfather, was spent on the family farm outside Boone. But farming had changed, and economic conditions forced her to take a job as a bookkeeper in town. She viewed politics with typical suspicion. "We need some people we can trust," she said, "but I don't know how we can tell who it is. I don't know if what we see is real. How do you know what to believe?" She had watched Ford in the first televised debate say that more Americans were working than at any point in American history: "Well of course that has to be," she said. "There's just more people." She thought Carter was honest and sincere, "but then you don't know what to believe." Yet she was leaning toward him, because as she said, people were ready for a change.

What was most impressive about Boone was that its citizens were exceptionally well informed. They were not apathetic. They paid close attention to the election, watched the national news programs on television, read their daily afternoon paper *The Boone News-Republican,* and took *The Des Moines Register and Tribune* (an excellent paper). As the presidential campaign progressed, they became increasingly negative. They were, they'd tell you, highly suspicious about everything they were seeing and hearing—the news reports, the frenzied, disembodied and disconnected scenes of far-off candidates, the slick political commercials, the personal styles of the candidates themselves. Their distrust was deep. "The political rhetoric is almost too smooth, too persuasive," one person said. Another said, "You need a Ph.D. in public relations to know what to believe."

Every day groups of citizens gathered in coffee klatches at a downtown drugstore to discuss everything from sex or football to business affairs or politics. Word-of-mouth gossip, shared information, and opinions were the essence of their sessions. What Johnny Carson or Walter Cronkite said were passed on, but not as revealed wisdom. They were aware, as one said, that "They're giving you *their* version." Distrust of politicians was equaled by distrust of the news media. It wasn't so much political bias in the news that disturbed them, as Spiro Agnew had thought. Their view of what they saw and read was more sophisticated, and generally not colored by fears of ideological manipulation. "I read the *Boone News* and watch the Cronkite news," Pat Olafson, a twenty-five-year-old insurance agent, said, sitting at the table in the back of the drugstore drinking coffee. "I don't know how factual it is. I guess you have to have some background to actually know the difference between what you see and what's really there."

Fred Doxsee shared this confusion—and the common search for something to believe in. "One thing television has taught me," he said, "is to be more analytical. I pick up the paper and I find myself analyzing it. I never did this before they did a lot of analyzing on television. I find myself reading an article three or four times. I can't do this with radio or television news. I'm afraid somebody's going to try and put something over on me."

In traveling extensively throughout the country reporting on five other presidential-election campaigns, I had never found such pervasive distrust. I had never met so many people anguishing about how and why they were going to vote—or whether their votes meant anything at all. And not only was the wariness in Boone similar to that being expressed nationally: serious attention to the issues shown by individual citizens there was the same as I had encountered everywhere else. Ed Smith, turning to his neighbors in Fred Doxsee's living room that night of the last debate, confessed he had never had so much trouble deciding how to vote; then, an afterthought: "I wonder if that's what's happening to the mass humanity of America. If it is, if they're actually thinking, well, that *is* a change."

By the time I reached Boone, after months on the road, I had formed several generalizations about the electorate. National politics was more irrelevant to more people's lives than ever before, and politics itself was viewed with much greater sophistication. Everywhere one saw a drawing inward, a rejecting of old prejudices and passions. In other years you'd meet true believers; they were still around, but even they didn't speak in such strident, dogmatic tones. If my ear was accurate, I heard many Americans doubting one of the nation's hoariest, and naïve, assumptions—that there must be an answer to every question. In the 1976 election I didn't meet as many people who blindly believed that America could solve everything . . . or that the American system was uniquely blessed . . . or that America had been endowed with a mystical mission in the world . . . or that Americans, almost alone, were nearly incapable of doing wrong.

But the strongest impression of all was what Ed Smith and others in Boone demonstrated—Americans had not stopped thinking.

◻   ◻   ◻

Understandably, the dominant feeling in the election year of 1976 was a desire for something new. Certainly the events of the past years gave little reason for confidence: change had occurred of such magnitude, at such an accelerating pace, that it almost defied understanding—the space age, the drug age, the sexual revolution. And all of this during a protracted political crisis beginning with Vietnam and ending with Watergate. Those years were full of turbulence and terror. Assassinations reminded us that no man, no matter how high or well protected, was safe. Riots raised questions about the survival not only of our cities but of our political system. A power blackout that plunged the densely populated eastern seaboard into darkness reminded us how dependent we had become on systems beyond the control of most of us—and then beyond the control of anyone. An oil embargo shattered the comfortable complacency about our accepted way of life. National leader after national leader—liberal and conservative, Republican and Democrat, black and white—was removed suddenly, tragically or in disgrace: the Kennedys, Martin Luther King, Malcolm X, Johnson, Nixon, Agnew, Wallace. Each time the nation showed a basic resiliency, but the price it paid was high, of course. Distrust in leaders and institutions ran deep. Citizens voted less and less. Many found themselves fearful of committing themselves fully to another potential leader: they guarded against giving themselves again, fearful of being disappointed once more.

While voters were looking for leadership, they no longer expected some presidential father-figure to solve their problems. They knew there were no miracle rulers. Indeed, they didn't expect nearly so much from their politicians—or from anyone else. To many, the national government, as they perceived it functioning, was becoming incapable of significantly addressing their individual problems. They began to look to themselves.

Carter, better than any of his opponents, sensed these feelings early, and swept up from nowhere to become the Democratic nominee. For Jimmy Carter of Plains, Georgia (population: 300), one-term state legislator, one-term governor, to win his party's nomination was a testament both to his tenacity and ability and to the extraordinary set of historical circumstances.

Carter's precipitous drop in the polls between his nomination and election day was expected—in part, at least. After their experience with recent candidates, notably Johnson, Nixon, and Agnew, voters were going to examine an unknown carefully. And they did. What *was* surprising, though, was how quickly the initial enthusiasm for Carter turned sour. In every section of the country that I traveled I encountered growing suspicions about him. Only blacks remained ardent on his behalf, and black support for him, whether

in Harlem or the rural South, more than anything else distinguished the 1976 election.

The Democratic convention in New York that summer, a dull affair, had enjoyed one dramatic moment that symbolized the political significance of the party of the urban masses' being taken over
by a white man from the rural South. At the very end, "Daddy"
King, the father of Martin Luther King, Jr., stepped to the podium
to deliver the convention benediction. His appearance was a surprise to most of the delegates; there was a stir in the crowd as his
name was announced. Slowly, almost painfully, he advanced to the
microphone, grasped the lectern, and called out in a booming
voice for silence. Then, his words pitching and rolling over the audience, Daddy King began preaching extemporaneously. He had
come there, an old, graying black man from the Deep South, bent
with sorrow—his son and wife murdered, and another son dying
tragically—to celebrate the nomination of a white man from
southern Georgia. "Surely the Lord sent Jimmy Carter to come on
out and bring America back to where she belongs," he called out,
keening. As he preached on, his voice rising and falling, flailing his
arms, throwing open his coat, showing his galluses, the thousands
in the hall stood transfixed. Many wept.

Out on the convention floor the Georgia and Minnesota standards were entwined, reminders, for the moment at least, of the
binding together of North and South, of blacks and whites. Painful
national history and personal experience brought those erstwhile
irreconcilable forces together in political alliance. Illusory though
it might prove to be, on that night and for the rest of the campaign, blacks gave their hearts to Carter.

You could go into a housing project in New York and hear fervent, unanimous praise for Carter. "If he don't make it, man, the
whole United States gonna go down the drain," said Plent Pratt,
who worked days in the Post Office and nights as a security guard
to support his family. Julius Manning, another Harlem resident,
who like hundreds of thousands of blacks had moved north in the
early 1940s, said: "I respect a good Southern white man because
he's not a hypocrite. He won't lie. I think Mr. Carter, he's a religious man. He comes from a Baptist church. I only wish it was
possible for him to get Mrs. Lyndon Johnson as his vice-president,

but that would be impossible. He should take that black woman [Barbara Jordan of Texas] for his vice-president."

And in the Mississippi Delta, in a white frame house in the middle of a cotton field, there was Hartman Turnbow. Seventy-one years old, raised by grandparents who were slaves, he had spent his life in the heart of Holmes County, as black and rural a part of Mississippi as you'll find. Turnbow had led other blacks in the first voter registration drives in the early 1960s. For his efforts his home had been firebombed, his animals slain, shots fired into his windows at night, he was arrested on trumped-up charges, convicted, and later became the centerpiece in a Justice Department case that led to his exoneration, with all charges dismissed. There were no further attempts to bar blacks from voting in that part of the rural South. Turnbow, a modest man, spoke in the old dialect of the cotton fields: "The votin', that's the only thing the Negro really won out of the civil-rights struggle; they can vote for who they wants and I likes that. You take Jimmy Carter and Mr. Ford, why every Negro I ever met's goin' for Jimmy Carter. And that includes me. We just think he's the man. One reason, he seems to be a Christian man and then on top of that he's a Democrat and the mostest money that the po' folks got on to was under Democrats. He gonna get all the black votes. Just everywhere you go and talk to a Negro about the two presidents they say Mr. Carter is the man. They goin' for him in a big way."

But blacks were the only group that remained constant to Jimmy Carter, and even in the South, his candidacy created ambivalence and doubt. Hardly a Southerner existed who didn't feel an initial surge of pride in his prospects; defensiveness about Southern stereotypes and resentment about national beliefs in Southern inferiority were common, and for generations the South *had* been regarded as inferior, brutal, backward, ignorant, impoverished. In literature, in language, in national mores, the South had been ridiculed and scorned. Southern politicians were portrayed as bombastic, bumbling Senator Claghorns, either venal wheelers-and-dealers or ignoramuses and bigots.

"Like many Southerners, I was emotionally caught up with the idea it was going to be great to have the opportunity to vote for a Southerner," said Berkeley Grimball, whose family has been in

Charleston, South Carolina, that citadel of Old South pride and prejudice, since 1690, and who heads an Episcopal school there. "Being a Southerner and having felt defensive for so many years about the South, I suppose I got a vicarious pleasure out of seeing some of the pompous people being drawn to Plains, Georgia, swatting gnats. Seeing some of them squirm, you know. They just couldn't see this peanut famer. And then when they began to attack him personally for his life-style, his accent, things like that, they were picking up more votes for Carter from people like myself."

But in the closing weeks of the campaign Grimball and others like him were having second thoughts. Some were offended by Carter's repeated references to religion; others found his message unclear; he appeared tentative, indecisive. Was he a progressive or a conservative, a populist or small "d" democrat? As Gedney Howe, Jr., a white-haired lawyer in Charleston and long active in Democratic politics, said:

> Carter says, "I don't like Washington." That's fine. He says, "I've been born again." And that's nice. But then he says, "I'm going up to Washington and put on another two hundred million dollars' worth of government programs." That's got to be something of a calamity. That's what comes through to me. Carter's got himself too far out. He can't explain where he stands. I guess the greatest speech in the history of America was when Roosevelt got caught trying to give fifty destroyers to England, which was of course an act of war. This was pointed out to him and he answered by saying, when your next-door neighbor's house caught on fire wouldn't you lend him your garden hose? It was a classic speech because it oversimplified an awful issue. Carter has got to get back to saying that people are unemployed and doing something about that is a function of government. That fighting inflation is a function of government. That fighting both inflation and unemployment are functions of the *national* government. And he's got to be unashamed to say that absolutely and completely. And then he's got to say that, to a large extent, the programs now in the hands of Washington are going to be turned over to more local forms of participation.
>
> I think he's in the process of blowing it. And that takes some real doing on his part, because frankly he was in a position where he almost couldn't lose.

Just before the election, George Gallup reported a surge of Southern voters away from Carter toward Ford—the largest regional
shift ever recorded by the Gallup poll.

Carter's strength in the rest of the country was never so solid. In
Eastern cities cynicism was pervasive—yet that was the primary
political battleground. Carter could carry all the Southern states
and still lose (Adlai Stevenson did just that in 1952), but every
Northern state was important. Ethnic voting blocs, Catholics, and
Jews obviously posed a special problem for the Southern candidate. "Religiously speaking he's foreign, and ethnically speaking
he comes from the wrong part of America as far as they're concerned," said Father Peter Paul Pollo of Our Lady of Pompeii, a
church that since the nineteenth century has served a large Italian-
American parish in New York's Greenwich Village. "I don't know
whether it's only a Village attitude that's creeping through or a
typical Italian-American attitude. I can only tell you that individual
Italian-Americans show a nose curled up about this election. They
are not enthusiastic about Ford at all, but they distrust Carter."

For generations the imposing old church with its tall steeple
towered over the houses nestling about its little park. Down
through the years the church, the community, and the park were
inseparably linked. By the 1970s, like New York itself, they were
all struggling to survive. In the old days, when the park was the
glory of the community and doors were never locked, you could
stroll safely through the streets at all hours. At night people would
congregate on park benches to talk and sing, and during the day
clusters of old men and women sat together in the sun. But now
the park was a danger zone, a place of muggings, robberies, and
drug sales. On all sides the neighborhood people were threatened
by forces they couldn't control. Who became president had little
effect on their lives. No one they knew, at any level of politics or
government, could or would change those conditions. As the Italian-Americans would say with a sneer, *governo ladro*, thieving government.

In ministering to his parish, Father Peter found that younger
Italians, particularly recent immigrants, were no longer so certain
that they would give up their national identity or even their Italian
citizenship. Many were returning to Italy. Older Italian-Americans
were wrestling with more painful and personal questions. "The

system seems to have collapsed around them," Father Peter said. "It doesn't afford them the type of security they ought to have. Certainly they come out of their long experience as immigrants in this country as bitter people. They're disillusioned."

Americans have always distrusted their political leaders, and belief in government's ineptness and corruption is an old national habit. But new factors distinguished political attitudes during the 1976 election year. People asked more questions, asserted themselves with less assurance, had more appreciation for the complexities of life, both theirs and their country's. They recognized their own limitations, as well as the politicians'.

"Sometimes I feel I could be as corrupt as the politicians are," a California man in his early forties said, "just as corrupt as the whole Watergate bunch—being manipulative and all. People are becoming more aware of that part of themselves. It scares me. That's the part of me I don't like, and I have to watch myself."

Personal judgments were given more tentatively. The martial, moralistic, or jingoistic words about communism or "Americanism" heard so often in other political years were notably absent. People articulated, with greater insights, their notions about what life in America was becoming—and whether they thought anything could be done to change it for the better through politics.

I recall two people out of many I interviewed—one was a Southerner:

> The birth of Jesus starts with the scripture telling us the times were tough. They were numbering the people. Now people have never liked to be numbered. The first thing a sovereign does to show his complete mastery is to give you a number—when he puts you in prison, when he calls you into the army. We don't like numbers, with all they symbolize. And we're living in a society in which we're becoming permanently numbered.

The other was a Midwest businessman:

> The question is asked: Well, why don't we just throw all the rascals out? Well, that's fine. And who are we going to get to take their places? Okay, why don't *I* run? Why don't *I* be a better practicing citizen? Well, I have a salary, but I don't have any money. To unseat our congressman would take half a million dollars. Where the hell's

the money going to come from? If it comes from big business, I'm beholden to them. If it comes from labor unions, I'm beholden to them. It's not going to come from you and me and my friends at the Rotary Club. We seem to be stuck with the system, and the only alternative—and of course some people have been espousing this—is some sort of revolutionary process. I can't figure out an alternative other than something drastic. And I'm no revolutionary.

From that kind of thinking it wasn't hard to move into the increasing ranks of the nonvoters. Nonvoters tended to be well educated and well informed, and often young. They were the political future, and they usually could explain specifically why they were going to abstain. For many, their decision came after careful deliberation. Their explanations became familiar; they were the same everywhere: *No matter who's president, the real problems aren't going to be solved. . . . there's no major difference between either one; it's all personality. . . . Politics is corrupt. . . . The presidential candidates are always captives of hidden forces—business, labor, what have you. . . . And where do they get all that money to run on, anyway? . . . Promises are all you get, and the promises are never kept. . . . All they're in it for are power and glory. . . . They don't really care about people. . . . And even if they do believe what they say, they aren't going to be able to do anything when they get in office. . . .*
Beneath this litany of quick answers, two principal themes were expressed. One was skepticism about ever being able to know the facts. With all the massive outpouring of political rhetoric month after month, and all the conflicting claims coming from the candidates and the press, how could a citizen determine the truth? In the end, weren't they forced to take the candidates on faith? Look where faith got them in recent presidential elections. The other theme was related: the people saw politics and politicians as ever more hypocritical. The candidates' lavishly produced, studiedly casual television commercials, the synthetic speeches, the phony rallies, the unreality of it all—they were, in the vernacular, a turnoff. "I hate it, I hate it," said a young Southern woman, well educated, concerned about issues. "The bullshit. The secrecy. The manipulation. It just makes me ill. Everybody's negative about politics—and they have a reason to be."
On the West Coast, a group of residents sitting on a beach look-

ing out across Tomales Point and the surrounding hills, covered with tall, dark pines, were talking about the election. A young woman was speaking: "It seems to me the most important thing a president can do concerns our economic foundation," said Elizabeth Whitney, who edited a small paper near Inverness, California. "The cost of living goes up, therefore workers want to get more money because they can't cope. So the cost of labor goes up, so the cost of living goes up. There's no way to stop it, and everybody's trying to figure out just how to stay in the same place. But I don't know if any president can turn any of it around. It has its own perpetual motion machine. I can't imagine if I had the power what I'd do first, and that seems to be the same way with the president. Who really knows what to do?"

Listening quietly was an older woman who lived nearby, in retirement with her husband. "I try to read and analyze the issues," Dorothy Johnstone said, "but I just get lost. Does everybody else? The more you know about something, the harder it is to know what you know. It's like what happens when you are bird-watching: you learn one bird, then you find that there are thousands of birds flying around that you haven't even noticed and don't know. I read all the League of Women Voters' material that comes in the house. I read *Skeptic* magazine. I read *Harper's.* I read the *Saturday Review.* I read—oh, well, I guess we'll survive regardless who's elected president."

These kinds of conversations made ridiculous all the talk about an "apathetic America." Apathy—indifference, and the absence of caring—wasn't a characteristic of the citizens you'd meet. They *were* concerned, but their problem was in finding political leadership.

What people were looking for was hard to define. The most popular model of a president seemed to be Harry Truman. Songs were sung about Old Harry—the blunt, decisive, plain-talking man of the Midwest who could plow a straight furrow and get his history and perspectives right. Politicians of both parties praised him. Presidential candidates tried to emulate him. He was a *real* leader: strong and compassionate. In fact, to me the great irony was that people seemed to be seeking the personal qualities they admired in Truman while rejecting the political reality that Truman and so many of his successors represented.

At the Truman Library, outside Independence, Missouri, you'd see crowds approaching the exhibits in an atmosphere of reverence. But what they saw and heard were hardly memorable—were, in fact, all the things people were now reacting against. *The glorification of the leader:* "Citizen, Statesman, Soldier," the legend under Harry's oil portrait read. *The rewards of political power:* "These swords and knives were given to the president by the royal families of Saudi Arabia and Iran," the inscription on a glass-enclosed case housing jewel-encrusted weapons informed you. *The paucity and cheapness of political rhetoric:* Tom Dewey, his voice droning on from a recording of the 1948 campaign, his tone insufferably pompous: "Let us move forward out of the desperate darkness of today into the bright light of tomorrow." Truman, speaking in that flat Missouri drawl, but far more vibrantly and self-assured, saying the choice was between the party of the people and the special interests, and adding: "We will win the election and make those Republicans like it. Don't you forget that. We'll do that because they're wrong and we're right."

No one you'd meet, in any part of the country, spoke of politics in such starkly partisan and simple terms. Farmers in Truman's home territory showed a shrewdness and sophistication far exceeding the level of Carter's or Ford's speeches—whether about foreign or domestic policy, about oil and the Middle East, wheat and the Soviet Union, productivity and the government—federal, state, and local. Gene Palmer, a farmer who lived in Platte City, just north of Truman's home, raised two subjects on a common theme when I talked to him—cynicism about government and political privilege:

Two or three years ago when wheat was four or five dollars a bushel, the powers that be just panicked and predicted a dollar a loaf for bread. How horrible that was going to be! Well, today the farmer gets less than half of what he did then for wheat, and the cost of bread is higher. If every farmer that owns or controls wheat today could say, "Okay, I don't want two dollars and fifty cents for my wheat, I don't want five dollars, I don't want anything for my wheat. There'll be no charge. We don't want these farm products getting this high so just take this wheat free"—without a doubt in six months bakery products would cost more than they do today.

In Kansas City, the residents of Jackson County were asked to approve some municipal revenue bonds to build those sports complexes we have out there. And we've got Mr. Lamar Hunt that's come in from Dallas, Texas, and brought us professional football games. But there's no way for the average person to go see a football game. The reason is, they have 'em all on season tickets and the tickets are held in very tight hands. The average person is never eligible, or ever given a chance, to buy season tickets even if he could afford to. The banks, all the major corporations, the utility companies, everybody in politics from the state level on down—they all have lots of tickets. The county court has one whole side of the stadium. And the public is paying whether they go or not. Every little guy that's got a three-bedroom house or any Goddamn thing that's taxable, he's paying for it.*

People saw—or wanted to see—something special in Jimmy Carter. Certainly they were ready for something different. They sensed integrity and simplicity. He was critical, but caring. He was competent. He seemed able to address the real questions troubling people—power and powerlessness, size and functioning of government, energy and environment, equity for the small as well as the large. (He makes his own bed, they said in surprise after he stayed at someone's home on an early New England trip. Later it was Jimmy Carter carrying his own suit bag wherever he went. That these symbols of informality and unpretentiousness impressed people—and they did—showed possibly naïveté, but also how desperate people were for a different presidential style.) And they also wanted to believe Carter was as capable a manager as his campaign made him out: zero-base budgeting (no one quite knew what it was, but supposedly it had worked in Georgia), make every program accountable, start fresh, shake things up, level with the people, cut out the pomp and artificial trappings of power.

People were willing to take a chance on a political novice. If they thought about it all, they knew that no president in the twentieth

---

*This kind of thing is of course not restricted to Kansas City. Nothing shows more clearly the nature of Washington relationships—professional, social, political, and economic—than the scene on any Sunday at RFK Stadium (built by public funds) when the Redskins play: about fifteen thousand season-ticket holders—newspapers, law firms, advertising agencies, and political offices—control the fifty-five thousand seats. Entertained in the owners' box are presidents, Supreme Court justices, cabinet officers, members of Congress, editors, columnists, commentators, and wealthy Georgetown hostesses.

century had had such limited exposure to government—and especially to Washington—as Jimmy Carter:

Theodore Roosevelt came to the presidency after considerable national and international experience, and long exposure to Washington. Aside from family and political connections there, he had spent six years in Washington directing the fight against the spoils system while on the Civil Service Commission before becoming governor of New York, and then he was back in the capital as assistant secretary of the Navy and vice-president. William Howard Taft, too, grew up in politics. As the son of a cabinet officer he became solicitor general of the United States and then served in Teddy Roosevelt's cabinet. Woodrow Wilson's lifetime study of government and politics had been crowned by his governorship of New Jersey; his book on congressional government was still considered a classic half a century later. Even Warren G. Harding, probably the most ineffectual of presidents, was a Washington figure: he had served in the Senate and knew the city and its politics well. Calvin Coolidge had spent his life in politics before becoming vice-president, and then president. Herbert Hoover was perhaps as well prepared for the presidency as anyone—through his service in cabinet and subcabinet positions for several presidents. FDR, like his cousin Theodore, was an important figure in the capital before going back to New York politics and thence to the White House. Harry S Truman, a veteran senator; Dwight D. Eisenhower, the only nonprofessional politician in this group, nevertheless understood well the way power worked in Washington from his military service in the city dating back to the early 1930s; Kennedy and Nixon came to the Congress the same day, and thirteen years later competed for the presidency; LBJ had been congressional aide, congressman, senator, most powerful of Capitol Hill leaders, and vice-president; Ford had been in Congress a quarter of a century before becoming vice-president and then president.

The idea that Jimmy Carter, the only member of his family in two hundred years to go to college (his father was the only one to have gotten as far as the tenth grade; and few, it seems, ever left the state of Georgia) could become president was extraordinary by any measure. His election would signal a radical departure in the kind of person Americans chose as their president. In background and experience he would be different from any president any American had known. But by the time they voted in 1976, Americans already were moving in different directions. They were in the midst of a period of revolutionary change. As someone said to me, "The real revolution is how we're going to live our own lives." It was political change that was lagging behind others transforming the country.

□ □ □

A friend of mine came home to America after an absence of five years just in time for the Bicentennial. It was an uneasy homecoming, for he had been away, as a consultant to another government, during all the turmoil of the late 1960s and mid-1970s: From what he had heard, he was prepared to be pessimistic. The country had changed all right, but, to his delight, not in the ways he had feared. Instead of the tense, poisonous society he expected to find, the atmosphere was more relaxed, even casual. In dress, in manners, in attitudes about sex and work, people's lives had changed and, from what he could see, changed positively.

A paradox existed. Americans were becoming more cynical: the better educated they became, the less they voted; the more they read, the less they believed; the greater their awareness of national problems, the less certain of any real solutions. At the same time they were re-examining some of their most deeply held values— about the worth of their material comforts, their desire for their children to "succeed" or even automatically go to college, their old vision of the good life in the city or suburbs, their supreme confidence in their country's inevitable rightness—and they were qualifying, or rejecting, many of them.

That didn't mean some syrupy "greening of America" was finally occurring, a cultural flowering led by affluent and supposedly superior young people. A strong reaction to problems of the immediate past, including the overblown rhetoric extolling the "unique" virtues of the young as national saviors, was coupled with an awareness of the insolubility of complex problems. Many Americans I met were withdrawing into their own lives, leaving the great questions of state and nation, and often job and community as well, to others. A muted, more reflective tone came through their conversations: they spoke partly out of a new sense of realism, partly out of a reaction to events, partly out of fear for the future, partly out of uncertainty for the present. They had survived a difficult period, and were facing less material abundance.

Accompanying the distaste for politics, and intensified by the climate of cynicism and uncertainty about the future, was a get-mine-while-I-can public attitude. It was easy—too easy—to look out on the America at the end of the 1970s and see a selfish, vain, narcissistic, insecure society—one that cared nothing about politics or public issues and one in which self-improvement was the national preoccupation, hedonism its philosophy, looking out for Number One its theme. And surely these traits were present.

One only had to gaze out the window to see the explosion of the physical self-improvement culture passing by. At almost any hour, in any town or city, joggers dressed in expensive and colorful athletic equipment were earnestly puffing along highways and neighborhood streets. Even the language, halting and inarticulate though it was, spoke to that personal point: People were, "Like, *into* it." They were, "Doing *their* thing." They were "laid back."

The pages of the best-sellers reflected the trend. Carefully compiled from computer-processed sales figures covering fourteen hundred bookstores in every region of the country, and published each Sunday in the authoritative pages of *The New York Times Book Review*, the best-seller list provides a guide to mass tastes—and to part of the politics of the day. For more than a generation, nonfiction books had been the big sellers in the hardcover business and there, dominating the lists in the late 1970s, were what passed for self-improvement-at-any-price volumes. In the months after the election I checked the best-sellers and found three on cosmetics and clothes: *Adrien Arpel's Three-Week Crash Makeover/Shapeover Beauty Program*, a winner at $11.95, offered advice from the head of an international cosmetics corporation. It stood alongside *The Woman's Dress for Success Book*, a guide to tasteful apparel, and *Designing Your Face*, on how best to use cosmetics. In keeping with their appeal, and message, was the number one best-seller, *The Complete Book of Running*, which competed with *Inner Skiing*, about improving your mental attitude, and *Arnold: The Education of a Body Builder*, which gave personal tips from the superstar of the film

Pumping Iron, celebrating muscles, lots of them. Five of the remaining nine best-sellers qualified as escapism, while close to the top was a mod bit of introspective wrestling-with-self from an author who had previously cashed in with an account of women's sexual fantasies. Nancy Friday's latest, *My Mother/My Self*, examined how mothers and daughters "relate." But the book that had been on the best-seller list twice as long as any other spelled out a symbolic message for the times. It was entitled *Looking Out for Number One.**

At the end of the 1970s, you could make a case that it was the façade that counted. Tom Wolfe gave the age a name and the attitudes a value. We were, he wrote, living in the "Me Generation." Later, the scholar Christopher Lasch wrote about contemporary America and called it a "culture of narcissism."

While undeniably accurate in part, these failed to take into account a greater truth, or at least a "truth" I had been learning—and that was the new degree of tolerance. "People are more realistic now," a black man told me in Selma, Alabama, once the very symbol of racial strife. "They're willing to let the law handle things, and believe the law will be fair. Nobody, black or white, wants trouble again. It isn't because of love, you understand, and it isn't the millennium, but there's been a remarkable change here."

During the late 1960s and into the 1970s many Americans saw moral decay: sexual promiscuity and drugs were common themes. But those fears seemed to disappear—what was abnormal, if not illegal, only a short time before was accepted with barely a question. Porno shops and porno movies were not a serious public issue. Turn on a television set and you'd find network daytime shows, which had once been filled with frivolous women's gossip and fashions, discussing the quality and variety of orgasms, kinds

---

*During the Kennedy years strong topical themes, with a flavor of reform and exposé of public problems, were nonfiction successes. James Baldwin's *The Fire Next Time* called the tune on black unrest and the prospect of urban mass violence, while Rachel Carson's *Silent Spring* sounded an alarm on man's abuse of his environment. Best-sellers of the Eisenhower era had clearly reflected current fears about atomic weapons and imminent doomsday: religious and spiritual themes won their way to the top with such saccharine books as Norman Vincent Peale's *The Power of Positive Thinking*, Fulton Sheen's *Life Is Worth Living*, Fulton Oursler's *The Greatest Faith Ever Known*, and Catherine Marshall's *A Man Called Peter*.

and uses of contraceptives, patterns of male and female homosexuality, the problems associated with abortion, adultery, interracial marriage. Nowhere in this once Puritan land were serious protests made against the airing of such subjects. At night, family television fare rehearsed many of the same subjects. Archie Bunker and the members in his family dramatized the changes in life-styles and the conflicts over values in a working-class neighborhood of "hard hats," "Middle Americans," and the "Silent Majority" of Nixon-era politics. A new soap opera shown in prime time—in which Mary Hartman and her husband, Tom, a factory worker, smoked grass, had affairs, got VD, rejected their parents' standards, had a grandfather who was a "flasher," and constantly worried out loud about their lives—was an instant critical and commercial success.

Changing sexual mores inevitably attracted the most national attention, but a more significant change was within the family structure. Women married later, had fewer children, and were divorced more frequently. As their career opportunities improved, more and more women were not planning on marriage at all. And of all young Americans in elementary school, about half would live part of their childhood with only one parent.

American life has always been marked by a restless, often frantic, quality. People constantly move, seek new experiences.* But in the early 1970s I saw a different type of movement. People gave up urban jobs and homes to start life anew in small towns. At first I thought this was either a reaction by a few to the stresses of the times or a banding together by the youthful survivors of the sixties to celebrate their uniqueness. But a more fundamental change was taking place. In the spring of 1975 the Census Bureau reported for the first time in the twentieth century people were moving *into* small towns and the countryside and *away* from cities: "The vast rural-to-urban migration of people that was the common pattern of United States population movement in the decades after World

---

*Tocqueville, in his travels across the country fifty years after the American Revolution, was struck by this trait: "In the United States, a man builds a house to spend his later years in it, and he sells it before the roof is on; he plants a garden, and lets it just as the trees are coming into bearing; he brings a field into tillage, and leaves other men to gather the crops; he embraces a profession, and gives it up; he settles a place, which he soon afterwards leaves, to carry his changeable longings elsewhere."

War II has been halted and, on balance, even reversed. In the eyes
of many Americans, the appeal of major urban areas has diminished and the attractiveness of rural and small-town communities
has increased." At the same time, the government reported another major change. The United States was experiencing "major
slowdowns in growth" in all its largest metropolitan areas except
Boston.

Take, for example, the Bob Sandell family. By the time he
reached his forties, Dr. Sandell had built up a successful practice
as a chiropractor in Camden, New Jersey. His wife and children
had all they wanted in a material sense. Then they broke with their
past and moved into a rural community in the West Virginia
mountains, where they found others like themselves. "We had everything that in the eyes of the world is a success," Natalie Sandell
told me. "A beautiful house, the Cadillac, the thriving practice,
healthy children—and yet we didn't have any time. We didn't have
time with each other, we didn't have time with the children, we
didn't have the satisfaction of being outdoors when it was nice. We
were always stuck in the house doing one thing or another, or parties or conventions or smoke-filled rooms. Just a lot of things that
really didn't seem to be satisfying. The children couldn't relate to
us as parents as well as they can here where we're working together for the basics of life. We're working together in the garden—on
the basics, their food, and they can see it from seed right on
through to eating it on the table. And they're able to learn so
many lessons that schools can't teach."

Bob Sandell, who kept up a small practice in addition to the
farm work, offered other explanations: "There are many, many
reasons why we made the move and you could talk about it for
hours. The main thing is, what do you want out of life? Security is
something that you obtain when you can do more things for yourself."

Creativity, security, safety, simplicity, and a sense of community—these were among the attributes the Sandells and their new
friends from other sections of the country had sought when giving
the reasons for their moves. If that sounded too pure to be true, it
was. A darker side existed among many new homesteaders I met.
For all their surface optimism, a strain of pessimism and withdrawal ran through their conversations. In one way or another, they all

expressed a deeper belief—that American life was deteriorating, that they had to learn to be self-sufficient in order to survive. They spoke in apocalyptic terms. Disaster lurked over the horizon. A worldwide depression, food crises, ecological disasters—these were the doomsday portents.

"We're coming to the end of an age," Natalie Sandell said. "There are so many factors pointing downhill, for this country and for the world. But at least from a temporary standpoint, we have the security of providing for ourselves, and we also have time to orient ourselves to the larger picture, to find out where are we going and how are we going to meet the crises as they come."

I found the political attitudes of these new migrants confounding. One couple who moved near the Sandells in West Virginia came out of corporate life; they had been members of the John Birch Society, and they said they were fleeing from the blacks. Another couple, political liberals, were trying to escape the John Birchers. Now these erstwhile political opposites were finding common interests. "Conservatives and radicals have a lot of things in common, actually," said one resident of that West Virginia community. "The conservatives seem to want to hang on to the eighteenth century. Louis XVI. And the radicals say this technological stuff hasn't worked—let's go back to when Mommy and Daddy ran a little family farm. They say we can do with less, and they do."

Although such people obviously weren't "typical," their doubts, their self-examination, their recognition of their own changing attitudes were shared by many more than the relative few who actually moved. A Harvard law student who had been committed to liberal causes said, "I'll tell you one thing: liberals in this country are bankrupt." A radical friend of his, who had been listening to us, nodded in agreement. "The radical leaders copped out, too. They left and never came back. Where are they now?" A third young man summed it up for all of them: "You know what I think? I think we're all jaded."

There lay the other side of the culture of narcissism. Along with a numbing of the political process and a state of national cynicism about politics was the rise of a belief alien to the American experience. For the first time in their lives many Americans were fearful that the best times might be behind them. They no longer believed that tomorrow would be better than today, as today was better than yesterday.

Perhaps the country had passed through its most prosperous period, they would say—these automobile factory workers, housewives, machinists, farmers, and waitresses. Perhaps their children would never have it as good. Perhaps the next generation would not be able to afford to own a home, or one as good as theirs. Perhaps they would have to forgo college for a trade. Perhaps they would face a permanent change in their standard of living, a world in which shortages would be the norm, not the exception. Perhaps they would have to lower their aspirations, to learn to live with less.

"I feel awful bad about the children," said Bernard Beauvais, an auto worker in Detroit. "We want 'em to go to college, but I don't see how they're ever going to do it. These young people starting out today—well, I don't know how they'll have a home. We're very fortunate because fifteen or twenty years ago you could buy a beautiful home for fifteen or eighteen thousand dollars for no money down or a hundred and fifty or three hundred down, as most of us did. That's impossible today. If we were starting today, I don't know how we'd do it. I'm awfully concerned about what's going to happen, not so much for ourselves—we're going to make it, our home loan is on the way to being paid—but for our kids going out into the labor force. I don't think they'll ever be able to live like we did."

Politically, the most striking changes were at the state and local levels. The great story of the 1976 election, I came to believe, had nothing to do with Jimmy Carter or the presidency or Washington—it was about the way citizens were responding to *local* politics. At the grassroots, the practice of politics had changed, and for the better. The statehouses, long and deservedly the object of political scorn and ridicule, were now characterized by legislative innovation and reform. And state legislators had changed. In the past they were poorly paid, unprofessional, and dominated by special interests. By 1976 they included fewer farmers and lawyers, more blacks, more women, more suburbanites, and professionalism had increased along with pay.

New state programs in health, criminal justice, personnel procedures, and economic development were found all over the coun-

try. Laws compelling open government sessions were enacted.
Codes of ethics became commoner. The statehouses took a hard-
nosed approach to fiscal matters and federal programs, but they
proceeded with a humane, reform-minded attitude toward social
problems. They fell into no definable political category, no neat
slots of liberal or conservative. In Washington, the antiabortion
right-to-life protest movement captured headlines and stirred political controversy; but in towns and cities around the country a
dramatically different issue—the right-to-die movement—quietly
won support. A landmark law passed by the California legislature
permitted terminally ill patients to order removal of life-sustaining
equipment, and in the following year eight states enacted similar
legislation while similar bills gained momentum in others. In Mississippi, the legislature, once conservative and reactionary, passed
a law easing criminal penalties for possession of small amounts of
marijuana. It was the eighth statehouse to enact such a law—and
no regional or ideological pattern could be found among them:
California and Maine, Colorado and Mississippi, Ohio and Alaska,
Minnesota and Oregon. In Florida, another supposedly conservative state, representatives at one state convention endorsed the
equal-rights constitutional amendment, went on record as approving abortion, and asked for the decriminalization of marijuana.
Only four years before, in the 1972 presidential election, Nixon
and his strategists had aggressively campaigned against the so-
called "three A's"—amnesty, abortion, and acid—in the belief that
the "new" and "silent" majorities were moved by a conservative
tide in such states as Florida and Mississippi. Now, it was difficult
to make any generalization about national political currents of
"right" and "left." Practicality, realism, an absence of ideology—
these were the new hallmarks, along with a desire for change and a
willingness to try something new.

□   □   □

It's fair to say most Americans were disappointed when they exercised their franchise in 1976—or deliberately chose not to exercise it. They had wished for something better and they didn't think
they were going to get it. Neither Ford nor Carter succeeded in

convincing them that his presidency would make a difference in the way they lived. Neither was able to summon the eloquence to inspire confidence. Neither gave a clear call for future action.

One result was certain: the next president would be watched more critically than ever before. Voters on election day already were highly critical of both candidates. Ford the man was warm, decent, earnest, trying hard, but Ford the president was considered a lackluster, negative leader. Carter the man was a puzzle, stirring unusual doubts and hopes ("I think there's a lie behind the smile"; "Watch out for a man who says he'll never lie to you"; "He's a very impressive man—a nuclear scientist, a military officer, a farmer, a governor"), while Carter the president was a risk.

Given the fragmentation of the country, the preoccupation with self, the complexity of the problems, the volatility of the electorate, the general disaffection with politics, the next president faced formidable challenges. Another failure in the presidency could be disastrous. But the future also held great promise. The next president would be starting fresh, backed by a citizenry ready for a new brand of leadership and tempered by realism.

Whether it would be progress or more pessimism no one could say. That the country would not stagnate was certain, for the changes were accelerating.

□ □ □

Election night, on the large national map shown on the television screen, Carter's color, red, was lighting up quickly and early. Georgia and Alabama and South Carolina and Florida, after stumbling in their support for their fellow Southerner, were falling into line behind him. Other Southern states were moving in the same direction, back to their old home in the Democratic Party, trying to give their native son a springboard for victory.

That wasn't true of larger states in the East, Midwest, and West. Even New York was in doubt. From the early hours of Tuesday evening, on through the night and long into the next day, uncertainty hung over the nation. Television, with its whirr-whirr-whirr of changing computer numbers, its "decision desks," its "projected winners" in flashing lights, its roaming cameras picking out candidates voting, smiling, waiting, was recording an unusually close election.

The first projections, an hour and a half before the polls closed in the East, called two states: Indiana, with thirteen electoral votes, was placed in Ford's column; Kentucky, with nine, in Carter's. As the night wore on, the changing computer numbers spelled out an extremely tight race. State after critical state was deadlocked—49 percent for Carter, 49 for Ford.

In their last surveys, the pollsters had found an extraordinarily large number of voters undecided. Perfect weather on election day had graced the nation from coast to coast, and at first a record national turnout was projected. But 65 million people eligible to vote for president—nearly 46 percent of those entitled to cast ballots—did not go to the polls.

The way the states were going reflected the national doubt and indecision. As Tuesday turned into Wednesday a number of key states—Ohio, Illinois, Texas, California among them—were still undecided; for several agonizing hours the returns slowed down, as if the nation were still weighing the choice, still wrestling over its decision. Carter's expected electoral vote total had crept to 267 on the CBS projections, three short of the necessary majority. Then CBS retracted an earlier call for Carter, and Oregon seemed uncertain. He had only 261 electoral votes—nine more to go. Hawaii, always so strongly Democratic, should have been assured for Carter, but it still had Ford leading. Then it slipped into the Carter column. Now it was 265—only five more.

On the East Coast the clock was inching past three o'clock in the morning. Six states remained in doubt—Maine, Ohio, Illinois, Oregon, California, and Mississippi. Maine, with only four votes, wouldn't be enough, and Ford was leading there in any case. The spotlight fell on Mississippi. It was Mississippi, a state that had seen such strife in the last decade, and a state that had been a center of Republican strength in the South, that put Carter into the presidency. In the end the South stayed loyal to its own. It had done more than that; it had made it possible for Carter to win. And it was the votes of Southern blacks in particular that gave Carter his base. They made the difference between victory and defeat in seven Southern states—Alabama, Florida, Georgia, Louisiana, Mississippi, North and South Carolina—and thirteen in all. In

Florida and Texas, black voting increased by 12 percent. In Alabama, 14 percent more blacks turned out to vote. And in Mississippi, the increase was 22 percent. Carter carried Mississippi by only 11,537 votes. He received nearly 90 percent of the 140,526 black votes cast there. The Hartman Turnbows of Mississippi propelled Jimmy Carter into the White House. Carter didn't carry a single Western state, although he came within an eyelash of winning some, giving him an opportunity to establish a solid constituency. In Iowa, for instance, where he lost by barely a percentage point, he already had a core of supporters. Among them was Fred Doxsee of Boone. Along with many of his friends and neighbors, Doxsee had decided to take a chance for change with Jimmy Carter.

BOOK TWO

GOVERNING

5

THE FIRST YEAR

WHEN HE came to Washington as a young professor, the same sight always stirred him: the plane would come down the Potomac, the wing would go up as it banked over the Jefferson Memorial before landing, and there below was a glimpse of the White House. His pulse would quicken, he remembered. And now, amazingly, here he was, walking through the White House gates for the first time, actually going to work there. It was an emotional experience that he had difficulty expressing in words: "I was feeling a tremendous excitement, and I had a feeling we had a chance to change things and do it for the public good." Then he was rudely awakened to find himself sitting in a small, cramped office amid a sea of confusion. "It was just chaos. Those first few weeks we were just swirling around. It was sort of our day in the sun, and we tried to go everywhere at once."

Steven Simmons' experience as a new member of the Carter White House staff was in many ways typical, as excited, nervous, eager, earnest Carter people began attempting to take control of the government. Like all presidential appointees, they brought a freshness and intensity to their jobs and, with many, awe. Jody Powell, Carter's press secretary, took his mother, an American history teacher from Vienna, Georgia, to the southwest side of the White House after the inauguration. As they approached, the Secret Service detail swung open the massive iron gates and the Powells found themselves inside the grounds, strolling up the winding driveway to the White House ahead. What are we doing here? Powell thought. Once inside, they found a friend from Georgia; it didn't seem quite so strange. But it was all so new, and they were all so untried.

They were determined to be different. That was why Carter had been elected in the first place, and they were going to help him fulfill that promise. The president was going to cut back on the ceremonial trappings of his office—no ruffles and flourishes, no fanfares. They and the cabinet officers would forgo the customary chauffeur-driven executive limousines. And if there were not enough people to answer the White House phones, or process the mail, or respond to the congressional requests for information or for favors or for patronage, well, that was the price of keeping the presidential staff small, as promised—the price of a less imperial presidency. Carter was serious about cutting back on the bureaucracy, and his example began at home, with his own official family. If it meant turning over much of the decision-making authority to the cabinet officers, in both determining policy and making political appointments, and if it meant no single vested authority in the White House staff to give centralized direction to the presidential effort—well, that was the price of bringing real democracy into the White House.

To sour cynics, all these plans were signs that the Carter people didn't know how to operate, and they quickly judged Carter long on symbolism and short on substance. When a reporter, a few weeks into the new term, obtained and published a lengthy private memorandum to Carter from his personal pollster, Patrick Caddell, the suspicions seemed confirmed. Caddell spelled out "stylistic points" he said Carter should emphasize immediately after taking office: cutting back on limousines for the brass, giving fireside chats, making presidential visits to the various government departments, et cetera. "Too many good people have been defeated because they tried to substitute substance for style," Caddell advised. "They forgot to give the public the visible signals it needs to understand what is happening." From Vice-President Mondale had come similar advice. Project "the image of a 'can-do' president who has taken charge in Washington," Mondale said.

So when Carter in fact did give his first fireside chat in front of a crackling White House fire, casually wearing a cardigan sweater; when he made much of eliminating the rituals and privileges of his office and reducing the size of his staff; when he visited the government agencies personally; when he participated in carefully staged "town meetings" away from Washington and in a homey "Call President Carter" nationwide phone hookup from the Oval Office, critics were convinced he was simply following a public-relations script. Before long Garry Trudeau's popular comic script *Doonesbury* was featuring a "Secretary of Symbolism" who charted Carter's moves.

But much of this reflected a genuine desire to set a different standard. Those whom Carter appointed felt that responsibility strongly. His first two presidential appointments, for instance.

□   □   □

The sounds of the last band to march by the inaugural platform were echoing off the brick walls on Pennsylvania Avenue when Max Cleland went inside the west wing of the White House. It was four o'clock, January 20, and Cleland was thinking, This is extraordinary, I'm going into the White House even before the parade is over. Some minutes later Hamilton Jordan asked him to come into the Oval Office to see the new president. "Max, you're my first appointment," Carter said. "Mr. President, I'm honored," Cleland replied.

Only once before had Cleland been in the White House. That had been two days before John Kennedy's assassination, during a brief visit to Washington while a senior at a small Southern Baptist college. Cleland had had a glimpse of Kennedy's office that day thirteen years before, and seeing Carter walk toward the big desk in the Oval Office gave him a strange feeling. The desk looked like the one his idol Kennedy had used; but Cleland was too struck by the moment to dare ask. (In fact, he learned later, it *was* Kennedy's old desk. Carter had requested it be put in his office that day.)

He was thinking about making Cleland head of the Veterans Administration, Carter said as he sat down behind the desk. Cleland, at thirty-four, would be the youngest person to hold that post, but Carter could think of no one with better credentials. They had known each other in their native Georgia, where both had entered politics after military careers. But Cleland's had ended differently from Carter's: he had been a small-town, all-American star athlete and honor student who had gone on to Vietnam and become a hero, bronze and silver stars to pin on his Army officer's tunic. Then, at Khesanh, there had been the grenade and the wounds. Max Cleland came home a triple amputee; he lost his right arm and both legs at the knees. Many years passed, and, as he said, "a lot of pain and a lot of effort and a lot of proving to yourself who you are and what you are and where you're going," before he began to recover from his wounds. It wasn't until he recognized that his artificial limbs were indeed psychological as well as physical crutches, and literally cast them aside, that he felt at peace with himself.

Sitting in his wheelchair in the Oval Office, waving the stump of his right arm as he talked, Max Cleland frankly thought of himself as a man with a mission, not the least of which was symbolic: he wanted the job Carter was offering "not so much to dredge up old wars and old wounds, but by sitting in my wheelchair and through my speeches and appearances, and general leadership, to be a public reminder of the price that's been paid in Vietnam." They talked about the job, and then Carter got up and walked alongside as Cleland wheeled himself, with his left arm, to the door. "Mr. President, I'll do a good job for you," Cleland said, as they parted. "I want you to do a good job not only for me," Carter said, "but for the veterans in this country."

Cleland was emotional as he left. "I was the first outsider, I was his first official appointment," he said. "That was a very signal honor for me. And in a strange way I had a feeling of picking up what had been left, a sense of purpose and idealism—moving on after a hiatus of some thirteen years."

The next appointment was another outsider. When he was in Washington in the late 1960s, Sam Brown had led antiwar demonstrations against the government. He organized the Vietnam moratoriums around the White House in the Nixon era, and before that had directed the students who left their campuses to campaign for Eugene McCarthy in 1968; at that time Brown was a Harvard Divinity School student. The 1960s left a certain bitterness. "Some of us who came here at one time with a pure burning sense of changing the world went through very cynical times—about the country, about other people, about the world in general," he said to me. "At least in my case, I lost a lot of that early faith in some larger possibilities, and about what the American people are like." Brown didn't drop out, but he did leave national politics and Washington. In 1974 he went to Colorado, ran for the state treasurer's office, and won. By 1977, when Jimmy Carter called him to Washington on January 20 to talk about working for the new administration, Brown was thirty-four and had a promising political future in Colorado.

Carter wanted Brown to take over as director of ACTION, the umbrella agency that housed what was left of the liberal, idealistic, and perhaps naïve governmental impulses of the 1960s—the Peace Corps, VISTA, and the War on Poverty. During the Nixon administration ACTION had become perhaps the most politicized and dispirited of all government agencies: it was a prime target for Nixon's attempt to impose ideological conformity on the bureaucracy. Make ACTION what it should be, give it a new sense of idealism, Carter said.

Brown's friends uniformly counseled him against taking the position. It was a time of cynicism now, they said. People were out for themselves, and not interested in volunteer governmental efforts. And Brown had his own doubts: "One of the things I know about Washington is that it eats people up," he said while thinking about the Carter offer. But he also knew that for a dozen years he'd been the critic, always calling for change. If he passed up a chance to see if he could make government work better in Washington, he'd probably forfeit a future national political career. And he had ambitions. Sam Brown took the job.

Walking into the lobby of his new office building, just a block from the White House, instantly made Brown uncomfortable. A guard was posted behind a desk, monitoring sign-in and sign-out forms, and around him were stanchions and ropes to cordon off the public. Why was all that necessary? the new director asked. Why didn't they scrap all those officious and uninviting trappings? Simple enough, he was told. It was to keep "them" out. In the past, "they" had tried to take over the building during demonstrations; "they" were still out there today. They and they and they. Brown listened long enough, and finally snapped: "Look, I don't think you understand. *They* are now in charge around here." He ordered the stanchions and ropes removed, the check-in and check-out books eliminated. The building was opened up.

Similar scenes were occurring throughout Washington as the Carter people took over. Several days after the inauguration Bert Lance met privately for the first time with a group of Washington reporters in his expansive office next to the White House. Lance had driven to work himself that morning, he said. That was how he intended to get around in Washington. He wanted to meet regularly and at length with the reporters, he was saying, and he would let them tell him how best to set up that working arrangement. The relationship with the press was terribly important, he knew, and he was determined to be as open with the news media as possible. That's how he had worked in Georgia, and that's how he intended to work in Washington.

As the president's new budget director, Lance immediately became a figure of power in Washington; next to the president himself, the head of the Office of Management and Budget exerted enormous influence by determining what the government would spend, for what and how. In addition, Lance was close to Carter personally, perhaps more so than anyone except Carter's wife, Rosalynn. For years they had been political and economic allies in Georgia. When Carter became governor in 1970, on his second try, Lance became his highway director. Four years later Lance was Carter's handpicked choice to succeed him as governor (a position that Carter himself had to relinquish because the state's constitution prohibited a governor from serving two consecutive terms). Lance lost, narrowly, and became a banker, helping to finance, among other businesses, the Carter warehouse and peanut operations in Plains. After Carter won the national election, Lance became his first choice for a high-level appointment.

Big, flamboyant, affable, a six-feet-four, two-hundred-forty-five-pound package of earnestness and guile, his disarranged black hair setting off a moonlike face, Bert Lance was a gargantuan figure among the often rather colorless Carter crew—part Babbitt, part Gantry, part disarming prototype of the good old country boy. He had presence.

"I do return telephone calls," he said now to the reporters, "even on Saturday afternoons, Sunday night, or whatever the case may be. I don't mind you calling me at home. I would prefer you do it when I'm there and not asleep—and I sleep from, you know, about twelve-thirty to four-thirty. So if you would just observe those hours. The rest of the time doesn't really bother me."

This was extraordinary. High public officials didn't act that way in Washington, and here was one of the most important of them telling the press he was going to lay himself open to their questioning at all hours.

Lance was no less open than President Carter. For someone who was supposed to be elusive, Jimmy Carter was remarkably expressive and revealing during those early weeks. His was not a conventional political message. Indeed, not wishing to sound political was central. Carter was sounding a *moral* theme, and accompanying it with a philosophic, even fatalistic air about his own presidential future. Nor did he seem interested in making news in the normal sense—to give the journalists something "hard" to lead their daily reports. If you listened closely, what you heard was a consistent espousal of a deeply held religious conviction. Here, truly, it appeared, was a Christian in the White House trying to relate his religious experience to national political life.

A week after his inauguration he spoke at a national prayer breakfast in Washington. In his original inaugural address he had chosen a different Biblical verse from the one he finally read, he recalled. The first verse he had incorporated into his speech, from Second Chronicles, 7:14, read: "If my people, which are called by my name, shall humble themselves, and pray, and seek my face, and turn from their wicked ways; then will I hear from heaven and will forgive their sin, and will heal their land." The American people would misunderstand what their new president was saying, his staff objected. But in his second draft, Carter again included the same verse. This time his staff was more adamant. People would think the president was putting himself in the position of Solomon and saying all Americans are wicked, they argued. Reluctantly, Carter changed the verse to one from Micah about justice and mercy ("To do justly, and to love mercy, and to walk humbly with thy God"); but he still thought he had been right from the beginning:

Sometimes we take for granted that an acknowledgment of sin, an acknowledgment for the need for humility, permeates the consciousness of our people. But it doesn't. But if we know that we can have God's forgiveness as a person, I think as a nation it makes it much easier for us to say, "God, have mercy on me, a sinner," knowing that the only compensation for sin is condemnation. Then we just can't admit an error or a weakness or a degree of hatred or forgo pride. We as individuals—and we as a nation—insist that we are the strongest and the bravest and the wisest and the best. And in that attitude, we unconsciously, but in an all-pervasive way, cover up and fail to acknowledge our mistakes and in the process forgo an opportunity constantly to search for a better life or a better country.

It was the sin of pride, both personal and national, he preached against:

Sometimes it's easier for us to be humble as individuals than it is for us to admit that our nation makes mistakes. In effect, many of us worship our nation. We politicians, we leaders, in that sometimes excessive degree of patriotism, equate love of others with love of ourselves. We tend to say that because I am a congressman, because I am a governor, because I am a senator, because I am a cabinet member, because I am a president of the people, and because I love the people and represent them so well, then I can justify their love myself. We tend to take on for ourselves the attributes of the people we represent. But when the disciples struggled among themselves for superiority in God's eyes, Jesus said, "Whosoever would be chief among you, let him be his servant." And although we use the phrase, sometimes glibly, "public servant," it's hard for us to translate the concept of a president of the United States into genuine servant.

He repeated this message as he attempted to indicate the direction of his presidency. He was modest, almost to a fault, understated, soft-spoken, never ranting, never pejorative, but withal quietly evangelical. To a group of Labor Department employees in Washington:

I am no better qualified than you are to address the problems of our country. We are partners in a process. . . . I hope, working closely with you, to bring about a structure of government . . . [and] to make your one life—like mine, which is very valuable in the eyes of God—be meaningful, because each career represented here can either be fruitful or it can be wasted. . . .

I also want us to realize that we are no better than anyone else. Just because I am president and because you work for the federal government or hold, even, an exalted job, doesn't make you any better than the unemployed American in Dallas, Texas, that you serve. . . . We are here to serve and not to be served. And we are not masters of anyone, for we represent a government that wants to make other people more independent, more free, more able to make the most of their own talents and abilities. That is all I have to say to you.

Invariably, he stressed how new and unfamiliar and untested he was with his new job, and how he needed people's help to succeed. He didn't claim to know all the answers, he said, again and again. As "an embryonic president who has never served in Washington before," he knew he had a lot to learn. To the workers at the Commerce Department, advice, and a plea:

Arrogance is something that is a temptation for us all. I have tried to remove as much as I could the trappings and pomp and ceremony that has in the past followed presidents. I don't want ruffles and flourishes played when I walk into a group like this. I am just one of you. . . .

I am going to make some mistakes. I hope you will forgive me. You are going to make some mistakes, and we will be in it together.

To the workers at the Housing and Urban Development Department, the stating of a presidential wish and the pronouncing of a sermon:

I want to make sure that whatever I do as president of our country in changing the structure or the priorities in our government, it makes your lives and your professions more meaningful. If I fail in that, then I've not only insulted you and your integrity as an individual but I've also caused to suffer the people who elected me to office and whom I love very deeply—as do you. . . .

I might add one other thing that has just come to mind. I have asked my own White House staff, and I've also asked . . . cabinet members to protect the integrity of their own family life. I think it's

very important that all of us in government not forget that no matter how dedicated we might be and how eager to perform well, that
we need a stable family life to make us better servants of the people.
So those of you who are living in sin I hope you'll get married.
Those of you who have left your spouses, go back home. And those
of you who don't remember your children's names, get reacquaint-
ed. But I think it's very important that we have stable family lives.
And I am serious about that.

This last, now-famous admonition about living in sin made national headlines. Set on paper, his words seem stiff, if not patron-
izing, and they contradicted a national trend away from the kinds
of life-styles Carter was advocating. Yet *seeing* and *hearing* Carter
deliver his little speeches—talks really, for he always spoke extemporaneously—gave a different impression from the sometimes
stern-sounding moralist. When he walked to a microphone set up
in the middle of a crowded Health, Education and Welfare Department basement cafeteria, and began speaking, slowly, in soft sing-
song cadences, he instantly captured everyone's attention—not
from the power of his oratory, but there was something about that
slight, serious earnest figure that commanded respect. As only one
person standing nearby, I found myself strangely moved.

Quoting Kierkegaard—"Every person is an individual"—Carter
reminded his listeners that presidents and politicians come and
go; but he hoped they would "let the one life that you and I have
to live on earth be expanded in a maximum, beneficial way toward
others." Setting a new moral standard in government dominated
everything he did. "I want to see our country set a standard of mo-
rality," he said. "I feel very deeply that when people are put in
prison without trials and tortured and deprived of basic human
rights, that the president of the United States ought to have a right
to express displeasure and do something about it. I want our
country to be the focal point for deep concern about human beings all over the world." If people had been listening closely during his campaign, these views shouldn't have come as a surprise.
They were consistent with his beliefs as he had been stating them
all along. (In his celebrated *Playboy* interview given during the
campaign, while speaking about foreign policy he had said something similar: "I don't ever want to do anything as president that

would be a contravention of the moral and ethical standards that I would exemplify in my own life as an individual.")

In private, or before small groups, Carter's command of information and his manner of explaining his views on issues were almost always praised. But the public Carter was so soft-spoken, so soothing in speech and manner, that it wasn't long before he was being criticized in the press for failing to inspire people. (That criticism—an oft-repeated one—faulted Carter for "swallowing" his best lines and lulling his audiences when he meant to stir them. Privately, some of his staff—and particularly his speechwriters— agreed.)

His work habits as president were prodigious. He left orders with the Secret Service for a permanent wake-up call at six o'clock each morning. But he usually was up long before that, a normal day beginning at five o'clock. First he would spend hours reading papers, dealing with memorandums and various policy proposals and alternatives, preparing himself for the making of decisions. "I'm learning, I'm studying," he'd say. "I get over here every morning at the latest by seven o'clock, and go home in time for supper at seven, and then I spend two or three hours a night working and studying and reading. It's not a laborious thing for me because I really enjoy it."

He took a speed-reading course and urged others on his staff to do so. His mastery of the information absorbed was an obvious source of pride. In the manner of the quick student, anxious to show how much he knew, he could be boastful. "You may be surprised," he told a group of State Department officers several weeks after his inauguration, "to know that the last three reorganization proposals sent to the State Department I have studied myself."

He was methodical. Next to his chair in his office was a large globe. When a dispatch from a country with which he was unfamiliar—like Gabon, in equatorial Africa—would reach his desk, he'd check the country on the globe and then study about it. When Secretary of State Cyrus Vance would cable back reports on a foreign trip, Carter instructed his staff to keep a careful log listing the principal attitudes of the various national leaders Vance had met. He wanted, he said, "to see if I can understand compatibility among them and what the remaining differences might be."

And, always, he had a hunger for the flow of information, on paper, from his staff. Those unfamiliar with his working style quickly learned that he personally was reading their policy memorandums, and swiftly responding to them.

"It's almost like we're pen pals with the president," one staff member told me, after getting back another memo underlined and with marginal comments written in Carter's small, careful hand. *Yes. No. Sounds good. Proceed. What does this mean? I don't agree. Check on this.* "It's almost as if you sent it to the Delphic oracle for the answer and the Delphic oracle checked the right box."

That the Delphic oracle was a remote figure, someone you dealt with by paper instead of personal contact, were facts that had to be learned by those new to Carter's service. When the president gave orders that the family quarters upstairs at the White House were to be strictly off limits, when it became known he gave little lectures about the virtues of marriage to people thinking of separation or divorce, even some inside the White House began to wonder just what Carter was about. For all his revealing remarks about his own personal beliefs, Carter remained distant. But that he was a worker, possessed of a first-rate mind, they were certain. It was as if, someone said, you suddenly had an engineer occupying the White House, opening up his big blueprints, and pointing out where to start. The way he worked quickly became legendary.

Carter's manner of drafting memos and letters was a departure from normal executive practice. He didn't dictate his material; instead, he wrote it all out by hand on one side of one sheet of a five-by-eight-inch pad. "I can write it very quickly, send it out, and it's done," he explained. Besides, it cut down on paperwork, a personally desirable goal.

The volume of work and the personal pace he set were remarkable. He demanded action on a huge number of vexing national issues—advocating not merely the beginnings of policy initiatives but "comprehensive" (to use his favorite term) solutions to longstanding and complicated problems. He wanted everything done, and all at once. Within three weeks of taking office, he told a small group of journalists about his determination to have an aggressive and dynamic administration. "There will be a constant stream of comprehensive suggestions going to the Congress," he said, "which in my opinion, are long overdue: a complete reform of the welfare system; for the first time a comprehensive policy on energy; a tangible addressing of the problems of equity in our tax laws, trade laws; interrelationships with our friends around the world and our potential adversaries around the world."

Did he *really* think he was going to be able to keep all his presidential campaign promises? he was asked. Unhesitatingly, he replied: "My determination is to keep *all* those promises." Spurred on by his demands and example, his staff and cabinet labored to meet his deadlines for action on energy, on welfare, on tax reform, on dozens of other major promised changes.

His determination to be different, to live up to his promises, was admirable—and also disastrous. He set impossible deadlines and standards, and created problems for himself and his staff. When he traveled away from the White House, to a town meeting on March 16 in Clinton, Massachusetts, he became so caught up in the moment—and, it would seem, his message—that he urged the people to write him personally. "I'll tell my staff to bring those letters directly to me," he said over the radio and television. ". . . You need not say that you were glad to have me with you and what a good job I did and so forth. Just say, 'This is what I think you ought to do to be a good president.' " The response was overwhelming. In one week alone, 87,000 letters poured into the White House, four times more than normal. They swamped the already taxed White House facilities and added to the enormous backlog. At one point there were 315,000 unopened letters at the White House. Included in them were not only letters from average citizens but important correspondence from Capitol Hill, corporation executives, and other "elites" in the country. The same was true of phone calls. Between twenty and thirty thousand calls a day were flooding into the White House, in large part due to Carter's wishes to have the people let him know what they thought. They did, but important political messages often went unanswered—and important political figures wanting to reach the White House couldn't get through. Many simply gave up in anger and frustration.

Carter also went out of his way to repeat his determination to impose more rigid standards on the government. He was not going to indulge in politics as usual or, as some began suggesting, politics at all. He was going to see that federal judges were ap-

pointed on the basis of merit and ability "instead of [as] a cheap
political payoff," he said, at one point. And, to the State Department, a similarly unequivocal pledge: "I am determined that every
single appointment that I ever make . . . is on the basis of merit
and nothing else. And I want to root out once and for all the cheap
political appointments that sometimes in the past have been an
embarrassment to our own country and sometimes an insult to the
nations to which we send diplomatic officers to represent us."

As in the campaign, he showed he was still capable of excessive
political promises. When a minister asked him about the prospect
of passing consumer-protection legislation, he instantly shot back:
"If we don't do that, Reverend Baker, before I get out of office, I
will consider my administration to be a failure."

                          □   □   □

Mr. President, the booming voice of Speaker Tip O'Neill called
out, the word "confrontation" is not in our lexicon—at least for
another six months. There were smiles around the table, and anyone looking on would have thought that political harmony prevailed. And would have been wrong.

The Democratic congressional leaders had just concluded a
breakfast meeting with Jimmy Carter, upstairs in the White House
family dining room, the first of many private sessions they would
have. It was five days after the inauguration.

On the surface the meeting had gone well. Carter had begun by
offering a blessing, which prompted the Senate majority leader,
the impeccably formal Robert Byrd of West Virginia, to commend
him. That was the first time presidential prayer had been heard in
all his long years of attending such White House meetings, Byrd
said. And Carter had conducted himself well, if stiffly, as he outlined his goals for Congress and himself in the coming session. He
wanted to work closely with them, he said, and hoped that such
private and informal meetings could help to resolve any differences between them.

His cabinet would be playing a different role, he explained. He
was going to use them as a collegial body and had asked them to
contact the appropriate congressional committee leaders to work

directly in the drafting of legislation. That's the way he had operated in Georgia, he said.

The president had one major request of them: to give him authority to reorganize the government. It was the most important
of his pledges to the people; he thought he was elected president
because of that promise, and he intended to fulfill it.

That was familiar to the congressional leaders, as were the rest
of his remarks. They, in turn, wanted to make sure Carter understood their concerns. As Byrd reminded the president, it was vital
that he let them know what he was planning and working on.

The president seemed to brush the point aside, until O'Neill
spoke up forcefully: You, Mr. President, should keep us posted on
what the White House is doing on legislation, so that if we have
responsibility for moving it, we know what is going on. When Byrd
concurred, Carter agreed. He got the message, he said.

The conversation came back to government reorganization.
Now Hubert Humphrey spoke up. There had been a total break-
down of the bureaucracy, he began. No matter what anybody
thought, the real bureaucratic problem wasn't in Washington. It
was in the federal government's regional and district offices. Chicago and Duluth were bureaucratic bottlenecks, Humphrey said.
They were dead on their tails. And take a look at Social Security. It
was disgusting, we keep getting the same old shuffle. You will reorganize here in Washington, Mr. President, Humphrey went on,
but out there they will still grind it out.

The president listened intently. Give me reorganization authority as soon as possible, he said, in a hurry; it's the thing that concerns me most.

Then he challenged them directly. He threatened to take his
case to the public, against them, if they didn't act. Once more
O'Neill's voice filled the room. That would be the worst thing you
could ever do, he told the president to his face.

Moments later, after O'Neill told him that "confrontation"
would be stricken from their dialogues, this first meeting ended.

Too many differences and too many doubts existed between the
president and the congressional leaders for their relationship to
begin smoothly. And the early weeks were anything but smooth.
Already, there were angry grumblings on Capitol Hill about the
inability to reach anybody at the White House. Democrats in Con-

gress were embarrassed and angry to learn only after the fact and through the press that Carter was appointing people from their states to positions in his administration. Liaison between the White House and the Hill (a task that Frank Moore was in charge of) clearly wasn't working. There was no patronage. To many Democrats, the Carter presidency was repeating the mistakes of the Carter presidential campaign.

The next private White House meeting between the president and the congressional leaders, on the morning of February 8, quickly became acrimonious—even over the food, for only rolls and coffee were served instead of the full breakfast the congressmen evidently expected. Carter ran through a list of items. The last and most important point, as far as Hill-White House relations were concerned, he said, was this: his cabinet officers were spending so much time testifying on Capitol Hill that it was almost impossible for them to administer their departments. Much more than half their time was being taken up with Capitol Hill. It was damaging to the government, the president went on, for cabinet members to spend so many hours preparing for congressional testimony when they were new in office and their assistant and deputy secretaries had not yet been chosen.

Immediately, the dissents began.

O'Neill: This is a part of congressional life that we have always had. I have not heard this kind of complaint before, Mr. President.

Congressman Dan Rostenkowski, of Illinois: Mr. President, you will always find this is the way it is at the start of Congress. Committee chairmen take pride in having new cabinet officers testify, especially when you have an important question like energy. There is even a jealousy quotient here, with respect to who testifies before which committee first. This is not a problem you can therefore really resolve.

Carter disagreed. It was a real problem, he said, and nothing he heard in the next few minutes while the leaders explained the process changed his mind. They told him that the newness of the president's programs made the cabinet testimony necessary; the entire congressional schedule had been changed to accommodate the hearings; Congress was hard at work considering the new ideas, new presidential messages, new budget resolutions; everything would iron itself out in time.

But Carter was determined. He wanted his cabinet officers just three days a week, he said coldly, he didn't think that would be asking too much. Now, it seemed, they were over on the Hill all the time.

Again, the leaders began explaining. Senator Abraham Ribicoff, who had been HEW secretary under John Kennedy: Mr. President, as a former cabinet officer, I know you just can't avoid this. With a major presidential policy, a cabinet officer will get television attention to the president's policy and other officers won't. There is no problem sending an assistant or deputy secretary to the Hill on routine bills but not on major bills. The system of having cabinet officers appear before congressional committees, therefore, works for *you.*

Carter was silent a moment, before saying: I'll speak frankly, if you don't mind. I don't want to stroke you. You say that you will get television attention with the appearance of a cabinet officer but with *one* appearance he can get television attention. Some of those meetings and appearances by cabinet officers happen seven different times. I am not trying to change the historic pattern of Congress, but perhaps you can let two committees meet together and let deputy or assistant secretaries meet before subcommittees.

Senator Byrd attempted conciliation: They'd think about it, explore it, and if there were some way of coping with the problem, they'd do it. Humphrey also struck a moderate note: We're governed a lot, Mr. President, by the media, he said. And the media made them all hostage. Congress had learned that if hearings were scheduled in the late afternoon or night, the media wouldn't come. That's why most committee chairmen wanted meetings in the morning, to give their sessions a better chance to get on the evening network–news shows. But perhaps that pattern could be broken and cabinet officers could appear at the end of a day. Others, in a similar vein, told the president they needed to hear from the cabinet officers, but that the momentary problems would abate.

Once again Speaker O'Neill cut through the conversation. In effect, he was throwing down the glove for the new president to pick it up, if he chose.

O'Neill: Mr. President, the history, the style, the dignity of the Congress *must* be preserved. We are an equal branch. *When we need*

*your cabinet secretaries we will send for them, and we will not do so unnec-
essarily.*

Contentious as that meeting had been, far greater damage occurred little more than a week later. The president—fully aware,
he later said, of the political consequences—suddenly and without
prior consultation with anyone in Congress announced that he
was considering cutting funds for nineteen water projects around
the country. This action stunned and angered the Congress. For
Carter not only had failed to consult with and in most cases even
notify House members about what he was planning but had intruded where presidents historically had not stepped: he had violated the unwritten Washington political agreement that allows
members of Congress to trade off benefits for their home areas—a
dam for my district, and a river-dredging project for yours, no
questions asked—pork-barrel politics, pure and simple, sacrosanct
over the decades. The wail from Congress—and from the governors and state legislators of the areas affected, none of whom had
been consulted or notified either—was deafening.

You didn't have to follow Washington politics for decades, as I
had, to know that Carter was right in calling many of these water
projects wasteful and largely unnecessary: the Corps of Engineers
had fashioned a notorious record of intimacy with its political
sponsors in Congress at the expense of the true public interest.
There was no doubt in my mind about Carter's sincerity.*

The way Carter acted, and why, went to the heart of his idea of
how he should function as president. While he never made reference to it himself, so far as I know, Carter had faced a similar situation in Georgia, had been decisive, and had prevailed. In 1971,
during his first year as governor, he received a midnight call in-
forming him that the Corps of Engineers was dredging in a legally
protected wildlife marshland creek near Saint Simon Island, off
the southern Georgia coast. Immediately Carter began rousing
people by phone, and then dispatched a boatload of Georgia
Rangers to stop the engineers, forcibly if necessary. By 3:00 a.m.

---

*I was impressed with the writer John McPhee's favorable comments about Car-
ter after he took a canoe trip with him during Carter's governorship to inspect environmental conditions in Georgia. McPhee described the trip in his book *The
Survival of the Bark Canoe* (1975).

Carter had delivered an indignant phone message and warning to the colonel in charge of the project: halt the work or the Rangers would do so themselves. The dredging ended. Throughout his term as governor, Carter continued to move vigorously against Engineer Corps works that would either create environmental damage or mar a place of scenic beauty. He intended to operate the same way in Washington.

His plan to slash federal money from the water projects was set in motion almost as suddenly as the Georgia stream episode. On February 14, just a week before his deadline for changing the final 1978 federal budget requests (which had been prepared by Ford), Carter asked for a review; within twenty-four hours an Interior Department team had given the White House a list of likely pork-barrel water projects that should be reviewed with an eye toward possibly terminating them. The White House called back: add more projects to the list.

Carter convened a small group of advisers, including Bert Lance and Interior Secretary Cecil Andrus, on the evening of February 17. By the next day, word of their decision to strike the projects from the budget was out.

Congress erupted. A private session with the president, demanded by some of the angriest senators, such as Russell Long and Gary Hart of Colorado, led to a scene—accounts of which quickly made the rounds. Long, the wily senator from Louisiana who had learned his political lore from his father, the fabled Huey Long, the so-called Kingfish, in his time perhaps the single most powerful man on Capitol Hill, stood up before a group of White House aides and, his voice dripping with sarcasm, introduced himself: "My name is Russell Long, and I am the chairman of the Senate Finance Committee." Long, whose state held five of the projects marked for extinction, proceeded to shout out his objections to Carter's decisions.

Carter was adamant: "My own judgment is that none of these projects are worthy and that none of them ought to be completed or continued," he told a small group of journalists in his office shortly afterward. It was, he said, "a gross waste" of the taxpayers' money. Somebody had to bite the bullet, and he was the one. Besides, he was totally committed to balancing the budget by 1981, and that couldn't happen if he submitted to Congress proposals that kept on wasting money. He would take his case to the people, if necessary, he said.

But he didn't, and he lost without a public fight. The Senate, by a vote of 65 to 24, added an amendment to the public-works bill with the president's proposed legislation to stimulate the economy—a bill strongly favored by the Democrats—that required continued spending for all money appropriated for the water projects. The president could veto it all if he dared, the Senate was telling him. Carter didn't; for he quickly knew that the water-projects issue was jeopardizing the rest of his program. At another White House–Congressional leadership meeting in early April, he asked how his economic package would fare in Congress. Senator Byrd, chin tucked down, looking right at the president, spoke deliberately:

I can't tell you, Mr. President, how much damage the water-projects list [nineteen dam projects scheduled to be killed] is doing to our efforts. Some senators aren't going to come around so long as those water projects are on the list. It's a battle you don't need. It will cost you—and us—here and on other, more important battles. Its timing was one hundred percent off. Senator Long won't put his arm around any other senators so long as water projects in his state are on the list. If we lose, it would be a defeat for the president and for the Senate Democratic leadership. I want to be very honest with you, Mr. President. I'd be very insincere and dishonest with you if I didn't say this. The president's decision on the water projects, Byrd continued in the same slow style, was the most stupid he'd ever heard of since he'd been in Washington, and he'd been there for twenty-five years.

Carter declined to veto the congressional requests, and the water projects went forward. Later, he and his aides told me, he deeply regretted not carrying the fight on through a veto; he remained convinced he was right and the Washington politicians wrong. But the view of him from the Washington insiders was different. "That water-projects fight was a perfect display of everything that was wrong with Carter's coming to Washington thinking he had the expertise," one Democratic congressman said to me. "He came in determined to balance the budget and prove he was fiscally tough. That feeling was compounded by his fascination with briefing papers. You know, here's the paper, check the appropriate box—(*a*) do nothing; (*b*) check with Congress; (*c*) take it out of the budget. So he checks (*c*). Even though I had to fight him on this, there was a lot of merit in what he was trying to do. It's the *way* it was done that was the trouble. I hope this will be a great learning experience for him, but I don't know that it will be."

As events soon proved, the president didn't draw the lessons the congressmen had hoped. Only one more week passed before again he took the Congress and the country by surprise.

A key element of his economic program, as he had announced and propounded it publicly, was that a fifty-dollar tax rebate would be granted to Americans. It was a promise he had made firmly, and in Congress Democratic leaders and organized labor were working hard to carry it out. At a breakfast meeting with the leaders on April 5, when he had been told that opposition was developing to the rebate, Carter strongly defended it. Losing the rebate, he said, would wreak havoc with working and poor families. This rebate should not go down the drain, he added, for unemployment is still high.

Over the Easter recess, Carter began going over the figures on his economic forecast. Economic conditions were already improving and another stimulus such as a tax cut wasn't necessary, he concluded. In addition, he was concerned about the inflation rate increasing more than he had anticipated. A tax rebate would exacerbate those conditions.

At six o'clock on Easter Sunday night, at his home in Plains, the president made his decision without consulting anyone. He was going to withdraw the tax rebate, and announce it immediately. He called Senators Byrd and Long and some others to tell them, but many other leading members of Congress never got the word until the news was in the press. Several days later Carter apologized to the Democratic leaders for not adequately consulting with them, and a couple of weeks after that he apologized again: I think I've been culpable in recent weeks in this lack of communications. I want to prevent a recurrence of the mistake.

But that didn't quell the discontent. The Democrats in particular were concerned not only by policy changes and lack of consultation but by what they saw as a rejection of Democratic Party positions and the espousal of highly conservative ones.

These feelings reached a peak—a crisis point, almost—after the
president convened a special White House meeting on May 2 to
which he invited the vice-president, the cabinet members, the
House and Senate Democratic leaders, members of his staff, and
Dr. Arthur Burns. (So many attended this "private" session that it
was held in the East Room, locus of official state dinners and most
solemn ceremony.)

Burns, the stolid, graying, pipe-smoking pillar of conservative
economic Republican orthodoxy, had long reigned as chairman of
the Federal Reserve Board. As such, he was one of the last of the
"whales" who could dominate Washington events that influenced
the nation, no matter what administration held office. The purpose of the meeting, President Carter explained, was to examine
the federal budget projections and the economic outlook over the
next four years—and for him to learn from Dr. Burns. He asked
Charles Schultze, chairman of his Council of Economic Advisers
and long associated with Democratic policies under past presidents, to give the administration's views. Schultze delivered a message that stressed balancing the budget, restraining government
spending, and counting on increased business investment gained
through greater business confidence in government policies—a
page straight out of the traditional Republican book. And he
topped it off with an optimistic prediction that by 1981 the gross
national product would rise 22 percent, generating some 10 million new jobs, cutting unemployment almost in half, and reducing
the inflation rate to 4 percent.

Some of the Democrats were openly critical; they didn't believe
the forecasts and said so.

But the president, and his budget director, Bert Lance, were optimistic. As the president said, with normal economic expectations
we could balance the budget by 1981. But, Lance warned, if we
were to achieve this goal there could be no new federal programs.
Carter underscored the need for frugality, and gave a personal example. The week before, his wife, Rosalynn, had gone to the hospital to have a tumor removed from her breast. She was there for
two hours and then returned to the White House. Had she spent
the night, he said, the cost would have been much greater. Lesson:
he had saved, and so could the nation.

When the president turned to Arthur Burns, Burns praised

Schultze's economic presentation for its forthrightness and reasonableness. It accorded, he said, with his own judgment that business investment was gathering strength.

The idea of Arthur Burns, nemesis of Democratic liberalism, endorsing this Democratic president's economic policies left other Democrats deeply disturbed. When they got back to Capitol Hill that afternoon, their resentment boiled over. Not only was the president's congressional lobbying effort inept—Frank Moore "couldn't be elected dogcatcher," someone said—but the thrust of Carter's programs was all wrong, they thought. Here he was, asking Congress to raise defense spending by $4 billion, contrary to his own campaign promises to cut defense by at least $5 billion, and coming out against the kinds of Democratic social and economic programs they all had fought for and still supported. And Carter himself was racing around in all directions at once. They were going to meet with the president for breakfast at the White House the next morning, and they agreed to give it to him straight.

And they did.

O'Neill: Mr. President, we had a little meeting yesterday afternoon to talk about yesterday morning's meeting. You have an awful lot of balls in the air at the same time. Your programs are unmindful that [Democrats] have always been the champions of the poor and the indigent. Twelve million people are on welfare, seven million of them children. We have had a lot of programs to help them, and I see no desire in this Congress to cut back. The base of our party is liberal, and you are going to have to appeal to it. If we are going to have cooperation and put your programs through, it must be a two-way street. We must have the Black Caucus, the support of cities, for those who are dependent on us and on what the government does. I can read this Congress, but if there is no move to serve those who need compassion, we'll run into a bag of troubles.

The Speaker was just warming up. With his huge frame, his shock of white hair, his forceful tones, he could be a powerful figure when aroused, as he was that day:

When Arthur Burns starts praising Charlie Schultze, then somebody's changed, and it isn't me. . . . Mr. President, there was no dialogue yesterday. Please don't think that silence meant consent.

I wouldn't want to lead you down the road. You won't have a better champion or friend than us, as time will show you. But we left that meeting yesterday, and—sure, we want a balanced budget, but I know I am expressing the feelings of Congress. . . . I hope I won't be the only fellow to throw the brick.

He wasn't. Robert Byrd immediately spoke on behalf of the Senate. He hoped the president didn't flood them with too many proposals for new legislation, he told Carter. The Senate already had its hands full, and Carter shouldn't expect too much too soon. If he put too much into the mill too soon, it would later look as if Congress were dragging its feet, and that would be difficult. It would not help the Democrats maintain their present majority in next year's elections. Besides, what O'Neill was talking about was right. They *had* to get young people and blacks off the unemployment rolls. They *had* to help the young, the blacks, and the Vietnam veterans.

Then Humphrey had his chance. He disagreed with the estimates Schultze had presented. Carter's budget office, the congressional budget office, the Federal Reserve, and the other bureaus that made economic projections couldn't even agree on the figures. It was ridiculous. And as for Arthur Burns, he remembered telling Burns once, Arthur, you've got theory and I've got history. He talked about social needs in America, about the national shame that functional illiterates were graduating from school, about the need for health care and the obstructionism of the medical-association lobbyists, about building child-care centers and not letting children run the streets. And, his main point:

Now, Mr. President, there is no way to balance the budget in 1981. You inherited an eight percent unemployment rate, six percent inflation, a seventy-five billion dollar deficit, and a poorly managed government. If you can balance the budget, you deserve a special chapter in the Good Book.

Tip O'Neill had the last word: Mr. President, the family that prays and talks together gets along pretty well together.

To a reporter who later that day asked Hamilton Jordan what had happened at that meeting, Jordan, who hadn't been there, replied: "They gave him a lot of stuff about acting more like a Democrat." That was a serious misreading. Blunt speaking and frankness had not been the hallmarks of the congressmen's private sessions with other presidents—indeed, one of the problems had been obsequiousness—and the bluntness that morning was far more than "a lot of stuff," just as the difficulties between Carter and the congressional leadership of his own party went beyond pique over "inadequate" breakfasts or fancied individual slights, though those were present. The legislators were genuinely appalled at what they believed to be the political incompetence at the White House. The president and his people didn't seem to appreciate the realities of political operations—of compromise, of courting individuals, again and again if necessary, of preparing the politicians first and then the public next for new laws and new legislative action. Seeming trivialities made a difference. In those early weeks you'd hear members of Congress complaining repeatedly about the White House's not even being willing to send the traditional birthday greetings to important constituents. That always had been done, but the White House reply to such requests now was that it didn't have time for such old political acts. They *were* old political acts, and Carter seemed to view politics as unworthy.

This was strange, for Carter's congressional-liaison people had been carefully taught the importance of traditional politics in Washington. Frank Moore, for instance, had consulted with Lawrence O'Brien, who had successfully run congressional-liaison operations for John Kennedy and, later, briefly, for Lyndon Johnson. A president can't whip members of Congress into line, O'Brien had explained. All he can do is work out a relationship that's comfortable for them and that keeps lines of communications open. It's all terribly fragile; it can break apart irreparably over the most trivial incidents. That was why the small things were so important, he had said—returning phone calls promptly, setting time aside for informal off-the-record meetings, aiding congressional constituents whenever possible, whether setting up a VIP tour of the White House or dispatching speakers to help in local political battles.

And Tip O'Neill had personally explained to Carter how the LBJ and JFK congressional-liaison systems had worked. Every Friday President Johnson would meet with his liaison staff, he told Carter, and he'd go over pending legislation point by point. They'd discuss the various members of key committees, plan who should talk to whom and how, and report back. LBJ was intimately involved every step of the way; the liaison people worked around the clock for him.

In the end the problems were personal, Hubert Humphrey told me one afternoon that spring. The senator had slipped into a small private office in the Capitol, closed the door and talked with me for several hours:

> You see, part of Carter's problems is that he really doesn't know the little characteristics of our colleagues up here. You've got to know what makes 'em tick, you've got to know their wives, you've got to know their families, you've got to know their backgrounds. You know, I used to say Johnson was a personal FBI. The son of a gun was incredible, but so was Kennedy, and so in a sense was Ford. All of the last four presidents were creatures of Congress. Kennedy, Johnson, Nixon, Ford—when they went to the White House, they had connections up here, buddy-buddy connections.
>
> There is a fellowship in the Congress which is unique. It's different and better than anything that you ever have in lodge or even a church. Now that changes when you go down to the White House; even as vice-president, I experienced it. But still, you've got the connections and you still know a lot about the members.
>
> But here comes Carter, and he's a new boy in town. Institutionally, Congress hasn't sized him up yet. And he still doesn't know all the players here—their idiosyncracies, their characteristics. He gets the stereotypes: he knows that Humphrey is garrulous, for example, or that Russell Long can be a good storyteller, and so on. But he doesn't know all the little things that make 'em tick. And that's the key around this place.
>
> How do you learn to handle people up here? I mean, how do you learn how to understand them? I'll give you a little example. [Humphrey named a certain Democratic senator with a fondness for taking late-afternoon drinks.] Now you've got to watch that like a hawk if he's got an amendment. And I never let him get to the point of getting to the floor with that amendment until I get a smile out of him. I work on him until I get that face loosened up. And then I say, 'Look at that countenance of that little friend of mine from _____'—just a little joke, to kind of soften him up a little bit.
>
> You've got to know each one of these people. Some people are no-nonsense. Some people like a little nonsense. . . . A lot of cloakroom talk. Now, you see, Carter has never engaged in cloakroom talk with us. Cloakroom talk is like in a golfer's locker room. It's

bawdy. It's rough and risqué at times. Lots of storytelling, laughin' and hootin' and hollerin'. That's when you get to know people.

Hubert Humphrey had reached the stage of his life where he was truly free to be himself—free of the constraints of political ambition, free to talk about the realities of political life with unusual candor. "This is the first time in my life that I am not a contender," he said, "nor do I have any reason for ambition." Yet he felt himself "a piece of the history of this capital . . . part of the history of some of the most turbulent years in this country," and he hoped other people would think of him that way, too:

> What I want more in life than anything now is respect, which I think I'm beginning to earn and get. I don't want to be president. I don't want to be vice-president. Or secretary of state. Or majority leader. I know that these things are not to be mine, and I have put them very neatly aside, without remorse. But what I do want to be known for in the history books—and I am interested in that—is that I was an effective man in government. That I was a decent man, and that I knew my job. That I knew how to get things done, and that I did important things in government.

That afternoon, while we talked, Humphrey was nearing the end of a typical day: two congressional leadership meetings, a leadership meeting with Carter in the White House, a luncheon with the president's national-security affairs adviser, Zbigniew Brzezinski, two congressional committee meetings, leadership of a key administration bill on the Senate floor, interviews, a speech, and a private dinner.

To Humphrey, as to nearly everyone of long Washington political experience, Carter was still something of an enigma. "I started out not understanding this man at all," he said, "but the more I've been around him the better I'm feeling. I think he's trying desperately to learn. He's really trying to get the feel of us." But that in itself was made more difficult than usual because of the structural changes in the political city:

> Up until the time of Woodrow Wilson, with the exception of Teddy Roosevelt, we had *congressional* government. Congress was the

predominating influence. Now Congress has asserted itself again. I
can't overemphasize the importance of this. Congress is no longer
afraid of the executive—particularly when you look at things like
the budget. I've heard dozens of people up here say, "Well, I know
that Carter's got that in *his* budget, but what's *our* budget say?"

And I'll tell you something I hear people say now that you never
heard before: "I've seen them come and go, and I'm still here."
They're talking about presidents, you know. I've run through seven
of them myself.

In all his years of private dealings with presidents, Humphrey
never had heard such blunt speech as that being used in the leaders' meetings with Carter. "I think he responds pretty well to what
we say. His demeanor invites candor, but I also think you've got to
be careful how you present things. I usually give the benediction
at these meetings, and I always try to give it with a little twist of
humor. I don't want to get too pontifical with him, because I think
he'll dig in. He's stubborn."

Looking ahead, Humphrey foresaw more problems for the new
president. Carter's method of operating, of letting his cabinet
members deal directly with Congress and the agencies instead of
asserting tight presidential controls through his own personal political staff in the manner of Kennedy and Johnson, spelled greater
trouble.

"You've got to run this government," Humphrey added. "If you
don't run it, it runs you. It'll run you down, too. And it'll run you
right out of town." So it was essential to create the impression of
strong leadership. There, Carter was in danger. Already, the private view was that the Carter administration was incompetent. In
the incestuous "city of conversation," as Henry James called
Washington, private judgments quickly became public ones—and
were quickly transmitted to the country at large.

☐ ☐ ☐

Immediately after the Bay of Pigs invasion in 1961, John Kennedy was discussing that disastrous failure with his aide the historian

Arthur Schlesinger, Jr. Kennedy was bemused. He had just completed his first hundred days in office, that arbitrary figure that supposedly marks the end of the presidential honeymoon with public and press. If he had been a British prime minister, he said, he would have been thrown out of office after such a defeat, yet the political reaction at home seemed only to have enhanced his prestige. At that point his secretary, Evelyn Lincoln, entered the presidential office carrying an advance copy of the latest Gallup poll, the first since the humiliation on the Cuban beaches. It showed Kennedy's popularity had jumped: an unprecedented 82 percent of the public backed his handling of his job. "It's just like Eisenhower," Kennedy said. "The worse I do, the more popular I get."

During his entire first year Kennedy's popularity-approval rating averaged 76 percent. No small part of his success came from the laudatory treatment accorded him by the press. His inaugural address was judged historic, eloquent, wise, confident, stirring the heart (*Time*), and bespeaking a quiet confidence (*The New York Times*). After a week in office, he was hailed as extraordinary. "President Kennedy seemed almost to sail through his first week in the world's most demanding office, soaring from triumph to triumph with the ease of the daring young man on the flying trapeze," *Newsweek* proclaimed. After the Bay of Pigs and his hundred days, *The Washington Post* editorialized: "He has presented an impression to the country and to the world of broad intellectual grasp, poise, vigor, and quiet competence." A bust of Augustus Caesar was the pictorial key for a *Time* assessment that said, approvingly, "There is an emphasis on style." And *Newsweek*, in another flowery appraisal, credited him with almost God-like characteristics: "Certainly the vigorous, sun-bronzed, young president—and his attractive family as well—already has become a dominant factor in the life of the United States."

That Kennedy's legislative record was slight at best; that most of his initial proposals were defeated; that his foreign-policy ventures in Laos and Vietnam as well as Cuba drew the nation deeper into cold war confrontation and, finally, active combat seemed not to matter. He was lionized by the press and applauded by the public.

None of these conditions prevailed in the early months of Jimmy

Carter's presidency, nor would they have for anyone taking office
in 1976, since part of the problem was historic—the poisonous
aftermath of Vietnam and Watergate. Another part of it was personality: the Kennedy charm, whatever it was, left an impression
of warmth, while Carter seemed remote. And part of it was the il-
lusion of performance: the martial fervor, the quick and restless
energy, the strident rhetoric made Kennedy appear commanding,
strong, "presidential," while Carter, soft in speech, gentle in manner, seemed "weak"—a peculiar judgment, given his political record of singleminded tenacious ambition, monumental self-assurance, and bold risk-taking.

And also, the press simply liked Kennedy. He had been a reporter himself, he knew journalists and flattered them, and he had
a finely honed sense of the news business, its pressures and problems.

Carter never seemed at ease around reporters, and he had been
unable to conceal his distrust, even disapproval, of the press while
campaigning. He felt, as he told a *Playboy* interviewer on his campaign plane, that the so-called "national" press still looked on the
South as a "suspect nation" and himself as a "secret racist." Moreover, "the national news media have absolutely no interest in issues *at all*," he said. "Sometimes we freeze out the national media
so we can open up press conferences to local people. At least we
get questions from them—on timber management, on health care,
on education. But the traveling press have zero interest in any issue unless it's a matter of making a mistake. What they're looking
for is a forty-seven–second argument between me and another
candidate or something like that. There's nobody in the back of
this plane who would ask an issue question unless he thought he
could trick me into some crazy statement."

Since many of those same reporters who had been on the campaign trail with him followed him to the White House, Carter's
press relations were strained from the start. Administration com-
bativeness, particularly on the part of his young press secretary,
Jody Powell, whom Carter regarded almost as a son, added to the
tension. And Carter's own promises, so many and so sweeping,
which he so steadfastly insisted he would keep, guaranteed that his
words and actions would be watched more closely than normal by

an already highly critical press corps. Carter himself had welcomed that scrutiny—and he got it, with predictable results.

During the campaign, for instance, he had spoken out strongly against abuses committed by the CIA. If he became president, it would be different, he promised. "If the CIA ever makes a mistake, I will call a press conference and tell the people," he pledged. Carter had been president less than a month when he ran head-on into just such a CIA controversy, and his first conflict with the press. Bob Woodward, of *The Washington Post* (and Watergate fame), had come up with an explosive story—that for years the CIA had been paying off Jordan's King Hussein under a top-secret project termed, with apparently unintentional but exquisite irony, "No Beef." Clandestine payments amounting to millions had been funneled to Hussein; but more than money was involved: the CIA had been providing Hussein women companions and bodyguards for his children.

After Woodward telephoned Powell to check out this story, he and Benjamin Bradlee, the *Post*'s editor and former Georgetown neighbor and close friend of John Kennedy, were invited to see Carter in the Oval Office. The president told them he hadn't known about the Hussein payments until he learned of the *Post*'s investigation, and he then immediately ordered them stopped. He hoped Bradlee and Woodward would understand the sensitive nature of this information, publication of which would be damaging to the national interest and highly embarrassing to the administration, for even then Secretary of State Vance was en route to meet with Hussein. Peace prospects in the Middle East could be seriously jeopardized if the *Post* ran the story. At least, he asked, the paper should delay until Vance's mission was completed. Bradlee told Carter he couldn't agree to such a request, but he promised to give the president notice when the story was published.

Woodward's banner-headline article ran, after due notification to the White House, the day Vance landed in Jordan to meet Hussein. Carter was furious. In his own hand, on White House stationery, he immediately wrote Bradlee a cold, terse "Dear Ben" note. Publication of the report had been "irresponsible," he told the editor. ("Irresponsible" was a word he would use many times privately to describe press behavior in Washington, and particularly the *Post*'s. Months later he would cite the *Post*'s disclosures—and those of some other papers—as being terribly damaging, as causing the loss of key intelligence sources in other governments, and as compromising spies and probably resulting in their deaths.)

While he confirmed the *Post*'s account in a secret briefing with congressional leaders, his public response ran contrary to his campaign promises. He had reviewed the matter, he said, and termed "some [of the revelations] quite erroneous, some with a degree of accuracy," but he hadn't found "anything illegal or improper." This complicated his problems: for if he had found nothing wrong with the secret payments, why had he ordered them stopped? Then, echoing every president before him, he pleaded: "It can be extremely damaging to our relationship with other nations, and to the potential security of our nation, even in peacetime, for these kinds of operations, which are legitimate and proper, to be revealed."

Well, then, he was asked, if erroneous information were involved why didn't he correct the public record?

"In some ways we are correcting the record," Carter answered, "but if I began to either dispute or confirm every individual story that's written, whether correct or erroneous, on every matter relating to the CIA, then these matters which are necessarily secret would no longer be secret."

In the days to come, Carter expressed continued concern about "the almost total absence of any sort of confidentiality around Washington on matters that I think sometimes we would like to hold to ourselves"; about the number of people on Capitol Hill who had access to highly classified information; about the old problem of congressional leaks of classified material; and about the classic American democratic dilemma given most eloquent expression by Lincoln: "Must a government of necessity be too strong for the liberties of its people, or too weak to maintain its own existence?" That was the way Lincoln voiced the quandary, in a passage debated by generations of American history students. Carter defined the ancient problem by wondering, "How to maintain in a democracy, truthfulness and frankness with the American people on the one hand, through the news media, and on the other hand preserve a mandatory degree of confidentiality about intelligence sources?" There was no easy answer, of course, as all his predecessors had learned. But excessive promises and moralistic rhetoric exacerbated his difficulties.

When he appointed Anne Cox Chambers as ambassador to Belgium (a woman who as owner of the Atlanta newspapers was a political and economic power in Georgia but who had no diplomatic experience or training), and Philip Alston, Jr., as ambassador to Australia (a wealthy Atlanta lawyer who had raised money and arranged important political contacts for Carter but who also had no diplomatic background), the press quickly pointed to his campaign promise to "root out once and for all the cheap political appointments." When the press learned that the White House staff had actually increased in size instead of being cut by a third as he had promised, he said that the reason for the "apparent increase, or actual increase," was because so many unexpected letters and phone calls had reached the White House. "I don't want to discourage people from staying in touch with me," he added, "it has taken a lot of struggle to do that." And when, months later, the United States attorney in Philadelphia, David Marston, a Republican, was removed from office after a Democratic congressman whom Marston was investigating protested to Carter's attorney general, Carter's words about insuring merit and ability and freeing the judicial process from "a cheap political payoff" were repeated—and repeated—and repeated. When his firm pledge to "come out with complete reform of the welfare system" and "do it by the first of May" was scrapped, he said the problem was "worse than we had anticipated" and would require greater analysis. But the deadline had been entirely Carter's own and, as Robert Shogan of *The Los Angeles Times* properly said, "made little sense to begin with." When he gave big pay raises to his personal staff after only two months in office (he had a choice of accepting salary increases voted by Congress for itself and ranking civil servants in full, reducing them, deferring them, or rejecting them totally), the press naturally cited the disparity with his campaign themes about living frugally, cutting expenses, refraining from dipping into the public trough.

Individually none of these episodes was of great consequence—insignificant, certainly, in the larger context of governing well and wisely. But collectively they were damaging, for they struck at a fragile, precious commodity Carter had brought to office—his difference, his freshness of promise. It was the *impression* of Carter that was being damaged. And for Carter the still unknown outsider, these impressions could alter his fortunes.

By the time Carter became president, daily journalism was exploring, with hitherto unheard-of frankness, a range of once taboo subjects. The intimate private lives of public people were being examined as never before. New techniques of psycho-history were in vogue, and they were beginning to be practiced in the print press as well as in the television "docu-dramas"—a dreadful genre in which it is impossible to know when the search for truth and fact ends and the fiction takes over, where actual conversations and meetings are enacted and when wholly imaginary ones are invented for dramatic purpose. At its best, journalists were producing notably more sophisticated work, offering better insights into, and explanations of, complex personalities and complicated issues. But at its worst, a journalism of mindless glibness, of vicious and destructive gossip was also at work. Washington had its share of both.

The lesson of the greatest publishing success of the 1970s, *People* magazine, wasn't lost on Washington. Founded in 1974 by Time, Inc., as the first new national weekly magazine in twenty years, at a time when general-circulation magazines were declining or dying, *People*'s advertising revenues, circulation, and profitability (it made money after only eighteen months, an astonishing feat for a new national weekly) climbed rapidly. In less than five years it had become the nation's second best-selling newsstand weekly. What was important was that *People* soared to the top by celebrating celebrityhood, and acting as a herald of the age of "personality journalism." *People*'s philosophy, as expressed by its managing editor, was simple: "We don't deal with issues; we don't deal with events; we don't deal with debates. We deal *only* with human beings." Reach the reader rapidly, say your say fast and provocatively, fill the need for gossip and entertainment and move on to the next subject before attention flags—that, in essence, was *People*'s formula. It quickly had emulators. Newspapers began featuring "People" sections, and gossip columns reemerged as forces in journalism.

The Washington Star, the smaller and less influential of the city's two newspapers, attracted attention by introducing a sprightly gossip column, "The Ear," which focused on political and media personalities. Its success led *The Washington Post* to hire a gossip columnist, who paid attention primarily to the Carter people, and particularly the Georgians in the White House. When the *Post* reported that Hamilton Jordan didn't use underwear, the White House response was lighthearted. But as Carter's troubles continued and the criticism and gossip items multiplied, White House relations with the *Post,* never good to start with and worsened by the Hussein-CIA story, became especially embittered. To the close-knit group of Southerners around the president, it seemed as if the *Post* were leading a vendetta against the White House. That was not true, but as the most powerful journalistic voice in the capital, as well as being influential nationally and internationally as a result of its work during Watergate, the tone of *Post* coverage had special political impact. White House suspicions that the *Post* was sneering at the Georgia innocents soon degenerated into a belief the paper was out to destroy them when, on successive months, in November and December, two lengthy articles by Sally Quinn were published. The first was on the president's personal secretary, Susan Clough, a good-natured and hardworking Southern divorcée.

Jody Powell picked up his Sunday paper at home early one Sunday morning in November, and then, as was his custom, took it back to bed to share with his wife, Nan. Mrs. Powell started reading what Quinn had written about Susan Clough:

> She's thirty-two years old. She is blonde, very pretty and single. And she is, except for Rosalynn Carter, the person closest to the president of the United States. Naturally this has led to speculation not only about her relationship with the president but about her social life in general. . . . She is aware of the winks and insinuations that continue to prevail not only among the staff but also the press, about her relationship with Carter.

Mrs. Powell read on, while chatting to her husband, and suddenly became still. What's the matter? Powell asked, glancing at her and seeing an obvious tenseness. She silently handed him the paper. He read:

> Clough was very close to Jody Powell, who had originally hired her when Carter was governor. So when at one point during the

campaign it looked as though Clough, who was based in Atlanta, might not get a shot at the top job, she appealed to Powell. She won. Powell, it is said, is still her protector. In fact, her detractors even hint there has been a relationship between her and Powell, but she maintains that if she were to have a relationship with a male staffer, not to mention the president, "it would have an adverse effect. I feel very strongly about dating among the staff. It would pose more problems than it was worth."

Several weeks later an even longer Sunday-morning Quinn article further infuriated the White House people. This one was on "The Carter Crowd and the Washingtonians," posting the at least arguable proposition that the Southerners were forfeiting their opportunity at national governance because they weren't getting along with the social and political pooh-bahs of the capital. She described the Carter group as arriving in Washington "like an alien tribe," and "confronting odd customs and taboos along the Potomac. . . . They were not, in fact, comfortable with limousines, yachts or in elegant salons, in black tie, with seating charts at the door, little envelopes with numbers in them, cocktail chitchat, place cards, servants, six courses, different forks, three wines, turning the table, fingerbowls, toasts, liqueurs and after-dinner mingling."

For many more columns the social gaucheries and insecurities of the Georgians were explored extensively. Her final words:

> At a recent dinner party in Washington given by Barbara Walters in honor of the Israeli and Egyptian ambassadors, Hamilton Jordan made one of his rare appearances, though without his wife, Nancy. Jordan, who generally holds court with other Georgians in the best Phi Delt tradition, seemed ill at ease during the cocktail hour, only relaxing when Bob Strauss was around to act as liaison. When he was finally seated for dinner he found himself next to Madame Ashraf Ghorbal, wife of the Egyptian ambassador. Henry Kissinger was seated on her other side. Jordan immediately unbuttoned the top button of his shirt and loosened his tie. Then, fortified with an ample amount of the host's booze, he gazed at the ambassador's wife's ample front, pulled at her elasticized bodice and was prompted to say, loudly enough for several others to hear, "I've always wanted to see the pyramids." Finally toward the end of dinner, he stood up and announced, "This administration has to take a p—."

This last anecdote, bitterly resented and passionately denied in
the White House, circulated throughout the country. Whether the
general public ever paid serious attention to such stories is prob-
lematical at best, but the articles did further affect relations between the *Post* and the White House, for not only was Quinn the
highly publicized star of the paper's widely read and emulated
"Style" section but, as everyone also knew, she was living with Ben
Bradlee, the *Post*'s editor (whom she later married). The White
House took her articles as further proof they would not get fair
treatment from Bradlee and his paper, a belief that intensified in
months to come.

Resentment over the idea that they could govern only if they
went to the right parties ran deep, and was bitterly expressed in
private. That was precisely the kind of attitude they had run
against, the Georgians said, and one of the reasons Carter had
been elected. Still, a serious rift was developing between the Carter group and Washington. It had less to do with the frivolousness
of going to parties than with the realities of personal contact and
personal knowledge.

All presidents bring a close group of advisers with them, and all
presidents discover they must broaden their circle. But that didn't
happen with the Carter people. "It took this group a long time to
stop being parochial," Tip O'Neill said later. It wasn't a case of
politicians wanting to have cocktails with the Carter group, but of
wanting to get to know them, to understand them, to exchange
political views, to discuss issues and ideas. Many Washington figures complained that they hadn't ever met important administration operatives, let alone talked to them. O'Neill didn't see Hamilton Jordan for nearly a year after the brief and angry encounter
over inaugural reception tickets. Then, at a diplomatic reception
one night, his wife asked if that weren't Hamilton Jordan across
the room. She'd like to meet him. "So would I," O'Neill replied.
They walked over, and he said, "I'm Tip O'Neill, and my wife
would like to say hello to you."

O'Neill's remark to reporters in the early days of the administration—that he'd never met Jody Powell, and all he knew about him
was what he read in the papers and that such a person was supposed to be the president's press secretary—was published, of
course. The next morning O'Neill was at the White House for a

meeting with the president. "This fellow comes over and says, 'Mr. Speaker, I'm Jody Powell,'" O'Neill recalled later. "I says, 'Nice to see you.' He has a shirt on. We're all dressed up. He shook hands and he walked out. I never knew where he went. I've never had a conversation with Jody Powell in my life."

Carter himself was familiar with the complaints about lack of contact between his administration and political Washington, and he appreciated the importance of personal relations. He set a good example himself, for he was meeting with members of Congress at least as much—and probably much more—than even those shrewd politicians Kennedy and Johnson. As for parties, he would say later, he couldn't care less. If other people wanted to spend their time socializing that way, that was okay, but he didn't believe his people were missing much by failing to enter the "right" salons. There was too much for them all to do, and not enough time to do it in. So he, and they, pressed on, and Washington be damned.

☐ ☐ ☐

Nothing better demonstrated Carter's determination to be a bold and different president in those early months than his zealous pursuit of a new arms-limitation accord with the Russians—and his equally zealous crusade for human rights around the world, especially within the Soviet Union. That the two might not mix doesn't appear to have entered into the president's calculations. Both human rights and arms reduction were noble goals, therefore both should be achieved.

In a president who was so often described as "passionless," these two subjects clearly struck an emotional chord. Listening to him, you came away strongly impressed by the depths of his convictions. "I want our country to be the focal point for deep concern about human beings all over the world," he said, in an extemporaneous remark at one of the "town meetings." "I am trying to search with the Soviet Union for a way to reduce the horrible arms race, where we've spent billions and billions and billions of dollars on atomic weapons. We are no more secure now than we were eight years ago or twelve years ago or sixteen years ago.

We're much more deeply threatened by more and more advanced weapons."

On both human rights and arms reduction, Carter was taking a radically different approach from his immediate predecessors, particularly the pragmatic policies evolved during the Nixon/ Ford/Kissinger years. Carter was repudiating Kissinger's theory of "linkage"—of always relating major foreign-policy issues to each other—which had been previously used to defend official American indifference to the lack of progress on human rights. The argument had been that the Soviet Union would not move to curb the growth in arms if pressed too hard about the well-known abuses of liberty inside its own borders and spheres of influence.

Not since Woodrow Wilson had so moralistic a tone emanated from the White House. Wilson, in foreign affairs, for instance, had reversed the American policy on recognizing other nations that had been followed by every president since Washington. The recognition policy instituted in 1793 by Thomas Jefferson as our first secretary of state was a practical one, carefully divorced from ideology. His policy stated that we would formally recognize, and deal with, any regime that was in fact in power, regardless of its form of government and internal practices. ("Everyone may govern itself according to whatever form it pleases, and change these forms at its own will," was how Jefferson spelled out the policy.) The sovereign *de facto* was the sovereign *de jure*. Wilson drastically changed that. The democratic *principles* of any given regime, as interpreted by *American* policymakers, were what mattered to Wilson. In 1913 he refused to recognize the Huerta regime in Mexico on the ground it was created by force, and continued to refrain from dealing with other countries which, by his test, were undemocratic. With some irony, it was another "liberal" Democrat, Franklin Roosevelt, who reversed the Wilsonian policy when FDR recognized the Soviet Union in 1933, thus returning American policy back to its beginnings.

Carter, like Wilson, was imposing moral values and judgments on the other nations. And obviously he didn't believe human-rights questions should—or would—affect such an issue as arms control. Eight days before his inauguration, at a private daylong Smithsonian Institution foreign-policy session with members of Congress and important officials in his administration, he had strongly emphasized both themes. Already, he said, he had been encouraged by the constant stream of messages to him from Leonid Brezhnev that asked for quick resolution of outstanding Soviet-American differences in the strategic arms limitation talks (SALT). Brezhnev was prepared to go beyond the treaty negotiations with respect to imposing limits on atomic weapons, he said. He also believed the Soviet Union would liberalize its policy on allowing dissidents to emigrate, "the less we coerce them." Yet literally seconds later the president-to-be was urging members of Congress to keep stressing human-rights issues!

Later that day Carter made a revealing remark about himself and his methods of operating. He had been explaining that Zbigniew Brzezinski was going to compile a list of the specific goals Carter wanted to achieve in each area of foreign affairs, a comprehensive, all-inclusive, far-reaching list. Then, his words: "If as an engineer I have something in my mind that I can work toward, I have a better chance of achieving it." Method and precision, logic and planning: he intended to achieve *all* those goals and fulfill *all* the promises he had made. He was confident in his ability, and confident his approach was correct. Human rights was correct, arms limitation was correct, better relations with the Russians was correct, and competition between the two superpowers was healthy, as each would understand.

Thus, when he first met with Soviet ambassador Anatoly Dobrynin in the White House, Carter immediately brought up the subject of human rights. "My position is strong," he told the diplomat. "It's not going to change." Thus, when the Soviet dissident and Nobel Prize winner Andrei Sakharov wrote him an appeal, he chose to answer it personally instead of letting the State Department handle it, and in the process made a strong pledge that infuriated the Soviet government: "We shall use our good offices to seek the release of prisoners of conscience and we will continue our efforts to shape a world responsive to human aspirations." Thus, when he prepared to dispatch Secretary Vance to Moscow at the end of March for the first meetings with the Russians, he continually reported good prospects and general optimism in his sessions with congressional leaders: the agenda had been carefully prepared, and after Vance went to Moscow, Brezhnev would come to Washington. Thus, when the Soviet government began to react against his human-rights assertions before the Vance trip to Moscow, condemning them as an intrusion into its affairs and—in Brezhnev's public words—making normal relations "unthinkable," if continued, Carter briskly and publicly replied: "I think it has been a well-recognized international political principle that interference in a government is not a verbal thing. There is an ideological struggle that has been in progress for decades between the Communist nations on the one hand and the democratic nations on the other."

Carter wanted not merely to continue the arms-reduction work accomplished between the United States and the Soviet Union before he took office. He was dispatching Vance with a proposal that he later described as a "radical departure" from the agreements reached between the two countries at Vladivostok in 1974: a steep reduction in strategic arms production on both sides and a new arms-control agreement that would "put a cap on the arms race." After that, he hoped, it might be possible to stop nuclear testing entirely. The proposal Vance was carrying was indeed new—and comprehensive. It would, for instance, put an absolute freeze on missiles—henceforth no new ones to be developed or deployed by either side; and there were many other technical and specific proposals, all new. Furthermore, it was a take-it-or-leave-it sort of thing. As Brzezinski explained it to Congress in a White House briefing, all the proposals were part of a package and, in his words, America was insisting on the whole package. (Vance did have a fall-back proposal: to ratify the Vladivostok agreements and then wait to solve the more contentious issues. Vladivostok, in that case, would merely become a point of departure, while the real resolution of strategic issues would be postponed.)

The United States had not dealt with the Soviet government in this manner before. Nor had an American president publicly laid out, as Carter did, the nature of the new proposals in advance of a key diplomatic meeting.

No sooner had Vance arrived in Moscow than Brezhnev voiced a strong attack on American policy. There could be no improvement in Soviet-American relations, he warned, unless the United States accepted the principle of "noninterference in international affairs." Within two days, the Russians had totally rejected all the American proposals and the diplomatic talks collapsed. For virtually the first time in memory Andrei Gromyko, the veteran Soviet foreign minister, held a press conference and angrily used this unprecedented event to denounce the United States. The Americans were trying to renege on the Vladivostok agreement, he charged, and their new approach was a "cheap and shady maneuver." The Moscow mission ended with Vance's hastily flying home while newspaper headlines trumpeted the breakup of the talks as a diplomatic disaster—a view, it was reported, shared by some of Vance's own aides.

President Carter minimized the failure—"I think the Soviet response has been predictable," he said—but in fact the damage was serious. Yet he rejected the argument that his human-rights policy had been instrumental in the breakup. Vance had hardly returned home when Carter was again stressing his determination to "reestablish the United States of America as the rallying point for human rights around the world. We've not enjoyed that position in recent years, but I'm determined that, once again, we'll be a beacon light for those who believe in human rights all over the globe." Nevertheless, many American and foreign diplomats believed he had bungled a critical first meeting with the Russians—and needlessly so. Sending his new secretary of state off with such peremptory demands was bound to fail, in the accepted view; Vance's first meeting should have been a quiet, exploratory one, affording the Russians a chance to get the measure of the new American team, and for the Americans to try to express what their new president was like, what they hoped mutually to achieve. "I thought it was disastrous," said one man who had handled delicate diplomatic missions for presidents over many years. "And it need not have occurred at all. It need not have ended that way at all. I can tell you ten people in this town who could have told Mr. Carter that that approach was bound to come a cropper, but none of them was asked."

It was true: Carter had not reached out to the old experts, but he understandably bristled at the suggestion that he and his team needed their counsels anyway. Several months later, when a reporter pointed out that the Soviet response had been predicted in advance from the beginning "almost without exception by people who had long experience in dealing with the Soviet Union," and wondered if Carter had ever consulted such "qualified, experienced people," the president icily replied: "I would guess that the secretary of state, my national security adviser, my staff, and others would be adequately qualified."*

There was, perhaps, another source for his early unyielding position. Once, at one of his meetings with Congressional leaders, he confessed to having felt frustrated during the presidential campaign because, as he put it, the Soviet Union and Communist China (his term) were getting credit for making nuclear nonproliferation proposals and for concern with human rights. He wanted the United States to take the lead and believed he was suited to make that move. Although Carter rarely sounded strident or ideological, such comments hinted at a cold war mentality that he normally rejected. In briefing members of the House once, he was capable of saying: "I believe that in the struggle for the minds and hearts of people for democracy against Communist totalitarianism we've made substantial progress." And again, at a closed foreign-policy White House session: "We've more to offer these [certain African] countries than the Soviet Union. We have in common with them a religious heritage and freedom. The insurgents don't want the domination of an outside, atheistic, Communist country."

The setback with the Russians after little more than two months in office did not much affect Carter's popularity. His popularity rating had climbed to 75 percent after two months in office, and was still in the mid-sixties a month later. The idea that his administration was inept, which was beginning to form in Washington and other capitals, had not yet been transmitted to the general public, where his standing remained high.

---

*Much later, though, he sat one night upstairs in his family quarters in the White House and said to me, with quiet detachment, that he had misjudged the Russians, had not understood their psychology, had failed to see how important the Vladivostok agreements were to Brezhnev, how the ailing Soviet leader regarded them with pride as a crowning point in his career and understandably reacted strongly when a new American group came in, swept the table, and demanded a new game. But this reappraisal came in a different period of his presidency.

□   □   □

Fred Doxsee turned on his television set after coming back from his regular Thursday night Elks Lodge meeting in Boone, Iowa. The closing minutes of a network special about a day-in-the-life-of-Jimmy-Carter were being broadcast. Doxsee found it boring and snapped off his set. It was the third week in April, and I had gone again to Boone to see how Carter's presidency was being assessed after his third month in office.

In Boone, Carter was getting no credit for having done anything significant yet about reforming the government. His foreign policy had aroused little comment. To people there, the issue of international human rights was of slight interest, and the questions about American relations with the Soviet Union or armed Cuban intrusion in Africa, so hotly debated in Washington, were barely discussed.

But Carter had developed a following in Boone. Citizens there spoke of him in favorable, and personal, terms. "He's kind of refreshing," Fred Doxsee told me. "You get the feeling that maybe something is going to happen, and maybe we can get the people to work together. People laugh at his informality, but deep down I think they kind of like it. I get the feeling that if Carter walked in this door I would walk over and I wouldn't have any fears of just talking to him." Via television, Doxsee and his friends had watched Carter closely those first three months. They saw him walk down the avenue to the White House on inauguration day, and applauded. They watched his first fireside chat, and approved. "I was just as scared for him as maybe he was," Doxsee said. They saw his early press conferences, and were impressed. "He's gotta be sharp, he's just gotta be sharp," one of them said. They listened to his nationwide telephone "call-in" one Saturday afternoon, and were less certain: "I didn't particularly care about the phone-in," Doxsee said. "I thought that was a big gimmick. I don't think he meant it that way, but that's how it came over to me."

But for the last few days people in Boone had been critical. They couldn't understand Carter's sudden dropping of the fifty-dollar tax rebate plan. "Not that it's too important, I suppose," Doxsee said, "but why did he promise it to us in the first place?"

Still, as Doxsee said, it wasn't that big a deal, and they went back to talking about other matters. By Monday morning, April 18, however, all of Boone was talking about Carter again. He was going to make a speech to the nation that night dealing with energy problems. People were uneasy. Obviously something big was coming: news of the speech was dominating everything. Doxsee's reaction before the speech was typical: "We're all scared to death. We don't think anybody can do too much about the energy thing, and we want to find out how much it's going to cost us." Once again, he invited some of his friends and neighbors to watch Carter in his living room that night.

In Washington, the president's advisers were telling reporters that with the energy crisis he faced "the greatest test" of his political leadership, a situation in which people would blame him even as they accepted his arguments. There was no inclination on Carter's part to duck the fight. The planning for the public appeals on behalf of his energy program was intensive. Within five days Carter would be seen again addressing the nation and the Congress—and twice more in televised news conferences. Then cabinet members and other administration officials would campaign across the country, giving speeches and making public appearances.

There was no doubt about Carter's sincerity of purpose on the energy question. As candidate and as president, in public and in private, Carter spoke repeatedly about energy problems. Next to human rights and arms reduction it was the topic that most dominated his thought—and politically, certainly, the most difficult.

For by 1977, the United States was finally beginning to see the effects of the inevitable depletion of its oil and natural-gas supplies. Supplies had been decreasing by about 6 percent annually for a number of years, while demand increased by leaps and bounds. By 1977 America was importing more than half its total oil. The nation's energy system was so complex and so massive that implementation of any major change in it could not be fully realized until years later. It took about a decade to design, retool, and deliver to the public a new fleet of cars, for instance, or properly insulate all the homes in America.

And this was assuming the people were prepared to act. The evidence was otherwise. After the fear and panic of the oil-embargo crisis of 1973–74, America swiftly returned to its old patterns of mass consumption, patterns based on the easy availability of cheap fuel. And people were demonstrating again that they were prepared to pay higher prices to maintain the accustomed ways of life. In 1973 the price of gasoline was thirty-nine cents a gallon. Four years later, as Carter entered the White House, it was sixty-five cents a gallon. Higher prices were making for grumbles, but not cutting consumption.

Other nations were right when they viewed America as a land of gluttonous appetites. The Swedes, Germans, and Japanese were using half as much energy per capita as the Americans, and every European country operated under stringent energy-saving programs. Small automobiles were an accepted way of life, for example; the average automobile weighed 2700 pounds, whereas in the United States, it was 4100 pounds. Detroit kept producing the gas guzzlers, the advertising agencies kept drumming home the message that bigger was better, and Americans kept buying them.

Their political leaders had failed totally to persuade Americans that the situation called for radical action and a change in living habits. No president had faced the problem directly, and none had proposed a sustained, long-term national effort to alter the pattern of energy consumption and conservation. They all tended to deal with problems on a day-to-day basis, operating from crisis to crisis, reacting to events as they came along, and not preparing the people for what might lie ahead.

Yet Americans were uneasy about it, groping toward a new understanding of the factors that affected their environment, health, and consumer products. Past assumptions were being challenged. Some were rejecting the old credo that economic growth was always a virtue. "Futurist" philosophers with computers, preaching the necessity for long-term planning and strong national policies to limit growth, thus making more tolerable the inevitable social traumas that lay ahead, were being listened to.

In Washington, people like Jay Forrester of the Massachusetts Institute of Technology conducted private sessions for members of Congress from both parties. Forrester's argument was arresting: in the United States the use of energy had been doubling every ten years. For the world, population had been doubling every thirty years. Any growth that repeatedly doubles will in time overwhelm its host environment. We cannot continue consuming and growing as we are, when natural resources are dwindling, population and industrialization are increasing, without facing serious dislocations. Our standard of living is bound to be affected, and the time to make those national choices is critically short.

Such prophecies went against the grain of traditional American optimism. But in a sense, the futurists were evoking Frederick Jackson Turner's thesis on the passing of the American frontier, Henry and Brooks Adams' fears about the tensions of the industrial age leading to colliding forces and eventual degradation and decline. While their words were esoteric, their conclusions were not. And citizens like Fred Doxsee were fully aware of the forces threatening their traditional assumptions.

Politicians understood this, too—though they didn't always show it. In the five years before Carter became president, Congress had enacted into law seventy-one energy or energy-related acts. But it still was far from enough, as the members knew best themselves. "The trouble," Senator Jennings Randolph of West Virginia told the president shortly after Carter took office, "is that we have not yet had an administration that has decided we must have action on the energy issue."

Hubert Humphrey had left a strong impression on several participants at that daylong Smithsonian session with Carter before the inauguration.

We cannot conduct a successful foreign policy until we devise an energy policy, Humphrey had said. Americans were gluttons for fuel, determined to waste it, and at the moment we were being held hostage by the Middle East. The development of a successful energy policy had to be linked directly to a successful Middle East policy.

As president, Carter threw himself into the energy question with characteristic intensity and with characteristic zeal to achieve a "comprehensive" new policy and achieve it instantly. His deadline of getting a new policy before Congress within three months was, like the others, arbitrary and his own. He worked intensively—and almost alone, with the exception of James Schlesinger, who was to be his secretary of energy (a newly created post)—spending probably more time on energy than on any other issue. It was, he told a small group in the White House one day, "one of the most challenging and in some degrees unpleasant undertakings I've ever assumed." But he drove on, and kept the details almost entirely to himself.

By February 22 he was telling a bipartisan group of congressional leaders that he had just about completed the outline of his overall policy, which he would present to Congress on April 20. And, he explained, he was thinking about a major speech, both on the policy and the basic legislation. It was the most important domestic issue of his administration, he said, and he needed their cooperation.

The trouble was, then and later, Congress was in the dark about what the president was planning. When Howard Baker, the Senate minority leader and potential Republican presidential candidate, asked for a chance to see a skeletal outline in advance so that he and his party wouldn't have to shoot from the hip on so important an issue, Carter confessed he was new at the job and didn't quite know how to proceed, but he would be glad to meet with members of Congress anytime. That wasn't Baker's point. Democrats felt equally uninformed—but, then, so did most of Carter's staff and cabinet.

Concern over this secretive approach began to grow as the deadline neared. When Robert Shogan of *The Los Angeles Times* was permitted to attend a meeting of Carter's senior staff on March 22 while gathering material for a book about the president's first hundred days, he found the subject touched raw nerves. Jack Watson, Jr., the cabinet secretary, complained that even the president's chief economics advisers hardly knew anything, either from the president or from Secretary Schlesinger. "What in effect is happening is that the substance of the energy plan is being put together independent of economic impact and analysis. And that can be devastating. Some of these people want to negotiate with Schlesinger before the plans go to the president, before anything is blocked in. There really ought to be some shirt-sleeve sessions."

But try as they did, the top Carter people could not find out from Schlesinger what specifically was in the works. A former head of the Atomic Energy Commission, former head of the CIA, former secretary of defense, Schlesinger did not want to have details of the plan leak out piecemeal, lest it be destroyed inch by inch by waiting lobbyists and special-interest groups.

Carter shared this fear, as he confided to the Democratic leaders when he met them on April 5. Robert Byrd had asked the president if senators were being included in the discussions on energy policy, adding that he wasn't aware that they were. A general discussion, critical in nature, ensued: people who considered themselves experts weren't being consulted. Others, who had worked with energy-related matters such as air pollution, had to know, and didn't, how it might affect their legislation.

The President: I understand. Here's the process. Dr. Schlesinger has met with me regularly one or two times a week. We have brought in forty-five people from government agencies with legal responsibilities in the energy field. We've had twenty-one mini-conferences with special-interest groups and ten hearings across the country. Dr. Schlesinger has given me memos and notes with alternatives. He is to give me a summary of the comprehensive energy proposal shortly. I've not seen it but I will, and I will see the draft speech, too. Once I sign off on it, within the next two or three days, I'll check with Senator Byrd and Tip on who in Congress should be brought in. . . . I'll have to admit, we've played the evolution of energy policy pretty close to our vest because if only parts of it were revealed, that would cause trouble. So neither Fritz, Charlie, nor Bert yet knows what it is.

In other words, less than two weeks before he was to go before the nation with his most important presidential proposal neither the vice-president, the chairman of the Council of Economic Advisers, nor his budget director knew what the plan called for—and neither, fully, did he.

The following day, after a personal appeal from a disturbed Hamilton Jordan, the president assembled Schlesinger, Lance, Schultze, Jordan, Powell, Frank Moore, Treasury Secretary Michael Blumenthal, and other key advisers. They discussed the energy program for hours, and this led to deletions of some proposals and alterations in others. But by then it was late; more than just a day was needed to examine thoroughly so critical a new program. And more than two weeks were needed for preparing the Congress and the public.

Everyone knew, of course, that the great test would come later. For Carter to win congressional approval for a complex new program dealing with the nation's most controversial issue, he had to achieve the widest possible popular support. Bold rhetoric alone would not suffice; other presidents had cried wolf too many times, and the public was weary and suspicious.

It was in this context that Fred Doxsee and his friends gathered to watch the president. For many reasons—the publicity, the air of crisis, the knowledge that Carter had promised to take perhaps unpalatable steps, the popularity he then enjoyed, the underlying fears about energy shortages affecting their lives—Jimmy Carter might never have a more attentive or receptive audience.

Carter was somber, and his listeners were silent as he spoke. He wanted, he said, to have an unpleasant talk about an unprecedented problem. War aside, we were facing the greatest challenge of our lifetime. The energy problem hadn't overwhelmed the nation yet, but it would, unless quick action were taken. It was no time for selfishness or timidity. We faced sacrifice, and a test of American character and the ability to govern ourselves. Then, borrowing William James's phrase, he said we were facing "the moral equivalent of war."

Carter then proceeded to lay out what was, essentially, a voluntary conservation program. America could avert an energy catastrophe by reducing demand through conservation, he argued. Protection from foreign oil embargoes would be achieved by switching to other abundant resources, such as coal. National goals would be set for 1985—among them, reduced gasoline consumption, a cutting in half of our imported oil, the establishment of a six-month supply of petroleum reserves, the insulation of all homes and new buildings, and the heating of some 2 million homes by solar energy.

The people in Fred Doxsee's living room thought the president had been impressive, but they were all bothered. They doubted whether Americans would all act voluntarily, and therefore they doubted that Carter's program would work. Controls or rationing might be the fairest answer, they agreed. They had expected something far tougher—and they felt let down.

Kenneth Walker, the high-school principal and member of the Boone City Council, like Doxsee a lifelong Republican who had switched to Carter at the end of the campaign, summed up their feelings best: "Much as I hate to think about it," he said, "I believe government controls are the answer. There's no convincing us—convincing me. Hell, I went out and bought a big car a month ago, and I know better. I think most people do. But the only way we're going to face what we have to face is when somebody slams it down our throats. We've never had shock enough. The situation wasn't bad enough. . . . I don't think we're going to do anything about it unless we're made to."

He told a story about the Boone City Council. In recent weeks they had tried to cut down on energy expenditures—and failed. When they tried to cut the streetlight wattage in certain sections of town, the merchants complained that it would hurt business. People would be afraid to come downtown at night, they argued, even in Boone, population some 13,000.

Gary Clark, a salesman who travels throughout Iowa, talked about the nation's mobility, about campers and campgrounds and how no one voluntarily would give up that life-style. "You're not going to go out and sacrifice, and neither am I," he said. "Hell, I just went out and bought a CB radio. You know why? So I can travel faster than fifty-five as I go around the state. If you ask me, we're not going to pull together as we did in World War Two. But you'll get some of that if the approach is fair, and the controls are fair."

Doxsee himself was disturbed. "Of course, we've known we've had a shortage but we haven't believed anyone yet," he said. "I believe Carter's laying it on the line now. But it's like the gas shortage before. When we finally got through with it we had plenty of gas at a much higher price. We've been misled for years, and they never do anything."

Someone mentioned waste in government. "Look at Uncle Sam," he said. "It used to be that postal workers carried the mail wherever they went. Now they ride around in little trucks before getting out to deliver the mail. Talk about waste, that's it. What's Carter going to do about that?"

Doxsee had the last word: "You've got to clean up your own house before you start on your neighbors'."

In Washington the next day, Carter met privately with congressional leaders. He asked Bert Lance to begin their meeting with prayer for divine guidance during a week when difficult decisions must be made affecting the nation's future. In similarly serious tones, he told the group that he'd been unable to find an easy answer to energy, or an uncontroversial one. They would have the draft legislation for a program in less than a week. He hoped they'd emphasize that the entire program was necessary. He couldn't turn over his responsibilities to a successor in good conscience without acting on energy. His program contained many politically difficult items—a stiff tax on crude oil, a levy on industrial use of oil and natural gas, national standards for setting utility rates, a tax on gas-guzzling cars, and an increase in the price ceiling on newly discovered natural gas.

But serious as he was in private and again in public when he addressed the Congress the next evening, Carter himself badly undercut his own position. At a nationally televised press conference on Friday he was sharply questioned about his new program. If the crisis were of wartime dimensions, why not immediate rationing? Why hadn't mass transit been mentioned in his speeches? What about costs? If people were supposed to sacrifice, what were the private companies going to be giving up? And what about the effect of his energy program on inflation?

Now Carter was more reassuring: things weren't so forbidding after all. The inflationary effect of his program would be minimal, for in fact, it would help the economy by creating several hundred thousand new jobs. "By increasing the costs of energy and returning the proceeds to all Americans we can save energy, save money, and continue to have a healthy economy," he maintained. "ENERGY PLAN NOW PICTURED AS CONSUMER BOOM," the page-one banner headline read in next day's *Washington Post*.

After all the buildup, the reality of Carter's program seemed tame indeed, not only to Fred Doxsee's friends but all over the country. The president seemed, Ralph Nader remarked, like a "sheep in wolf's clothing." Russell Baker, the *New York Times* columnist, dryly observed that Carter's "Moral Equivalent of War" speech could also be read as standing for "MEOW."

By June, when his energy program was beginning to run into serious trouble on Capitol Hill, Carter was sounding pessimistic. He was concerned and surprised, he said, at the extraordinary influence of oil lobbyists, and to see Congress already chipping away at the program. "Unless the American public can be aroused to help me and others who believe that this is extremely important, and that the American public is willing to accept some sacrifice if it's fair," he said on June 11, "I'm afraid we are not going to have an adequate program when it's over." But the president himself had not done much to "arouse" the public. After all the anticipation and attention focused on his April appearances, the president had not made another address to the public since then, and months would pass before he did. Yet already he seemed to be assigning part of the blame for failure to the public. "Unless the American people speak up," he said, "the special interests are going to prevail." Why or how they were supposed to speak up when he wasn't, was an unanswered question.

□   □   □

One day in the spring, when the Carter administration was fresh and its public approval rating remained high, Hubert Humphrey ended a meeting with the president by saying: "The Carter administration looks good in *The New York Times* and *The Washington Post*, and you are popular, too, Mr. President. But out in the country the HUD people, the FHA people, are zilch. They aren't producing. The best thing to do would be to get rid of all these people." Humphrey urged Carter to order his cabinet officers out "into the field," so they could find out for themselves what it was like dealing with the bureaucracy at first hand. It was familiar advice about a familiar subject.

Of all Carter's promises, none had been more strongly repeated than his pledge to reform the federal bureaucracy. Making government work better was above all else central to his presidency. It was the reason why he had been elected, he was sure, and he knew he would be judged on how well he fulfilled that promise. But the beginnings were bad. Government workers had supported Carter and were watching him closely for signs of a "new spirit." What the president had said in his round of visits to department headquarters had been fine, even moving, but what his administration was *doing* raised doubts and new fears.

Government employees from throughout the Washington area had attended a special symposium run by the Civil Service Commission on the workings of Congress and the federal agencies. For

most of them, it was a first chance to get a personal impression of
the Carter people who were scheduled to speak. What they heard
was chilling.

A Carter White House aide began by discussing the president's
plan to reorganize the government. It was the president's intention, the forum was told, to get people in the bureaucracy with the
same philosophy as himself. Dismay swept the room. When the
employees heard a reference about "no one was going to lose
their jobs until . . ." the murmur of disquiet was audible.

"The scary part is that this is what Nixon used to do," a government worker told his colleagues. Word of the session was carried
swiftly throughout the layers of government. It had been unfortu-
nate, for it had not accurately expressed administration policy, as
the president himself had stated it publicly; but it did reveal a genuine ambivalence about how to deal with the bureaucracy: should
one try to lift the *esprit* of government workers, or was it best to
take a tough, boot-'em-in-the-pants stand? Carter himself seemed
to hold both points of view.

Not long after the inauguration Hamilton Jordan had compiled
a series of charts. He set them up in his office (Haldeman's old
quarters) at the rear of the White House, and showed them to visitors. The charts listed the civil-service employees who had alleg-
edly been involved in the patronage scandals of the Nixon
administration, and what they had done. "We've got a bunch of
crooks over there that we're going to clean out," Jordan said to
me then, gesturing to the charts one night in his office. He and the
president had discussed those charts: Carter was going to clean
house at the Civil Service Commission by appointing three new
commissioners (the first time all three jobs would be filled by a
new president)—and then they were going to turn over the names
to the Justice Department for possible prosecution.

"The president has a general feeling there's a problem with the
civil service, and he's been given some of the stuff you saw on the
charts in Hamilton's office," Jule Sugarman, one of the three
whom Carter named to the Civil Service Commission, told me later that spring. "There have been some serious discussions about
civil-service reform with the president, but really only about what I
consider to be this narrow area of wrongdoing—not about what
the civil service is or should be. I don't think there's any depth of

understanding. At this point the civil service has about the same stature it's always had, which is not very high. It's the enemy, and it's never perceived as an institution that is there to help. We're going to try to do something about that. I hope we can recast the commission in a significant way."

Sugarman had been chief administrative officer to Atlanta's mayor after a long career in federal and local governments (he began working at the Civil Service Commission in Washington in 1951 and later created the Head Start program under Lyndon Johnson). He had vivid memories of his first meeting with Carter, which occurred in 1971, when Maynard Jackson, Atlanta's black mayor, asked him to attend a session with the then-Governor Carter. Jackson, as chairman of a group of Democratic mayors in the Southeast which had drafted a political platform, wanted to know where Carter stood on the issues.

"Give me a copy of the platform and I'll write you a letter," Carter said. Days later, back came a seven-page, handwritten letter, in which Carter spelled out point by point where he agreed with the mayors, where he disagreed, and where he believed compromise could be worked out. There was no equivocating, and clearly the letter was Carter's own. You knew precisely where he stood. Sugarman was impressed.

As president, though, Sugarman saw Carter as being torn between the two conflicting impulses toward the bureaucracy—to buoy it up, or to treat it roughly. "He comes at the issue from two points of view," he said. "One's that of every citizen who believes that the government employee is there to screw up. The best answer, of course, is to have [the bureaucrats] do their work competently, and eventually, that will begin to permeate the government."

Carter's new Civil Service Commission chairman, Alan Campbell, had a similar impression. Campbell, a political scientist who had been dean of the Maxwell School of Citizenship and Public Affairs at Syracuse University, was about to take over the LBJ School of Public Affairs at the University of Texas when he was called to Washington early in the winter of 1977. He first talked to Hamilton Jordan. Jordan asked "if I'm going to have guts enough to fire everyone," Campbell told me. If that's what they want, he had replied, I'm not interested. A meeting with Bert Lance was different. Lance was enthusiastic, helpful, persuasive—and told Carter they had to get Campbell. And it was Lance who had over-all authority for reorganizing the government, a task he approached with enthusiasm and energy.

When Carter and Campbell met before Campbell's appointment was announced on April 5, "the president perked up when I said there was a need for better management in government." But Carter did not show the kind of knowledge and enthusiasm about the civil service that Lance had revealed. "He did not have any very detailed understanding of the federal system," Campbell said, "and why the hell should he?" But then and later, the subject of management improvement most interested the president.

There was another need, of course, and probably no one expressed it better than Senator Charles Mathias of Maryland. "We have all heard horror stories of bureaucratic delay and inefficiency," he said, "and many of them are true. But the bureaucracy is made up of layers, like the volcanic ash that buried Pompeii and the blown dust that once covered the Parthenon. Stir it with good ideas and it responds. It will even produce some astonishingly valuable artifacts."

No one could fault the president for failing to work hard or lacking good intentions, for however much government reorganization receded from public notice as other issues demanded attention, the president tenaciously pursued his goal. Throughout his first year he met regularly with aides on their efforts to reorganize the government. Those who conferred with him found his interest, as one said, "intense to the smallest detail." But they were all, president and advisers alike, discovering just how difficult the task was, and what a large gap stretched between their erroneous impressions and the realities.

"It's very difficult for new people to understand the physical size of the government," Howard Messner, an energetic bureaucrat, said to me that spring, "or to realize there is no quick fix to this. A while ago we were giving the president a briefing about the size of government, and we were trying to describe GSA; we pointed out that the government has two hundred thirty-five million square feet of leased space. Well, he stopped for a minute. He was trying to size that back to his experience in Georgia. But two hundred thirty-five million leased square feet! You could see in his mind: What the hell do we need two hundred thirty-five million for? You want more, you're coming in for more, and you own almost everything in the United States! Or the same for numbers of people, or amount of equipment."

Messner was a perfect example of the unknown but indispensable bureaucrat. In fifteen years of government service, starting in the Eisenhower administration in the Census Bureau, he'd seen the nature of government change drastically. He remembered the excitement of the early 1960s, when he was with the space program and he and his colleagues volunteered their spare weekend time to help the new War on Poverty program get under way. His work had taken him from the big agencies to Capitol Hill, but hardly ever got his name in the paper. Now he was working directly for the president as part of a special government reorganization task force, looking for ways to reform the civil service. He had no illusions about the difficulty, or doubts about the importance, of the work. "The bureaucracy is serious and it's defensive," he said. "It is hard to penetrate. The bureaucrats say, 'Why doesn't the president say nice things about us? Why are the politicians dumping on us? Who is going to defend us?' That's circular reasoning. No one's going to defend them. You've got to be up and moving. You've got to do good things."

None of it was going to be easy, he knew, and he was watching the Carter group, as he put it, "learning to scale." That, by itself, was at times painful for all of them.

Messner's boss as head of Carter's reorganization effort was Harrison Wellford, a thirty-six-year-old North Carolina lawyer who had once worked for Ralph Nader and ten years before had been a Capitol Hill aide. Wellford thought he knew Washington well and appreciated the problems, but he was finding both far more difficult than he'd imagined.

"All of us, including the president," he said to me in June in his suite of offices in the OEB next to his superior Bert Lance, "are coming to a real awakening. The problems are so much harder than we'd been led to believe. The fragmentation in our governmental system is so extraordinary that it takes enormous agility to put together a coalition to get anything through.

"Being back in Washington has been a constant retreat from the premise that reason counts in the affairs of men. I used to think that if you were extremely well briefed and had all the facts at your command and put on a brilliant argument, success was assured. I realized there were political considerations, but I believed there were many opportunities to make things happen by just doing very good work. Well, I still believe you have to do good work, but it's not the substance any more that's so important. It's knowing how to manipulate. I'll tell you, nothing in the world is a substitute for experience on the Hill. Nothing. We can't do anything of substance without Congress, and there's no way to get the most out of our opportunities up there unless you have a feel for the system."

Wellford was beginning to have the sense they might be in Washington only a very short time. He was also struck by something else: the limitations of presidential power. He wasn't alone. Over at HEW a veteran bureaucrat, with a canny political sense, had been watching the Carter people as they tried to reform the government, colliding with interest groups and losing. "The old leadership is gone," he told me. "There is no central authority in the Congress anymore. There is no central core of authority in this country including the presidency, because the president's been denuded of much of his power. The lovefeast of the American people with the presidency is over, and Carter's finding that rough."

☐ ☐ ☐

Washington slumbered through June and July of 1977, stagnating in record heat and record air-pollution alerts, moving listlessly, after years of crises, through the first summer that seemed "normal." A revival of *Porgy and Bess* was coming to the Kennedy Center, bringing soothing lullabies about summertime when the living is easy. The papers, with a dearth of hard news, were finding space for the inevitable, daily "terrible problem" stories. There was a water shortage, but no one took it seriously. (Despite official appeals for water conservation, citizens used as much as ever.) There was an energy crisis, but no one paid attention. (The phlegmatic James Schlesinger, the new secretary of energy, studied the figures on national petroleum consumption and was dismayed. "In the first five days of July," he told me at lunch one stifling day that month, "the motorists of America used more oil and gasoline than Army ground forces in the whole year of 1944. In the first two weeks of July we used more gasoline than the U.S. Army Air Corps in all of 1944. Just blowing it away in the hundred million cars we have here.") Even the one subject that official Washington loved best, the character and actions of the president, was failing to arouse emotions. After six months of Jimmy Carter, the city still professed puzzlement about him. He was still getting high ratings in the opinion polls, but stirring little emotion. In a *Washington Post* column around that time, I wrestled with an interim assessment:

> Jimmy Carter, at this stage, stands as perhaps the most perplexing, and promising, president of recent times. By this point in office most presidents have left a distinct stamp on Washington, altering the pace and, to a degree, the character of the city. That hasn't happened in Jimmy Carter's Washington. . . . On any given day, on any given issue, he comes over as a liberal, or as a conservative. . . . But for all the contradictions, it just may be that Jimmy Carter perfectly suits the politics of the present. It's a present with problems, but no passion; a politics with issues, but no ideology. The most persistent question about Carter this summer is: is he drifting with the current, or leading the waves?

Those words were published on July 10. The next day the president sent a letter to the chairman of the Senate Government Affairs Committee—a seemingly routine letter making a seemingly routine request. Carter's budget director, Thomas Bertram Lance, had encountered a problem that, in the president's words, "has placed an undue financial burden on Mr. Lance." The matter could be easily resolved by modifying an earlier agreement which had provided that Lance would dispose of all his stock in a Georgia bank by the end of the year.

From these innocent beginnings in the sultry Washington summer flowed events that shook the foundation of Carter's presidency, struck at the core of his pledges, raised questions about his judgment and standards, laid bare weaknesses in his inner circle of advisers, lowered his popularity, stirred partisan discord, aroused passions against the press, and shamed Senate and federal investigatory processes.

Carter and Lance were almost inseparable—personally, politically, culturally. They were partners in the presidency. There were similarly close relationships in the past—Harry Hopkins and Roosevelt, Robert and John Kennedy—but certainly Carter and Lance were an extraordinary White House team. They were like the Corsican Twins; you could not cut one without wounding the other.

The story of how they met has been told often: Carter, the ambitious young south Georgia politician, speaking at some gathering under an oak tree; Lance, the ambitious young north Georgia banker, impressed by the speech and offering his personal support. That story, and accounts of how the two shared similar values growing out of small-town, rural Southern life and common Christian convictions, had the sweet flavor of a Sunday-school tale.

What the stories failed to explain was why Carter found Lance so appealing. For all Lance's demonstrated charm, gregariousness, and capacity for hard work, he seemed—by his own self-portrait and by the accounts of others—a thoroughly conventional type, an entrepreneur unencumbered by ideas in the grander sense, with no clear political or philosophical vision of a better America.

Lance himself gave perhaps the most intriguing clues into their relationship shortly after coming to Washington. Six weeks before Carter's inauguration, he said to a group of *Washington Post* editors and writers: "I think I understand him probably as well as anybody in the country, with the exception of Rosalynn. And I understand how he does things. We don't spend a lot of time talking about the weather and that sort of thing. . . . I like to beat him on the tennis court. He's a poor loser. . . . He doesn't like to lose at anything. I don't either, so that's the reason that we have a good relationship."

When, attempting to succeed Carter, Lance ran for governor in 1974, and lost, he spent about a million dollars and incurred a complicated series of debts that were never entirely paid off. That political race came back to haunt Carter. He felt responsible for pushing Lance into it, close aides said—and he believed that most if not all of Lance's subsequent financial troubles were a result of that campaign. (As president, Carter felt a similar responsibility in urging Lance to come to Washington; as he told someone else who was reluctant about serving in his administration, Lance's board of directors was against his taking the job.)

After Lance lost the gubernatorial race, he became a big-city banker. He moved from Calhoun, Georgia, to Atlanta in January 1975 and became president of the National Bank of Georgia. A few months later, along with several business colleagues and some multimillion-dollar loans, Lance bought a controlling interest in the bank.

Bert Lance was a promoter with big ideas. The National Bank of Georgia's executive committee was eager to get him, even to the point of agreeing to buy a plane for his use. Lancelot & Co., a partnership of Lance and his wife, LaBelle, just happened to have one for sale: an eight-year-old Beechcraft Queen Air which had been bought for $80,000 a year before and which Lance had used as a campaign plane. He rented it to the bank for a few months and finally sold it for $120,000 in July 1975.

In his own accounts of his business career, Lance depicted himself as just a drawling country banker following the American dream. He was Horatio Alger, working his way up, building the business, increasing the assets. He had been the ninety-dollars-a-week bank clerk working to support his wife. They had pooled their resources to buy their first stock in the bank, he said once—not mentioning that he had married the bank president's daughter. As he progressed, his horizons widened. "My plans for the bank included a program to develop a network of correspondent banking relationships, establish a national account department, conduct an aggressive agri-business program, and become involved in international banking."

Among the beneficiaries of his "aggressive" agricultural-loan program was his friend and political associate Jimmy Carter. The 1975 National Bank of Georgia's annual report, which looks like a garish news magazine, sums up with a startling centerfold display of a huge peanut and a boldface headline reading: "NBG GOES NUTS IN PLAINS." "Because of The National Bank of Georgia's aggressiveness in agricultural financing, it's not surprising that one of their clients is a major peanut producer in southwest Georgia," the report said of the bank's nearly $5 million in loans to the

Carter family businesses. "Carter's Warehouse in Plains, Georgia, produced 6,000 tons of peanuts in 1975, and expects, with NBG's help, to double that production in 1976. . . . According to Billy Carter, president of Carter's Warehouse, the future is bright indeed for peanuts in Georgia and the U.S."

Throughout 1976, during Carter's spectacular run for the presidency, Lance remained in the background, basically unknown to the general public. With the election won, Lance became Carter's first choice for an important government appointment. In mid-November they met at Carter's house in Plains. Carter wanted Lance to be either his budget director or treasury secretary; and, because of his concern about setting the highest ethical tone for his administration, he wanted Lance to divest himself "prudently and as soon as possible" of his huge stock holdings in the National Bank of Georgia so as to avoid any conflicts of interest.

Lance alluded to some problems he had had at the Calhoun First National Bank, where he was still chairman of the board, but, both he and Carter later implied, it was only a cursory account of those problems. What stuck in Carter's mind was that Lance had overdrawn on his campaign accounts at the bank during the 1974 governor's race. In fact, since April 1975 the Justice Department had been investigating the affairs of the Calhoun bank. A routine examination by the office of the Comptroller of the Currency (the U.S. agency that regulates national banks) showed serious deficiencies, including overdrafts by the Bert Lance gubernatorial campaign, company insider and family overdrafts, and numerous questionable loans. An FBI agent assigned that summer to an embezzlement case involving a Calhoun bank offical named Billy Lee Campbell had come across a "pattern" of other overdrafts on the personal accounts of Lance, his wife, and additional bank officials and relatives. In August the agent tried to subpoena those records, only to be put off by the bank president.

Lance himself was a target as the investigation widened. Over a four-year period, Lance, his wife, and family had run up as much as $450,000 in overdrafts on the bank they controlled.

Lance said later that he could not remember mentioning that to Carter. Nor could he recall telling Carter about a cease-and-desist agreement that the comptroller's office had insisted upon the previous December. Lance and other bank directors had signed the order as a "voluntary" agreement in the comptroller's regional Atlanta offices, and it was still in effect when he and Carter conferred.

Just before the presidential election in 1976 a federal bank examiner made a special visit to the Calhoun bank, Robert Ashley Lee found "some improvement" but not enough, in his opinion, to justify lifting the agreement. The bank's loan portfolio was still a "problem" and needed to be restructured, he told a special Internal Revenue Service team in an affidavit. Had he been asked, Lee "would have recommended the agreement be continued." No one asked him.

The discomfiting agreement was lifted anyway, immediately after a visit by Lance in late November—exactly a week after he met with Carter—to Donald Tarleton, director of the comptroller's Atlanta regional office. Another federal bank official there later testified that Tarleton told him of Lance's visit and quoted him as having said, essentially: "Jimmy wants me to be head of the OMB (Office of Management and Budget), and I want to go into it with a clear record, so I just wondered if you could see your way clear to lift the agreement on Calhoun." Tarleton moved quickly, formally rescinding the restrictions on the Calhoun bank the very day of Lance's visit.

In Washington, most senior officials of the comptroller's office were, by their account, disturbed by Tarleton's action, some quite angry. The then-acting comptroller, Robert Bloom, later said he was outraged—but not enough, on reflection, to try to countermand the move. Far from it. Bloom, who had hopes of becoming comptroller in the Carter administration, made a number of helpful gestures on Lance's behalf: he drafted an innocuous-sounding press release for Lance about the Calhoun bank's problems, which skirted crucial points (such as referral of the campaign overdraft case to the Justice Department); he kept the text of the cease-and-desist order from FBI agents conducting a background investigation on Lance; he consulted Lance and his advisers and even told him about a letter he, Bloom, was sending to the Senate Government Affairs Committee, which has to conduct the upcoming confirmation hearings. Although aides showed Bloom derogatory information about Lance's performance at the National Bank of Georgia even as he was composing his letter, the acting comptroller concluded by pronouncing Lance "well qualified to serve as the director of the Office of Management and Budget."

"Mr. Bloom . . . wanted to be kind to Mr. Lance," Lance's lawyer, Sidney Smith, recalled later. Bloom had told him "he was at a 'dead end' unless he could be comptroller."

The man who finally got the job, Comptroller John Heimann, remembered Bloom "chastising himself for what he had done" and "saying something to the effect that when he thought back as to why he did it, he guessed he did it to win some 'Brownie points.'"

Bureaucratic bowing and scraping continued. Alerted by a call from Bloom about the Justice Department investigation, Lance's lawyer found a sympathetic ear at the U.S. attorney's office in Atlanta. When on December 1 Smith asked the U.S. attorney, John Stokes, about the status of the Lance case, Stokes took the prosecutor off it the same day and pronounced the case closed the next day, an action that effectively squelched any thought of a parallel investigation into the personal overdrafts by the Lances, their relatives, and other officials of the Calhoun bank.

Stokes, like Bloom, had a powerful reason for acting on behalf of Lance. He had been appointed U.S. attorney by President Nixon, and at that point hoped to keep his job. If he stayed on for eleven more months he would become eligible for an $800-a-month lifetime government pension. And he knew who Bert Lance was, and how important he was to Jimmy Carter. After closing the investigation, one of Stokes's aides recalled that her boss told her that "he should call 'Jimmy and Bert' and tell them what he had done." In any case, he told Lance's lawyer.

On December 3, the day after the Lance case had been closed, Jimmy Carter announced his choice of Bert Lance over nationwide television from Plains.

From that moment, Bert Lance became a time bomb planted in Jimmy Carter's White House. The scope and seriousness of the investigations against him, the special treatment he received from compliant bureaucrats eager to protect their own special interests, the way he had handled his and his bank's affairs, when put against his new responsibilities as the nation's budget director leading a fresh crusade against waste, mismanagement, and unethical government practices—all would prove devastating when they became public. Jimmy Carter, of all presidents, had won support because of his promises to restore integrity to government. You can count on it, he had said time and again across the country. "All we see is waffling, inaction, attempts to shift blame and to talk problems away," he said as a candidate. "The confidence in our own government must be restored, but too many officials do not deserve that confidence." By the time the Lance case moved to its inevitable conclusion, those words would be called to account.

For Lance, who was probably alone in knowing fully what heavy personal and private liabilities he carried, those early days after his appointment were glorious. He sailed through his confirmation hearings. There was no inclination on the part of any major politician of either party to challenge him. Some unsettling questions about Carter's choice did find their way into print early the next year, before the inauguration—on January 8, *The Washington Post* carried an Associated Press story about the Justice Department investigation; on January 11, *The New York Times* reported that the inquiry had been dropped by U.S. Attorney Stokes the day before Carter's appointment of Lance; and five days later another *Times* story recounted the Calhoun bank's habit, as criticized by federal bank examiners, of permitting Lance's wife and relatives of other bank officials "to make repeated overdrafts of their accounts while continuing to honor the checks and not press for quick payment"—but the stories didn't make the front pages, and were not pursued.

Any incoming president gets a free ride for a time from the press, and often on issues that beg for scrutiny. It is regarded as bad form after a long campaign to suggest out loud that the winner might be less than perfect, and that was so even in the post-Watergate days. As Bloom said in his defense, "No one likes to be the skunk at the garden party." But the federal bureaucrats were not the only ones in Washington who fawned over the new regime. The Senate—whether individual members responsible for judging the fitness of a specific nominee, or the body itself, with its constitutional duties of advice and consent—almost always accommodates a new president at first. In the Lance case, that was notably so. As Republican Senator Charles Percy of Illinois said later: "Research showed the case closed. There were glowing letters from the U.S. attorney. If the comptroller of the currency gave him such a beautiful, glowing tribute, why should we complain? Our staff were not trained investigators [who could] go out and research deeply. The things we were told totally removed any questions of why we shouldn't go ahead and confirm." The senators ignored the newspaper accounts, and as for the FBI background report on Lance, it wasn't completed until January 31, after his confirmation, and the senators didn't read it until nearly eight months later, when questions about Lance had taken a different turn.

When the final Senate vote was called, only one man was curmudgeonly enough to cast a dissenting vote. William Proxmire of Wisconsin, chairman of the Senate banking committee and a Washington gadfly, opposed Lance because of what he called Lance's "appallingly barren background" in the federal government. "He has had none—zero, zip, zilch—not one year, not one week, not one day" of Washington experience, Proxmire protested of the man about to be put in charge of the $400 billion federal budget.

Lance was in, and few officials ever made as grand an entrance into Washington.

Someone who was to work closely with him on the White House team would never forget the first time he saw Lance. It was not long after the election and he was standing on Pennsylvania Avenue, in front of the Executive Office Building next to the White House. Suddenly, he saw people at the bus stop turning their heads, staring down the street.

"So I looked around," he said, "and there, proceeding at a stately pace, was an incredible black limousine. It must have been half a football field—forty yards at least. It had the Georgia flag and the American flag flying from the bumpers. My God, I thought, this must be an Arab potentate. As the car came by, I could see this big fellow with a large entourage inside, and the front license plate said, 'Bert.' As it turned inside the White House driveway, the back license plate said, 'Lance.'

"My God, here's Genghis Khan coming into Constantinople. No doubt about it, he was going to conquer this town, and do it with panache."

Lance fed something in Carter, fulfilled a need. They joked

together. They played tennis together. At times they prayed together.

Lance's political instincts were finely honed. His self-confidence was so infectious that he made others, far younger and less experienced, feel confident, too. He'd throw his burly arm around an aide's shoulder, and say, "Look, you work for me, and I'll be the most loyal boss you ever had. Sky's the limit, sky's the limit. We'll just wipe the bastards out." He had a bravado and a dash that the Carter group sorely lacked.

Yet "there was something sinister about Bert, too," an aide told me much later. "He had a bodyguard working for him who was a very sinister character. I was with him a few times, and what he told me gave me real pause. And Bert, too. For example, we'd be walking out of a White House meeting and Bert would see somebody on the domestic policy staff he had a particular dislike for, and he'd say, 'Sometime I'm going to run down that son of a bitch.' He was half joking, but it had kind of a menacing tone. And his bodyguard always talked that way—it was always, 'If they give us a hard time, we'll put an investigator on them. We'll destroy the sons of bitches.' I never was sure about it, and I never was sure how well Bert would have worn."

The aide recalled the first time he learned Lance was in real trouble. It was late spring, and there had been a small item in *Time* magazine about Lance's having financial troubles. Walking over to the White House with someone who had worked closely with Lance's bank he asked, What's all this about Bert? The reply shocked him. He'll be out of the government by Christmas, the associate said flatly.

(Several weeks after the inauguration a critical article about Lance by Alexander Cockburn and James Ridgeway had appeared in New York's *Village Voice*. Under the headline "Cracker Credit," the story spoke of "a possible scandal involving the Carter administration," and suggested that Lance's wife may have had bank overdrafts running as high as $250,000. FBI agents were vexed at being called off the case, it said. In Washington the article was dismissed by administration supporters as typical New York malice and not developed further. Then, months later, *Time* reported that Lance's National Bank of Georgia was writing off bad real-estate loans and facing the prospect of having to discontinue dividends. This jeopardized Lance's income, for his chief source was from nearly 200,000 shares of bank stock he had acquired.)

Still the Lance affair slumbered, just beneath the surface, as spring gave way to summer.

The catalyst came on July 11, in the form of Carter's seemingly routine letter to Abraham Ribicoff, chairman of the Senate Government Affairs Committee. Carter asked the committee's consent to set aside the December 31, 1977, deadline for the sale of Lance's bank stock. The stock price had dropped sharply since Lance acquired it in 1975 and 1976; in the president's view, a forced sale would pose "an undue financial burden" on Lance.

On July 12, a new comptroller of the currency took his oath of office. John Heimann had been, as he said, "aware of allegations from various quarters that T. Bertram Lance, Director, Office of Management and Budget, prior to his assumption of that office, may have committed infractions of laws or regulations relating to national banks." Heimann was a different breed from his predecessor, Robert Bloom, and on July 14 quietly ordered an inquiry into Lance's banking affairs. Still, Ribicoff's committee was expected to rubber-stamp the president's request to set aside Lance's deadline for the sale of his stock. Indeed, the committee scheduled a hearing to do just that—but here the press became a factor.

A number of news articles that raised serious questions about Lance began to appear. William Safire, the *New York Times* columnist and former Nixon speechwriter, was especially forceful and critical.* Then on July 24 *The Washington Post* began to ask about the timing of a loan of $3.4 million which Lance had obtained from the First National Bank of Chicago, and which Lance had begun shopping for on December 2, 1976, the day before his appointment. In all, Lance then owed a number of banks some $5 million.

In light of this fresh publicity, Ribicoff and Percy, the ranking Republican, said their committee should make an immediate investigation. But the committee was divided—Washington had

---

*Safire later won a Pulitzer Prize for his commentary on and reporting of this subject.

seen the press destroying people all too often, some felt, and Ribicoff agreed to hear Lance first, then decide on whether to have an investigation.

Lance turned up on Monday, July 25. He assured the senators, in his deep and resonant drawl, that there was nothing improper about the Chicago bank loan—and nothing to any of the other "unwarranted uncertainties" that had arisen. The questioning was gentle. Lance responded with generalities. "You have been smeared from one end of the country to another, in my opinion unjustly," Ribicoff finally told Lance. "We can just imagine what this has done to you and your family."

Ribicoff later came to wish he had never uttered those words, for they became a source of political and personal embarrassment, and he relished neither. Abe Ribicoff had earned a reputation over the years as one of the shrewdest Democrats. In 1960 he had helped to elect John Kennedy, having been floor manager for him at the convention, and later served in his cabinet. Now his committee was assessing some of Jimmy Carter's most cherished legislation—on nuclear proliferation, basic governmental reorganization authority, government ethics, consumer protection. But paradoxically, his criticism of the press probably led him to be especially critical of Lance when new evidence showed that much more than a smear was involved. As fresh questions about Lance arose, Ribicoff began to get queasy lest he be accused of having run an inept confirmation hearing and having condoned a subsequent cover-up. And soon there was more than press accounts to rely on.

Comptroller Heimann's completed investigation into Lance's affairs was scheduled to be made public on August 18. This softly, almost soothingly, worded document came with a stack of exhibits and records that pointed to improper, and quite possibly illegal dealings. It was devastating.

Ribicoff had gone to Miami to visit his ailing mother-in-law when he got the report. For four days he sat by the pool reading the exhibits. The more he read, the more disturbed he became. He called his committee staff and told them to get busy. "I felt his going was inevitable," Ribicoff said later, "when I came back from Florida from my vacation and talked to the staff that Saturday."

White House officials had an entirely different reaction to the Heimann report. They read it as a vindication of Lance. Jody Pow-

ell first learned that a potential crisis was building in a telephone
call July 22 from Joseph Laitin, press aide to Treasury Secretary
Michael Blumenthal. Powell was in New Orleans with Carter on
the last day of a three-day swing through the South, and the word
from Washington was blunt: Laitin told Powell the report was a
mortal blow. Powell passed the information to the president.*

From that moment, a small group of White House aides began
to work on the Lance case. It included Powell, Jordan, counsel
Robert Lipshutz, and Frank Moore. All were Georgians, all extremely fond of Lance, all intensely loyal to the president. None
brought a dispassionate view to the affair, none was capable of
coldly calculating the pluses and minuses. Powell and Jordan in
particular agonized over their dual roles: The president came to
them for advice; so did Lance. The two older men had always
done this, but now it was far more complicated.

Lance had one other important ally in the White House: Rosalynn Carter. Long after others realized there was no way he could
be saved, she passionately argued his case to the president. But
Carter didn't need any convincing: he wanted to believe in Lance's
innocence.

Now, the press was in full attack. The brushed-aside Lance story
of the winter became the sensation of the summer. In the summer
the news was slow, the Carter administration no longer so fresh,
and Lance a far greater figure in the capital. And, each day the
damaging facts that had been there all along were becoming
known, piece by piece.

Washington pretends to abhor public hangings. In fact, it rel-
ishes nothing more than good, gory bloodletting. To see the
mighty squirm, and perhaps fall, is an enthralling, if unseemly,
spectacle. Politicians, bureaucrats, and journalists strike a careful
note of dispassion as they go about their daily jobs, and then rush
to exchange the latest and juiciest gossip in private.

Nothing was juicier than Lance. Next to the president he was
the single most powerful person in town, and certainly the most
visible. He was Jimmy Carter's emissary to business, to Capitol
Hill, overseer of the administration's effort to reorganize the bu-

---

*The White House Georgians came to resent the way Blumenthal and his Trea-
sury officials proceeded against Lance, leaving ill will between them.

reaucracy. Next to the president, Lance's voice carried the most weight. Among the Georgians around Carter, he was first among equals. The Lance affair was about high stakes and high places, insiders and outsiders, people on the rise and fall, public arenas and private corridors, personal ambition and political advice, intrigue and influence. The figures that began to take public form were instantly familiar, even if the names were not: the tired bureaucrat trying to protect his job, or pension, by pleasing his political superiors; the earnest young governmental attorneys offended by evidence of favoritism; the confidants and counselors to the mighty, who make the wheels turn. And, in the end, it was about one thing—power, and how it affected the president. Because Bert Lance was introduced to the public as a "fiscal conservative" by a president promising new ethical standards and prudent management, his case struck at the new administration's credibility. That wasn't how the Carter group viewed it, though; to them it was a personal fight. Their man was under assault; they were going to defend him. They were coming to the aid of a friend. Lance's personal reputation was at stake, they believed, and anything less than a full presidential endorsement would undercut Lance's fight for his honor in public. They genuinely believed that Lance had been wronged, and they were not going to have political expediency force them to turn him over to a lynch mob of press and politicians.

The White House received Comptroller Heimann's report on August 17. Immediately Lipshutz and his lawyers went to work on it. The next day Jordan and Lipshutz took a helicopter to Camp David. Apparently the president didn't require much persuading that the report vindicated Lance. And Powell and Jordan encouraged him to return to give full endorsement to Lance in Washington that day. That should end the matter.

Back to Washington they flew and there, at a nationally televised afternoon press conference, with Lance at his side, the president said: "I have reviewed the report of the Comptroller of the United States, both personally and with the White House legal counsel, Bob Lipshutz, and my faith in the character and competence of Bert Lance has been reconfirmed. I see no other conclusion that can be drawn from any objective analysis of these findings." Lance was a man of honesty, trustworthiness, integrity, he said, who enjoyed his complete confidence and support. As far as he was concerned the comptroller's report had answered all questions about Lance. Then, turning to Lance, he ended; "Bert, I'm proud of you."

The incident *didn't* end. It grew worse. More damaging information came to light, and Heimann's report seemed to raise the interpretation that Lance had committed what might technically be criminal violations of the law. Criticism of Carter and Lance intensified in the press, on Capitol Hill—and now, for the first time, the White House itself. Outside the small group of Georgians around the president, many presidential aides I spoke to then were appalled. Mistakes made over Lance were stirring unpleasant memories—it was like the campaign, one aide said, when Carter's huge initial lead had melted away as mistake followed mistake. "It's either an error of naïveté or stupidity," another commented. "Whoever read that comptroller's report and declared it exonerated Lance was just plain stupid. There's no other way to put it." Even more perplexing was how Carter and his small circle of advisers continued to misunderstand how the Lance case appeared to the public. Overdrafts were common to small, rural banks everywhere—that was a standard White House reply to allegations about Lance. But "their putting on that 'everybody does it' song just doesn't play," was the bitter comment of one aide who expressed amazement at the evident failure to remember the lessons of Watergate. Most damaging, in their view, was an incident involving Senator Percy who had become one of Lance's strongest Senate critics. Jody Powell attempted to "plant" press stories saying Percy was guilty of unethical practices. The charge was false: Powell had to apologize publicly after stories appeared describing his efforts against Percy; and the tactic aroused more memories of Watergate.

Amid repeated new findings and allegations, official and unofficial, the ordeal continued through August and into September. The original agenda of the Carter administration was disrupted. In Congress, Democrats were saying that the president would be further damaged on the Hill if Lance remained: having lived through Watergate, the Democrats didn't need a major ethical impropriety case laid at *their* party's leadership. "Hell, yes, it's hurt

Carter," Senator John Glenn of Ohio said. "He's laying his reputation on the line for Bert." "If you ask the question, 'Why not the best?'" Senator Dick Clark of Iowa said, "it's hard to see Bert Lance's position as being the best." Privately, Senator Byrd told Carter that Lance had to go—and said the same to Lance.

Eventually the inner core of the White House came, reluctantly and sadly, to the same conclusion. Over Labor Day, Hamilton Jordan flew off to Sea Island, Georgia, where Lance was staying at his vacation home. He had decided that Lance had to resign, and he said so; Lance apparently agreed. But then a new round of newspaper allegations, which Lance felt to be the most irresponsible and inaccurate of all, appeared. He had to have time to clear himself publicly through the forum of a congressional hearing. Jordan and the others agreed. Perhaps it would still turn out all right.

In the end, it was death by accumulation. The longer Lance protracted his defense, the greater the attention paid to his misdeeds. Lance led the evening television news, commanded the covers of *Time* and *Newsweek*, dominated headlines everywhere. Still, his testimony before the Senate (prepared through the assistance of his lawyer, the wily Clark Clifford), carried live on television, aroused another glimmer of hope in the White House. On the morning of the hearing, Lance and Carter had met alone, with each saying a brief prayer. Later that day Carter told the columnist Jack Anderson how the Lance case had been one of the most difficult situations he'd ever faced. He was convinced of Lance's honesty and integrity: "I was talking the other day [with] just a group of us who have been close, and we all decided that if we could name two thousand different things that might have caused me any problem or any embarrassment, Bert Lance's character would have been the last thing we would have guessed about." At that time he didn't see any reason for Lance to resign, but if it came to that he supposed he and Bert together would make that decision.

That moment came the following week. At 6:00 a.m. Monday, September 19, the two friends met alone for forty-five minutes in Carter's office, with the president, as he later explained, "going over all the present questions that still remained, the prospects for the future." Lance had exonerated himself and had proven the

system worked, Carter said, but he asked Lance to think about
whether it wouldn't be better to resign, and make that decision
himself. The next afternoon Lance told Carter he was resigning.

Twenty-four hours later a tightly controlled but emotional Jimmy Carter went before the press to announce the departure. Tears
glistened in his eyes as he read Lance's resignation statement.
Lance was like a brother, without any doubt a good and honorable
man, literally irreplaceable: "I don't think there's any way that I
could find anyone to replace Bert Lance that would be, in my
judgment, as competent, as strong, as decent, and as close to me
as a friend and adviser as he has been. . . . There has been a special relationship between me and Bert Lance that transcended official responsibilities or duties or even governmental service over
the last six or seven years. So, he has occupied a special place in
my governmental career, in my political career, and in my personal life, and I don't think there's any way anyone could replace him
now."

It was a painfully old scene. Carter, like so many before him, was
trapped by a tangled friendship. With Warren Harding, he could
sigh and say, "It isn't my enemies who are causing me problems.
It's my friends that are giving me trouble."

On September 23, two days after Bert Lance resigned, the
White House announced that Carter would make a whirlwind trip
around the world, covering nine countries on four continents in
only eleven days, beginning on November 22. To Washington
cynics it confirmed an old adage about presidents: when in trouble, travel. And, in fact, the idea of a president racing around—
back and forth, in and out of time zones and climates—did have a
desperate air about it, particularly for a president who had said
that he planned to avoid making the many foreign trips his predecessors had enjoyed. But there was no way Carter could escape
from the disarray of his administration or leave behind the unre-
solved problems of Washington that had become worse during the
Lance affair.

□   □   □

In the closely connected tribal groups of Washington, judgments about the Lance case were delivered harshly, often gleeful-

ly, and often unfairly. After eight months in office the outsiders
had flopped after all, as people had guessed they might. And there
was enough substance to the complaints to raise genuine doubts
about the future. By now, the winter's bold initiatives in foreign
and domestic affairs were stalled. The fragile groups of traditional
Democrats that had tenuously supported Carter as he came to
power—blacks, liberals, labor, urban groups—were turning
against him. "Jimmy campaigns liberal, and governs conservative," Bert Lance had remarked, and Carter himself did not entirely dispute this. "I realize I'm taking a very conservative position,"
he once told a group of politicians in the White House. Jews, already uneasy about him, were growing more so over his Middle
East policy evolution. Carter's relations with George Meany of the
AFL-CIO were frosty at best. Labor had been incensed by a number of Carter administration moves—dropping the promised tax
rebate, refusing to raise the minimum wage standard higher than a
few cents, implementing what it called an ineffectual anti-inflation
program—and had not neglected to let the president know its reactions. After one session with Meany, Carter told his wife he'd
never been spoken to so roughly in his life. (It was to grow worse:
at a closed-door meeting with the president, one union president
employed flagrantly profane language to Carter's face in front of
other union leaders. "This is a very emotional man," a union official told me, "and when he gets worked up he can't think of another word for 'motherfucker' and he says 'motherfucker.' ") The
press, never close to Carter to begin with, had become more critical throughout the Lance matter, and the White House replied in
kind. Many of the top Carter people believed the press deliberately had conspired to "get" Lance and, through him, them and the
president as Southerners. As Alan Otten, a respected Washington
journalist, wrote in *The Wall Street Journal* in September, the Carter
people had failed to anticipate how Washington reporters would
see the Lance record and keep digging at it. "The Carter camp has
never remotely understood the press's view of its own role, perhaps vainglorious but honestly held, to act as surrogate for all the
citizens who can't be in Washington themselves checking on
government officials." And despite all the meetings over all
the months, the chemistry between Carter and Congress wasn't
working.

No president could have been a more patient or attentive listener, but Carter rarely gave back much in return—and when he did, it tended to come over as a long lecture. That, in the congressional view, wasn't consulting. For months the leaders had been saying the same things to Carter—he was trying to do too much, too fast, and without adequate preparation. In Senator Byrd's homely phrase to Carter, "you can't put a half gallon of water in a quart jar." As the problems continued, the congressional comments had become even more blunt. Just before the Lance problems began, following a detailed foreign-policy briefing, the Democratic leaders in both House and Senate had weighed in with frank advice.

O'Neill: What do you want done? There is only so much time. Give us about four priorities that you want between now and the rest of the year. You have four years here, Mr. President. You've made so many promises, and it's easy for you to get off the hook by saying, "It's up to the Congress!" But we have to deal with these various groups that want different bills. We've got to have instructions.

Byrd: Meetings like the one yesterday are of very little value. You need very small meetings and don't just brief [the Congressmen who attend] but get their advice and let them feel they have some input. You don't want them talking to the television cameras when they leave. You can't go for a kill on every bill. Work must be done in advance. The bill must be ready for the stomach, and the stomach must be ready for the bill.

Yet after Lance the same problems and same criticisms continued. September 27, another White House breakfast session, and Congresswoman Shirley Chisholm of New York is speaking: I hear many of the younger members in the Cloak Room and I know that they're so committed to human rights that they lose sight of the ramifications of their votes on other countries. So call us in, Mr. President. She's joined by the House whip, John Brademas, who had been a Rhodes Scholar before being elected to Congress from Indiana: If you bring in these members to talk, you can also have a chance to give them an idea of what you're thinking more broadly about foreign policy and give them an indication of what you're going to do. This may be one of the last opportunities before we adjourn for you to do this.

The Lance case had crystallized judgments about Carter throughout Washington, but, even among those who had been watching and dealing with him closely, he still remained an enigma. I was talking about the president one day with a member of Congress with a strong liberal and national following. He was saying how difficult it was for anyone to get close to Carter. Then he reached inside his drawer, pulled out a special file he was keeping about Carter, and handed over a memo.he had dictated to himself at the end of June setting down his impressions of the president after six months in office:

> He's now completed ten percent of his term. What are emerging as his basic traits? There are some surprises, particularly as he's one of the few presidents who went to the White House without being well known to the American public for a decade or two, and without having a chance to be evaluated. We're all subject to basic influences, products of our past. He's a small-town boy with eleven years in the Navy and twenty years as a medium-sized businessman. There's now little doubt that among his deepest and sincerest convictions are a set of beliefs on economics, fiscal and monetary policy based on the old small-town chamber of commerce virtues that are going to get him in trouble with liberals. His administration, compared to Ford, has been pretty good for liberals. He respects consumer agencies, human rights, amnesty, voting rights, stopping the dams, appointing liberals to key environmental positions. The common denominator of all this is none of them costs much money. Liberals should understand that he will give them some things, but money will not be among them.

Nothing had happened since then to change those judgments of Carter, he said, but the Lance business made him all the more doubtful about Carter's capacity for leadership in this most difficult period for governing.

Not long after that, a man influential in many previous administrations gave me the most dispassionate, disinterested, and shrewdest appraisal I had heard about Jimmy Carter and his administration to date. His was the view of the Washington insider who had weathered other presidential times of crisis and was still intimately connected to the centers of power. Typically, he would not permit me to use his name but his anonymous comments nonetheless reflect the reactions of many like him who had witnessed government close up over the years:

If they ever administered intelligence quotient tests to presidents, this man would rank very high—at least among the presidents I have known. I like the way his mind works. I like the quality of it. When a subject is being pursued, an effort is being made to elicit information without emotion becoming a factor. He does not view issues in an emotional context. That was never possible with President Johnson—good God, just the opposite. President Johnson brought a whole background of prejudice and emotion to a subject. This man doesn't and that's appealing to me. I like Mr. Carter's ability—at least what I've seen of it—to subject the problems to what I consider to be a high degree of objectivity. He's a seeker of information searching for an opinion. There's no pretense about it. He goes to the heart of it. If a different view is offered, it is considered.

It's my present opinion, after eight months in office, that he has the potentiality for an unusually successful presidency. I think he could turn out to be a very successful president. Could is the key word. Could.

At first I had the feeling of great rigidity on his part, and great sensitivity to what people thought were the ways he was operating. But now I find increasing flexibility. I believe he has the ability to learn and is a quick learner. And he's a good reader. Many presidents are not. This president reads rapidly and well, with understanding and with discrimination. As you know, some of our presidents are more industrious than others. This president is extremely industrious. He's up early, spends all day at his work, and goes on to the other functions and all these ghastly things they have to do.

What I am saying is here is the potentiality for excellent leadership. He is brighter than [the men] our political system usually offers up to the American people.

I should have said earlier that I have found Mr. Carter to be an honest man. He's been completely honest with me. I believe him to be a man of integrity. I believe him to be a man of patriotism. I believe him to be a man who genuinely wishes to bring the best and most honest government to the country. Most people outside of Washington believe that our presidents always feel that way, but you and I know that is not always so. Some of our presidents want to get more out of their presidency than just the opportunity to serve. I have not found that trait to be a part of this president in any way, nor in any of the men around him. In other words, they are not on the make. And again, that is more unusual than you would suppose.

Now we have been talking so far about the asset side of the ledger. Let me turn to the liability side of the ledger. I believe a major factor must be the way he and the small group of Georgians around him perceive themselves—that you could come out of a background of a small town in Georgia and with skill and industry and singular singleness of purpose run for the presidency and win, and that that success endows you with the necessary assets to run the country. They have no real understanding of the complexities, the nuances, the convolutions, the immense intricacies of handling the government.

It seems to me that the success or failure of this administration will depend to a considerable degree upon their willingness to alter that original concept. If they persist in the belief that they can continue to operate as they have in the past eight months, we're in for a rough time, because that will demonstrate [to me] that they are not the quick learners I had hoped them to be.

There is another factor. Intelligence alone is not enough. You could select the twenty most brilliant individuals in the world and put them in the White House and it would be the most unholy mess we have ever seen. There is no way to make decisions wisely, there is no way to make government work, based upon pure reason. I believe it was Immanuel Kant who wrote a book about pure reason. Pure reason will not work in the White House, and it will not work in Washington.

It's too bad President Carter could not have sat down with Lyndon Johnson or asked Lyndon to please come to the White House and spend a week talking with him about the Congress. Lyndon Johnson was the best president I ever saw with reference to understanding Congress and understanding how to achieve what he wished to achieve. I'm afraid Mr. Carter's relations with Congress have created quite a lot of problems. The idea that the president simply develops his legislative program and the party's supposed to go along with it and approve it—particularly this party, with the largest majorities in either house in history—is ludicrous.

The administration has gone through its first eight months, the ship of state has been buffeted about, it's hit some reefs and shoals,

but the hull is still intact. It is exceedingly clear that now is the time
to chart the course.

Right now they are hunkering down. They are in a circle. There is
going to have to be a very important period of serious contempla-
tion. The president has taken a serious roasting, his staff has taken a
severe roasting, and it has been deserved. A number of egregious
errors have been made. I consider them errors of experience. A
more experienced staff man, for example, would have looked at that
comptroller's report and rendered an entirely different verdict. Had
that been so, the administration would have been spared this recent
embarrassment and humiliation. But there was no objective reading. It was, "Here's good ol' Bert, and he's a good ol' boy, and he's
our good ol' friend, and we've got to do all we can to help him.
What are the most favorable conclusions to be drawn from the report to help him?"

Somebody else, with a long pointed nose and his eyes set too
close together from reading too much, would have stuck his nose in
that report and focused his eyes on the words of that report, and it
would not have been very long before he looked up and said, "Hey,
fellows, I don't know Bert Lance from Adam, but there are red flags
all over this damned paper."

There is apparently a great deal of soul searching going on. Now,
you know everybody goes through soul searching after a terrible
mistake. I've seen intelligent and able men go through a deep period of soul searching after a terrible mistake—and then go out and
make the same mistakes all over again. And I've seen some who recognize that some important changes have to be made in the way
they operate.

We have one human element involved here, and it is important—
the element of pride. This is a proud man. He got where he did on
his own. And the group around him are proud. My fervent hope
and wish is that he can sit back and take stock and think about what
has happened and what the real lessons are. He needs more than
just a group of good ol' boys. He needs more than the basic assumptions which he carried with him into the White House—that
the team that won the election is the team that can run the country.

If he recognizes and rectifies what I consider to be the glaring
mistakes of the past weeks, it will have been an exceedingly useful
incident. If, on the other hand, he doesn't sense the deep impact of
what has happened, then it will be quite a disillusionment, because
there is enough here to indicate that the attitudes, the assumptions,
the efforts of the operation were not equal to the task.

The office of the presidency is not only the most exciting, the most powerful, but also the most exceedingly difficult and dangerous office. That is hard for newcomers to understand. You see, they think they understand the presidency. They see the excitement of it, they see the opportunity to pull the levers of power; but it is very difficult to see the dangers of it, the deficiencies of it, the disappointments of it, the tragedies of it.

A president should be reaching out. He should be making new contacts. He should be making new friends. He should be making an aggressive effort to do so. It is my experience that the longer a president is in office, the narrower are the range of his contacts. Now in reaching out to some people, he will make some mistakes— some of his discussions will appear in some form in the media, some people might use their acquaintanceship for some personal gain. Those are some of the reasons why a president's circle gets smaller with each passing year. But this man must not permit that to happen.

He starts with a substantial disadvantage. Our last five presidents have had experience in Washington that adds up to more than a hundred collective years of experience with the national government—and each one of them had serious problems in office; this man does not begin from that base. You learn a great deal from reaching out—you learn not just how the legislative branch works but that there are people in this country and in this city who are worth talking to and worth listening to. If his predecessors came to understand that need, think how infinitely greater the need for this man.

□   □   □

"How quickly will the Senate pass the energy bill, Senator Byrd?" the president asked one day at the end of September. The majority leader ambiguously but accurately replied: "The Senate is a place of shifting moods."

Democrats in Congress were pressing for an adjournment by October 15 to get an early start for next year's congressional elections; more than two hundred separate pieces of legislation were still pending; frustration and frayed tempers were in evidence amongst them all as their long session lumbered on. But over everything hung the single issue of energy, dominating the discussions and debates, private and public; dividing the Democratic majorities; pitting regional interest against regional interest, Northeast vs. Sunbelt; arraying special interest against special interest, consumer groups vs. the oil companies; and attracting an army of powerful lobbyists to the legislative process. ("I have never seen so many oil people in my life," Senator Jackson told the president. "They are swarming all over me.") Hopes for passing the president's energy program were deteriorating. Selfish interests were prevailing over national ones, and not only on energy.

As the deadline for congressional adjournment neared and passed, and as the energy struggle became more embittered, the president kept pressing his case in meetings with the congressional leaders. Energy was a test of his leadership, of *their* leadership, of the capabilities of all American institutions, he would say. He recognized his own failings in persuading the public, but they had to act. Already the increasing dependence on oil imports had a devastating effect on American life—and it would grow worse. An already adverse trade balance was eroding—and that would grow worse. The dollar was weakening. Consumption *must* be discouraged, the shift to new sources of energy *must* be made. He recognized the power of the oil industry, but they *must* stand up to it. The oil companies were blanketing television with commercials, he said at one breakfast meeting, and what they were accomplishing far exceeded what he could do in a fireside chat. They were chipping away at the consciousness of the American people, making people believe the companies were correct in saying everything would be all right if only citizens turned off their lights. He'd respond favorably to any suggestions they might have. Tell him if they wanted him to call a particular congressman or senator—he'd do it. The measurement of his own success, and that of the Democratic Party, was riding on how effective the final energy bill was.

But the issue remained deadlocked. Irreconcilable forces were colliding. Over the months, painfully and laboriously, compromises had been achieved and from the summer on, a House version of his energy program had become a key in the struggle. There, through the efforts of Speaker O'Neill, a compromise had been agreed upon over natural-gas pricing, retaining the president's proposed increase in the price ceiling on newly discovered natural gas but broadening the definition of what qualified as new gas. Using that agreement as a base, Carter had designated the natural-gas–pricing legislation as the key element of his energy program. But the Senate was further from agreement than the House.

For months liberals had felt the emerging energy program was a disaster for American consumers and an unconscionable giveaway to the oil industry. In early October they seized upon attempts to remove federal price controls and deregulate the price of natural gas and began a rare filibuster. It was led by James Abourezk of South Dakota, a senator already marked as different by his announcement several months before not to seek a second term and by his candid criticisms of the way Congress functioned. Coming while the Senate was pressing for adjournment, and centering around the difficulties over energy, the filibuster shattered the carefully structured façade of the Senate. Personal assaults, alien to the Senate, flared into the open. Older members took to the floor to warn they would all have to live with memories of what was happening. Before the filibuster was broken it had affected the president and vice-president, the Senate leadership, liberals and conservatives. And, it left bitterness. The liberals felt betrayed by the president, who they believed supported their position. When the administration suddenly broke the filibuster by a ruling by the vice-president in the presiding officer's chair, this led them to condemn Mondale and the administration for having committed an "outrageous act" and a "brutalization of the rules."

After it was over I spoke to Abourezk. He was still weary from his long hours of filibustering as he talked about his impressions of the president. He didn't know Carter well at all, he said, but "it seems to me that on any number of political issues Carter will take a position that is not very well thought out, and suddenly when his shift comes it surprises everybody and angers others. He's done this several times, and he hurts himself when he does. The way this break in the filibuster was handled is another example."

And the energy issue remained as divisive as ever, while the battle continued over tax credits for energy consumers who practiced conservation and also large credits to energy producers and other businesses.

At one long breakfast with the president at the end of October, entirely devoted to energy, senators flared into open dispute. The protagonists were Russell Long, the ablest and most powerful spokesman for the oil-producing states and the oil companies, and Scoop Jackson, speaking for the consumers. Long had been soothingly saying they were going to get some kind of bill, when Jackson spoke up. He didn't want to throw a bad apple, he said to Carter, but he wanted to make a clear and simple point: the president's tax program contained a crude-oil tax designed to dampen demand and make the revenues go to the government instead of the oil companies, yet later that very morning, in his judgment, the Senate would face a bill giving $40 billion under Carter's program to the oil producers and not the consumers. This was a complete repudiation of Carter's program, the antithesis of what he had told the American people.

Long objected. He wouldn't call it something for the oil companies. It was merely a continuation of what the president had asked for in his energy speech to the nation, funds to allow business to develop new sources of energy.

Jackson struck back: That wasn't correct. What was happening was deeply disturbing. Those who were trying to get the president's program passed were being confronted with a bill giving it no money—it was all going to the oil companies.

Long: Aside from what the president mentioned in conference, there is nothing in here for the oil companies. But we say we ought gradually to deregulate. I don't think we are talking in terms of black or white but gray. I don't think the administration wants to keep controls until eternity. The oil industry should be free to sell in a competitive market.

Jackson: This is a tax bill, not price controls. Of forty billion dollars, not a dime in there is for the people. . . . It's really ridiculous. We're going to have a battle.

Carter intervened. He wanted three things: fair treatment for consumers without enriching the oil companies; to meet his April objectives of cutting back on oil consumption and reducing dependence on foreign imports; and not to destroy the budget. Jackson and Long immediately went back to their fight. After further lengthy but discordant discussion, Carter, somewhat wearily, said, Let's change the subject.

But the energy problem wouldn't go away, nor would it be resolved. A few days later Carter was musing before reporters about the changing nature of the criticisms of his presidency. "I remember in this room last May," he said, "someone asked me if my administration was all image, or style, and no substance. Lately the criticisms have been that there's too much substance and not enough style." It was in such a mood that the president spoke informally at the White House the night of November 1. He had invited the congressional leaders, and a few of his staff, along with the vice-president, to review their work that year at dinner. But it was also an occasion to pay private tribute to Hubert Humphrey, who had just returned to Washington.

Humphrey was dying, and he and the country knew it; his doctors, with his approval, had announced that his cancer was inoperable and terminal. He came back to Washington thinner and grayer than ever, but still exuberant.

The conversation had gone around the table, with the frankness that had marked almost all of the White House–congressional meetings, Carter listening quietly as usual, until his turn came. He was planning a fireside chat on energy, he said, perhaps next Thursday. There was so much confusion about energy—he'd try to bring the public up-to-date. It would be his second fireside chat on energy, and the first since April. It was overdue, he recognized.

Another problem he had been working on was the situation in the Middle East. It was a thankless task. He thought they'd already done a great deal; his only motivation had been to try to bring peace there and to protect America's special relationship with Israel. That very day, he noted, Howard Baker had attacked his Middle East policy by saying we were sacrificing Israel on the altar of expediency. Bipartisanship apparently was going down the drain, the president said. He hoped those present would speak out in support of his policies whenever they could, not only in domestic but in foreign affairs. He repeated his pleas: whenever they had a chance, he hoped they would give him some public support.

The conversation continued, until finally Carter turned to his vice-president. "Fritz?" he asked. Mondale had been Humphrey's protégé in the Senate and had consulted often with him about the experience of being a vice-president. But their relationship went beyond politics, and it was clear that Mondale was deeply affected by Humphrey's condition. He'd defer to Hubert, Mondale said.

"Mr. President, I have become more moderate," Humphrey said. "My brother used to say that you should never pass the mashed potatoes to Hubert first because there wouldn't be any left. Well, you shouldn't let me talk last!"

Hubert Humphrey had come to Washington nearly thirty years before; he had less than three months to live. Now here he was, at the end of his life, giving what amounted to his last speech in a place he had long vainly sought to reach, to the people who understood him best, his fellow politicians. But Humphrey was addressing not them, but Jimmy Carter. His theme was leadership, presidential leadership.

Humphrey spoke about the central problem before them—the division between Carter and Congress: If it continues, people will say the Democrats don't know how to govern. Why, even in Minnesota people believe Carter is going one way and Congress the other! Congress is its own worst enemy. Frankly, the senators had made jackasses out of themselves over their filibuster. Young congressmen are like sheep. They won't speak up.

The people are the key. The people have to be reached. Mr. President, you are courting the business community, and that's fine. But if you think you can woo business and make 'em Democrats, you will do something no Democratic president has ever done. When they talk about business not having confidence, confidence in whom? They don't know what OPEC will do and neither do we. The thing to do is take the Democratic course and work for the middle-income people and the poor. The business people have got to complain against you. Just like the Arabs have got to complain against Israel. When businessmen complain, tell them to go talk to Arthur Burns and make them show you their profit statements.

Humphrey was warming up. God knows, he went on, enough people had asked him to speak against the president's Middle East policy—and against him on this and that. *So here's where it stands, Mr. President: Put your program down on paper saying here is what we are for and here is what we are against. Lay it out in capital letters. Tell the American people what we have done. Stand up and fight. . . .*

Mr. President, when you go down the street, you have got to have the poor and the blacks thinking you are their savior, like President Roosevelt. You have got to have people saying of Jimmy Carter, "That's my man!"

□ □ □

Earlier in the year Jimmy Carter had said that he planned to stay at home; he didn't intend making the kinds of lengthy foreign trips other presidents had made. Yet, like those predecessors, Carter had been drawn more and more into foreign affairs. He liked meeting the foreign leaders, enjoyed giving state dinners at the White House, and found, after his visit to Europe in the spring, that foreign travel was bracing, a welcome change from domestic frustrations and squabbles. When President Valéry Giscard d'Estaing invited him to return to France later in the year, Carter liked the idea. The plan that eventually emerged, though, was more grandiose—allowing him the briefest look, and that was all it possibly could be, at Communist life in Eastern Europe, at the Middle East, India, the oil-rich African nation of Nigeria, and South America's largest country, Brazil.

The timing couldn't have been worse. The president's presence obviously was needed if his energy program had any chance of passage on Capitol Hill. At the strong urging of Vice-President Mondale, Carter postponed the trip. But November passed with the energy legislation as far from passage as ever. Leaving for the trip without a new energy law would be seen as the president's and the Congress's failure to work together effectively after what had been more than ample time for deliberation; but the president was committed to making the journey, and another postponement was dangerous. On December 29, with passage of the energy bill doomed for the year and his political fortunes at the lowest point of his presidency thus far, Jimmy Carter flew off on his exhausting journey. The first stop, Poland, was inauspicious. On the glistening black tarmac of the Warsaw airport, on a bitterly cold night of snow and sleet, the president gave the ritualized remarks of greeting while flanked by the leaders of the Polish regime, comments that are normally quickly delivered and swiftly forgotten. But Carter's translator, speaking into the microphone after every few sentences, had evidently mangled the president's traditional words to such an extent that even I standing far away, behind a line of police, could see stirs of consternation sweeping the line of troops in the honor guard. Instead of "leaving the United States," the translator had said, the president "abandoned" it; instead of "bringing a message of love and friendship from the American people," the president was "lusting" after the Polish people; instead of "revering" the Polish Constitution of 1791, Americans were holding it up to "ridicule." The embarrassment was not of the president's making, but it seemed to typify many of the blunders that had plagued his first year in office.

On New Year's Eve, in a blinding snowstorm, the president left Poland for Iran. Earlier in the year he had told Congress that among all America's allies, Iran was one nation on whom the United States could rely. That night, at a glittering state dinner tendered by the shah in his opulent palace, Carter stood to give a toast. When they were planning his trip, he said, he had asked his wife, Rosalynn, with whom she would most like to spend New Year's Eve. "Above all others," she had said, with the shah and empress Farah of Iran. "So," the president explained, "we arranged the trip accordingly and came to be with you." It was, he continued, "a good harbinger of things to come—that we could close out the year and begin a new year with those in whom we have such great confidence and with whom we share such great responsibilities for the present and for the future."

Jimmy Carter completed his first year as president by toasting Iran, through the great leadership of the shah, as "an island of stability in one of the more troubled areas of the world."

6

THE SECOND YEAR

HAMILTON Jordan was probably Jimmy Carter's best political strategist, the one whose judgment had been indispensable in the race for the White House. His manner was deceptive—so easygoing, so casual in speech and dress, so unlike the stereotype of the high-powered counselor charting the president's moves. When one of the congressional leaders had complained to Carter that most people on the Hill didn't even know what Jordan *did*, much less look like, the president had smiled and replied that Jordan was his number one man, superb, a logician who could look down the road and come up with ideas, someone too valuable to become immersed in details. "If no one told you he was smart," James Fallows, Carter's speechwriter, said of Jordan to me, "you might not know it for a long time. He's the kind of guy who will sit and ponder for two weeks, but when he does give you his answer his judgment is good."

As the end of the first year approached, Jordan had compiled a detailed analysis of what, in his view, had gone wrong—and what Jimmy Carter needed to do differently in his second year. Jordan took special pains with his analysis, working on it for nearly a month. One main point was stressed by Jordan: Carter was personally involved in too many issues. He was all over the lot, and had been unable to focus public attention on any one issue. The energy crisis was the only one that the public perceived as of paramount importance to the president, but even his work on that had been blurred by so many other undertakings. And also, the president was spending far too much time on foreign policy. Jordan

229

made a comparison, which he pictorialized in graphs, of how many times Carter had met with heads of state in his first year, and how many meetings his predecessors had held in the same time: Carter had had sixty-eight state visits, Gerald Ford twenty-one, Nixon forty-three, Johnson thirty-two, Kennedy forty-three. That wasn't what people had expected of Carter, Jordan concluded ("probably in error," Carter wrote, in longhand, when he saw that section later).

Jordan listed other problems—in personnel, on the White House staff, in congressional liaison, in the cabinet, in the way information flowed. Policies and programs lacked adequate direction and follow-through. And a failure to take political considerations into account when making decisions, whether on domestic or foreign policies, was harming the chances for congressional passage of the president's programs. Priorities needed to be assigned.

When his long random memo was completed, Jordan brought it to Carter, who approved: he would make the changes. The memorandum, along with an agenda for the administration's second year prepared by Vice-President Mondale, set the course for a fresh beginning.

□   □   □

No matter what anyone said, or tried to do about it, government in America kept growing. As Jimmy Carter's second year began, 43 percent of the total revenues collected by the United States was going for government—23 percent for federal, and 17 percent for state and local governments. State and local spending had increased more rapidly than federal: about twenty cents on each state and local budget dollar came from Washington—and that didn't include Social Security payments or defense spending.

The dollar figures had reached such astronomical sums as to be almost meaningless. The United States was crossing into a $2 *trillion* annual economy. While much was made of the increasing federal budget deficit, as a percentage of the gross national product the U.S. deficit was about the same as other industrial countries (except Japan, which was considerably higher). At the same time, American tax rates were the second lowest in the industrial world.

Americans kept asking more of their government but were still less willing than other societies to pay the price for it. Inflation kept rising, but attempts to control it remained voluntary. President Carter had also shunned another voluntary device, the practice employed by other chief executives of using the powers of government to "jaw-bone" companies and unions to keep wages and prices down. As the economist Walter Heller told congressional Democrats behind closed doors in January 1978, the administration's anti-inflation program "ain't much of a program" but it was the only one in town. (That program, too, relied upon the voluntary goodwill, and good efforts, of labor and business to hold their wages and prices below 1977 levels—and, it was hoped, the Carter administration would be able to achieve a half-percent reduction in the nation's annual inflation rate and also to cut labor costs by that same amount. Later, a set of government wage-and-price guidelines were promulgated by the administration, but these, also, were voluntary.)

Few presidents had been more active in their first year. Congress was unhappy, Carter knew, for his demands on it had been great. As Tip O'Neill pointed out to him in mid-January, seventy-one bills had passed the House but not the Senate, while eighty-one had passed the Senate but not the House. They were wrestling with seven bills in joint Senate-House conferences—and that included the critical one, on energy. The Senate faced grueling debates over the Panama Canal treaties and later on SALT, both of which were related and both of which were drawing heavy, organized opposition from the political right. Carter's intention to end an American era going back to the days of gunboat diplomacy and Theodore Roosevelt by turning over control of the canal to Panama—a move backed by his four immediate predecessors—had been high on his personal agenda when he took office; but in the press of other efforts his timetable for conclusion of negotiations with Panama had slipped beyond June, and by the time agreement with Panama was reached and the two treaties signed, much of his first year had passed.

The first of the agreements was a treaty which would guarantee permanent neutrality of the canal after the year 2000, while the second actually transferred control of the waterway to Panama that same year. There was more symbolism than sub-

stance in the debate over the treaties: the age of the battleships
had passed, thus negating the canal's previous strategic importance in giving the U.S. Navy quick access to both Atlantic and Pacific, and in the new era of so-called "super" oil tankers and
gigantic aircraft carriers, the size of the canal itself, a passageway
completed in 1914, had become obsolete. But the frustrations created by perceived U.S. weakness worldwide after American defeat
in Southeast Asia, had made the canal a symbol of American reso-
luteness and strength. Depending on the political point of view,
the canal was either a last vestige of American innocence—or arrogance. The debate over ratification proceeded on such terms; the
canal represented American daring and might, an embodiment of
the kind of thinking that had led Teddy Roosevelt to say "I think
the twentieth century will still be the century of the men who
speak English," or it was symptomatic of the lessons of the new international realities that dictated American approaches other than
the jingoism and armed interventions of the past. To the Carter
administration, ratification of the canal treaties had another significance. If they couldn't win the battle over Panama, they rea-
soned, they never would be successful in the infinitely more
complex, controversial—and significant—struggle over gaining
acceptance for a second strategic arms treaty with the Russians.
Debate over Panama in the Senate thus had become highly ideological and time-consuming, placing great strains on the Senate as
the new congressional year began. On top of all these activities
that had marked his first year, the president had sent Congress
sixty-six messages. They couldn't handle that volume again, the
leaders told the president, especially in an election year when the
members were determined to recess no later than October.

  Carter understood. Most of his major agenda already had been
presented. In 1978 he was going to concentrate on a limited number of priority items. The key to his legislative year would be the
implementing of his economic policy goals—again typical of Carter, a patchwork policy, without economic ideology but withal setting most ambitious goals of balancing the budget by 1981,
reducing national unemployment of the work force below 5 percent and lowering the inflation rate to 4 percent, all the while pro-
moting economic expansion and an annual economic growth rate
of 5 percent—but he recognized there could be no permanent so-

lution to the nation's economic problems until an energy bill was passed. He would take the advice of leading members of Congress and remain aloof from the legislative struggle over energy, although temperamentally that was difficult for him to do.

Reorganization of the civil-service system was critical to his promise to reform the federal government; he had a legislative package on that subject. And already before Congress was a bill about which he felt deeply, and which as both candidate and president he had strongly promised to achieve. It was to create a consumer-protection agency. An early vote on this bill looked possible, and Carter wanted it passed. If he didn't create such an agency, he had said in 1977, he would consider his administration a failure. That had been a bit excessive, but at the time there was little reason to doubt that his administration would get a bill passed. Twice before, Democratic congresses had passed laws creating a consumer agency with even stronger authority, but twice before they were vetoed by Republican presidents Nixon and Ford. With a Democratic president in the White House pledged to such a bill, and a Democratic Congress with big majority margins, there seemed no political likelihood of a block. As Carter said when he urged the leaders to push for an early vote, the administration bill was not costly in money or personnel, and it wouldn't limit business.

□   □   □

Consumerism was a political offspring spawned by the 1960s era of citizen demonstrations for civil rights and against the Vietnam war. Along with new environmental action groups formed to combat pollution of the nation's air, land, and water, consumerism in the 1970s had become a political issue, with national organizations boasting millions of members and Washington lobbying operations ready to fight for specific legislation. In a nation better educated, more affluent, less ideological, and more aware of health and environmental issues, the so-called consumer movement appealed to a wide constituency and had attracted articulate champions. Its emergence as a political force also corresponded to the decline of organized labor's influence and the rise of greater business power as companies and corporations. Organized citizen protests, it was believed, would check growing corporate powers. Along with that conviction was the belief that divided government—and differing philosophies—had been the greatest obstacles to fulfillment of consumer political goals. To people such as Ralph Nader, who had been in the forefront of the consumer movement since the early 1960s, when he successfully challenged the design of cars rolling off the Detroit assembly lines and the record of national auto safety, Jimmy Carter was the kind of president the movement had been seeking. Carter's stand on consumer issues during the presidential campaign led Nader to praise him as being better on the major issues than any candidate "in decades"—a point Carter quickly reinforced. When Carter spoke before Nader's Public Citizen Forum after winning the Democratic nomination, he had said he intended to challenge Nader "for the title of the top consumer advocate in the country." His record as governor of Georgia won him backing from other national consumer organizations and his presidential appointments placed vigorous consumer advocates in important governmental positions— Michael Pertschuk as head of the Federal Trade Commission and Joan Claybrook as head of the National Transportation Safety Board notable among them.

As his consumer-affairs adviser, the president appointed Esther Peterson, whose grandmotherly appearance and gentle demeanor belied a long and successful record as a liberal Washington lobbyist. Now seventy, she knew the Hill and she knew politics, as well she might after a career that spanned half a century in labor and government. In 1961 she had left the AFL-CIO to become Kennedy's assistant labor secretary and head of the department's women's bureau. Later Johnson appointed her his consumer-affairs adviser, and during three Democratic administrations—Truman, Kennedy, and Johnson—she had been instrumental in passing major legislation. Mounted as trophies of those years on a wall behind her desk in the Executive Office Building were the pens given her by those presidents for her work on behalf of bills giving equal pay for women, fair labor standards, highway beautification, fair packaging and labeling, and the presidential commission on the status of women.

Creating an independent body empowered to plead the con-

sumer's case within the government—cutting across the bureaucratic layers in other agencies and departments, helping to correct
inequities in programs designed to protect consumers, and serving as "the people's lawyer" by litigating on behalf of consumers—was meant to be the high point of Peterson's career, and of
the consumer movement. In the spring of Carter's first year the
administration began mobilizing its political forces. A high point
of its drive had come on June 1, 1977, a gray and humid day, when
the White House played host to a large gathering of labor, business, consumer, congressional, and high administration officials,
cabinet officers, and presidential staffers. They filled the audito-
rium where the president holds his news conferences and heard
speaker after speaker sound the battle cry—Ralph Nader, lean and
intense; Bert Lance, in his black suit, florid and commanding;
Mike Pertschuk, small and feisty; Frank Moore, hefty and self-ef-
facing. The meeting had the flavor of a revival. "We must show
this is a people's Congress and they can't buy it," New York representative Ben Rosenthal, said. The agency would be "a pain in the
ass [for us] in the [Federal Trade] Commission," FTC Chairman
Pertschuk said, "but it will keep us honest." Peterson spelled out
the prospects for the bill: "Now we have a president who will sign
this bill when it gets to his desk [applause]. And it will get to his
desk [applause]. Why are you here? I'll tell you why. To get in the
fight." She was excited, she said; there was "a great new swelling,"
all over the country.

A confident Jimmy Carter spoke that day, but he sounded a
warning. "Now when it's sure that the White House will approve
this legislation . . . the lobbyists have come out of the woodwork
and the Congress is under intense pressure." The business community, he went on, was forming "selfish . . . special-interest
groups" and spreading "misinformation" about his proposed consumer agency. Such rhetoric was common from Democratic presidents, but Carter was expressing a political truth more fundamental than perhaps even he recognized. This was a time when the
lobbying powers of big labor were declining and those of big business increasing. New special-interest groups proliferated—well organized, well financed, well staffed. In the past, corporations had
not pressed their case aggressively in public: the political climate
from FDR onward had been unfavorable, and they feared that the

appearance of collusion in exerting political influence could turn
the federal government against them. Big business money flowed,
of course, and often in cash. But now business political action
committees were matching, publicly, the sums spent by the
unions, and their campaigns were skillfully organized and fought.
America was in an antigovernment mood, and business thought it
had a better chance to succeed politically.

The very day that Carter was exhorting the White House gathering to fight for his consumer agency, Richard Lesher was looking out his window over Lafayette Park toward the executive
mansion—and expressing a different attitude to the political process. Lesher was the new president of the U.S. Chamber of Commerce, and he was talking to me about "the great untold story" in
Washington.

It was the beginning of a new era in American history, he explained; the forty-year period of big government was drawing to a
close:

> I believe that thirty to forty years from now people will look back
> and say, 'Those were the years when the transition took place.'
> Over that last period of time we've broken all the ground in all
> areas of human activity—the environment, outer space, human
> rights, civil rights, women's rights—right across the board. We
> know what the objectives are, and very few people in society really
> disagree on them. The arguments today are over the means toward
> the end. Now some of these means have been put into place very
> very carelessly; we've thrown up government as the catch-all solu-
> tion to all problems. We're just now waking up to the fact that gov-
> ernment is ill-equipped to deal with many of these problems. We're
> waking up.

Big business, he was saying, was going to be the spearhead of
that antigovernment drive, and Carter's consumer-protection
agency was a key target in their attack. The president was inadver-
tently helping them, Lesher thought.

And it was true that Carter's antigovernment campaign and the
central promise of his presidency—to cut back on the "bloated bureaucracy" in Washington—was used against him by business.
The business message for defeating the consumer-protection bill
was always the same—that Carter would be adding another bu-

reaucratic agency "costing possibly hundreds of millions of dollars, to a government already overburdened with such agencies," as a Washington advisory dispatched to Chamber of Commerce chapters nationally put the case. (In fact, the agency was supposed to be small—180 employees and an annual budget of less than $11 million.)

Esther Peterson found, as she traveled across the country building support for Carter's new agency, that she was continually being put on the defensive about Carter's own promises. Through the summer and into the fall of 1977, the corporate lobbying effort became more intense. But Peterson was having troubles of another, perhaps more serious kind.

Peterson thought that she was being kept away from the president and his Georgia group in their key planning sessions by Frank Moore. She began to wonder if it were her fault, for it hadn't been that way before under other Democratic presidents, when she had had personal access and was a vital part of the White House team that planned strategy in dealing with the Hill. Now, Moore obviously didn't want her as part of his operation; she could hardly get time to talk to him. As she saw it, Moore's lobbying operation was weak, and he himself clearly didn't have his heart in the bill. He didn't give a damn about it, he had told her bluntly at one point. It was a mistake for her to get the president involved in a controversial issue like that.

By October the consumer-protection agency bill was in trouble, as members of Congress found the anti-Washington, antifederal government mood in their districts running strongly against creating another federal agency that was surrounded by controversy— just as big business hoped and was working to achieve. The Rules Committee, which was to consider the bill in the House, was wavering. Peterson, working closely with Speaker O'Neill, proposed a compromise version of the legislation, one that appeared to have a good chance of passage. A floor vote was planned at the end of the month. But the business reaction was swift. From Washington Chamber of Commerce headquarters mailgrams immediately went out to every local office in the nation:

MUST ALERT YOU THAT ADMINISTRATION AND CONSUMER LOBBY-
ISTS PREPARING NEW EFFORT TO PASS CONSUMER PROTECTION

AGENCY BILL SO BITTERLY OPPOSED BY BUSINESS. WHITE HOUSE
AIDE ESTHER PETERSON CLAIMS SHE IS DEVELOPING REVISED
NEW BILL THAT WILL ANSWER CONCERNS THAT SO FAR HAVE
BLOCKED MEASURE. NO SUCH BILL YET AVAILABLE, ONLY
SKETCHY FACT SHEET THAT CLEARLY DOES NOT REMOVE BUSI-
NESS OBJECTIONS. NEVERTHELESS, INDICATIONS ARE THAT SOME
REPRESENTATIVES ARE SUCCUMBING TO PETERSON'S PERSUA-
SION.

STRATEGY IS TO GET MODIFIED BILL THROUGH HOUSE, THEN TRY
TOUGHEN IT UP IN SENATE. BUT WHATEVER THEY CAN PASS WILL
BE ONLY FIRST STEP. AGENCY POWERS AND PERSONNEL WOULD
BE ENLARGED IN SUCCEEDING YEARS.

GOOD CHANCE THIS WILL REACH HOUSE FLOOR OCTOBER 27 OR
28, OR EARLY FOLLOWING WEEK. REQUEST YOU PROMPTLY GEN-
ERATE AT LEAST 10 WIRES AND PHONE CALLS TO YOUR REPRE-
SENTATIVE, URGING HIM TO RESIST THIS MOVE. IF NEW BILL IS
TO BE OFFERED, IT SHOULD BE SUBJECTED TO FULL COMMITTEE
HEARINGS AND EVALUATION BEFORE GOING TO HOUSE FLOOR.

> HILTON DAVIS, CHAMBER OF COMMERCE
> OF THE U.S.
> WASHINGTON, D.C. 20062

Wires and phone calls poured into congressional offices, but Peterson still believed the compromise bill would pass. Then, on November 1, she was shocked to learn that the administration
suddenly had withdrawn the bill without putting it to the test before the House. Esther Peterson was stunned—and furious. She
had not even been consulted about the move by Moore; it was a
fait accompli.

The more she thought about it, the angrier she became. She left
Washington immediately and flew to her home in Utah, giving as a
public reason a death in the family. When she got off the plane,
she was still angry. She telephoned the president.

Carter was solicitous, gracious. He was sorry about the bill, and
knew she was, too. "Mr. President," she said, "I'm not only sorry,
I'm mad." Carter didn't understand. She hadn't even been consulted, she explained. Carter was surprised. She hadn't? No, she

hadn't. Perhaps it was right to pull the bill, she added—they weren't all that sure about the votes—but they hadn't even gone through the normal procedure of getting a good hard head count. Carter attempted to calm her down. She was upset, he could tell; try and tell him what had happened. For a moment, she hesitated and then, thinking, I don't give a God damn, gentle Esther Peterson told the president: "Mr. President, *I cannot do this.* Your people don't know how to get a bill through Congress. They don't know the basic tools of how to operate there, of using the powers we have there as a party. Maybe my techniques aren't right, but at least we used to pass some legislation."

As soon as she got back to Washington they should talk, Carter replied.

On her return, Peterson wrote a private memorandum which she personally gave to the president. Consumer protection was *his* issue, she said; it was what the voters had seen in him, something fresh, something for the people against the special interests; it was the kind of issue he could take to the public in a fireside chat. If they were going to win in Congress they would have to revise the operation there. Then she spelled out specific steps to take to reach the members of Congress. (The White House didn't even have their home-telephone numbers, she learned.)

When Peterson saw the president, she told him she wanted to resign, but before leaving wanted to do everything possible to help. What, Carter asked, did Frank Moore think of her suggestions? "He disagrees with me, Mr. President, and I think Frank Moore is wrong," she said. Carter didn't want her to leave, and asked that she please work it out with Moore. He wanted the bill passed, and he wanted her help. Peterson was a good soldier. She went back to battle.

O'Neill was especially helpful. He believed in the bill, he told her over the phone, it was a real Democratic issue and he would do all he could for it. Working with both O'Neill's people and the Moore operation, Peterson coordinated the new move to create a consumer agency. Carter, although busy on other issues, was also strongly supportive. To every memo she submitted, he instantly replied with directives to his staff or personal, handwritten notes of encouragement: "OK. Good luck. . . . Be aggressive. . . . This is good, Stu [Stuart Eizenstat, his domestic policy staff chief], trust

and back Peterson. . . . Use the VP, he has access. . . . I'll help
when needed."

By the time the issue was coming to a vote, early in 1978, the
president was calling members of Congress, personally lobbying
for the bill, and privately telling the Hill leaders that he had spent
as much time on consumer protection as he had on SALT and the
Middle East. But he never did make a special public address on it,
as Peterson had hoped. Meanwhile business lobbies, given a three-
month reprieve since the bill was withdrawn in October, and
smelling blood, intensified their campaign. They were demonstrating how much powerful national pressure could be applied to
Congress when organized aggressively around a single controversial issue. Tip O'Neill thought it was the most extensive lobbying
he'd seen in twenty-five years. And to Esther Peterson it was the
fight of her life.

Public opinion, as measured by the polls, was overwhelmingly in
favor of creating a federal consumer agency. On the eve of the
vote Lou Harris, the pollster, was saying, "We find by two to one
that the public wants such an agency." But public opinion, unor-
ganized politically, was up against the powers of a classic single-
issue business lobby.

Final debate in the House was scheduled for the afternoon of
February 8. That morning in Washington the National Association
of Manufacturers headquarters put out a final recorded telephone
message for corporate offices around the country:

> Yesterday the House began consideration of the consumer pro-
> tection bill HR 6805. Major amendments and final passage are now
> expected late this afternoon. . . . Administration lobbyists crowded
> the House halls yesterday and the president himself is making calls
> to wavering representatives. With a hard administration push, what
> looked like a sure defeat for the consumer bill is now looking like an
> exceedingly close vote today. NAM members should make personal
> calls immediately to their representatives to make sure that they are
> not caving in to administration pressure to create a new bureaucra-
> cy. Your efforts are crucial to defeat any version of the bill today.

Once more, the calls came flooding into the halls of Congress.

The debate began shortly after one o'clock. Tens of thousands
of words and several hours later the final votes were counted: 227

to 189 against the proposed new law. Crushing defeat for the bill, for the Carter administration, and for Jimmy Carter personally. In the first important test of 1978, the president lost decisively. At a time when he sorely needed a victory, his vulnerability was highlighted. The lesson was not lost on the lobbyists who filled the corridors of Congress—nor by the people's representatives who had followed, not the will of the people, but the power of the biggest lobbies. On the morning after the vote, NAM produced a jubilant telephonic message for its corporate members nationally.

> Business deserves all the credit for bringing attention to the expansion of the bureaucracy to Congress and making the House realize that red tape was not justified. It was a stunning defeat for the Carter administration and Ralph Nader, both of which have swarmed the Hill in recent weeks lobbying for the bill. . . . NAM has been in the forefront opposing the consumer agency for the past eight years. NAM members are commended for their efforts over the years working to defeat this bill. . . . NAM members are asked to thank all those representatives who opposed the bill by a letter or by phone.

Similar words were sent out by the Chamber of Commerce's headquarters. It was, the chamber proclaimed, "a remarkable victory" for business. And so it was.

Esther Peterson was devastated. It wasn't just losing, although it had been the worst defeat of her career. It was how and why they lost, and what it meant. The president had tried to call her that night after the vote, but she wasn't home. When he reached her the next morning, he confessed his disappointment. He was feeling low. "Mr. President," she said, "that's what bothers me the most. I feel we let you down." She didn't have the heart to tell him what Tip O'Neill had been saying. The vote wasn't against the president personally, O'Neill said. It was against his people. The hardest thing going against the administration was the way Congress felt the Carter people had been acting.

Problems between the Carter people and Congress were nothing new, but congressional resentment about the Carter operation was becoming even more serious. To Congress, Jimmy Carter was in enough trouble at home and abroad without continually adding to his woes—and theirs—by tolerating further internal *gaffes*. The president's second year had begun with his approval ratings dropping below the 50 percent mark for the first time and continuing to fall. At that point in office he stood lower in the polls than any elected president since the Gallup soundings began forty-three years earlier. Few kind words greeted him. A *Washington Post* editorial appraisal said: "The most tiresome cliché of the political season is the hearty comment that President Carter learns quickly. It's like saying that a pitcher going into the third game of the World Series is showing a knack for picking up the rules of the game." And a week later *The New York Times* was even more critical editorially: "Having tried however ineptly to rouse the nation only to be kicked for the effort, he invites us now to slumber on soundly, but to let conscience stir our dreams. He is a soothing flatterer and a sensible president, but not yet a leader, or teacher, even for a quiet time."

Indeed, the times did not really appear all that quiet: criticism against the president was extending beyond Washington to the published barbs of the foreign press and the mutterings of foreign leaders in other capitals. In Africa, new conflicts were rising as the Soviet Union boldly moved arms and advisers into the strategically important Horn of Africa; there, a war between Ethiopia and Somalia threatened the entire region, a situation complicated by the presence of Cuban troops. In Europe, and particularly Germany, members of the North Atlantic Treaty Organization were apprehensive about the American president's seeming indecision over whether to begin production of a formidable new weapon—the so-called neutron bomb.

Since the early days of the Kennedy administration, when the possibility arose of developing neutron weapons (miniature nuclear bombs that would produce less radioactive fallout, thus cutting down on blast damage), the subject had drawn lurid press attention—"death rays," they were called. To Pentagon planners, the merit of neutron weapons lay in the fact that one could consider using them in crowded-population areas that were facing a massive infantry invasion led by tank divisions—in short, precisely the situation NATO allies could face along the Soviet-German border. Radiation from the neutron weapons supposedly could penetrate through thick armor plate and concrete, killing the soldiers inside

the tanks without harming the civilians in the surrounding countryside.

By Carter's presidency neutron weapons had become a reality.
The question was whether to produce and then deploy them: early
in 1977 Carter had ordered modernization of U.S. weapons in Europe to allow the introduction of neutron warheads, but delayed a
decision on whether to develop and deploy them. That decision
kept being postponed, although both houses of Congress had approved spending money to develop the weapons for European
use. Back and forth went the administration stand on what to do
about the weapons; the president wanted the NATO nations to
declare their views on using the neutron warheads before going
ahead with production.

Early in April 1978 West Germany acknowledged what its highest officials had been telling the Americans privately for months—
it wanted the weapons produced and deployed in Europe. But
three days later Carter took them and all of NATO by surprise
when he said he was deferring a decision on producing the weapons. German Chancellor Helmut Schmidt was furious. His public
statement was restrained but pointed: strains had developed in
German-U.S. relations, he said, and he hoped the president would
have no more surprises for his European allies. Even some administration officials were perplexed. "At various times he has been
on various sides," an arms expert said of the president's ambivalent moves. Criticism in Europe was sharp. Coming to the surface
publicly were the kinds of private assessments that some diplomats had been making of Carter to journalists in Washington and
overseas: Carter was a weak president at a time when the national
will had been weakened by the Vietnam experience. A measure of
the severity of the criticism was a caustic attack on his performance
by the respected and normally circumspect *Financial Times* of London. The focus was on Carter's handling of the neutron weapons
issue, but the judgment was more general. "The Europeans must
now recognize President Carter as an erratic, if not unreliable
partner," the *Financial Times* commented. "The Russians, who
have led an almost unprecedented propaganda campaign against
the neutron bomb, must be further encouraged to think that they
can get their way whenever they wish. And the outside perceptions

must be that the Russians are right, even if—as is more than probable—Mr. Carter's refusal to order production was a result of his own peculiar conscience rather than of giving way to Soviet pressure."

On top of all these concerns, the president continued to find himself bedeviled by problems among his closest staff. A nasty and largely unsubstantiated gossip column item about Hamilton Jordan in *The Washington Post,* alleging that Jordan had spat ice cubes at a woman in a Washington bar, was treated as a major national incident by both press and White House: the White House, in an attempt to refute the account, responded with a thirty-three–page document that included legal depositions from the bartender and other witnesses—thus guaranteeing the elevation of a barroom incident onto page one and insuring further ugly exchanges between the press and Carter's press secretary, Jody Powell. And all the while Carter's popularity continued to fall. After fifteen months in office, Jimmy Carter's approval rating had dropped to 39 percent, the lowest for any president after such a time in the White House.*

Polls were not the measure of a president, of course, as Walter Lippmann had written years before:

> The notion that public opinion can and will decide all issues is in appearance very democratic. In practice it undermines and destroys democratic government. For when everybody is supposed to have a judgment about everything, nobody in fact is going to know much about anything. . . . Effective government cannot be conducted by legislators and officials who, when a question is presented, ask themselves first and last not what is the truth and which is the right and the necessary course, but "what does the Gallup poll say?" and "what does the fan mail say?" and "how do the editors and commentators line up?"

But the problems Carter encountered with his other partners in government, among his own party on Capitol Hill, clearly affected the success of his presidency. In the aftermath of the consumer-

---

*Comparably, Nixon's approval rating at the equivalent time was 56 percent, Johnson's 68, Kennedy's 77, Eisenhower's 68, and Truman's 57. Only Ford had dropped below the 50 percent level. Ford's popularity plummeted after he pardoned Nixon, but his rating of 41 was still higher than Carter's.

protection bill debacle, some thirty of the Democratic congressional whips met to discuss, often emotionally, their problems
with Carter's Hill liaison and lobbying efforts—but their criticisms
went far beyond any specific bill.

Out of that and other sessions a number of major problems
were pinpointed—each of which was communicated to the president personally, and in detail. They fell into three general catego-
ries. First, there was the simple nuts and bolts of politics—
returning telephone calls promptly, letting the members know in
advance about federal grants and projects being awarded in their
districts, and so on. These were so obvious they shouldn't have to
be stressed, but they still weren't working in Jimmy Carter's presidency. More serious was the matter of how the cabinet departments related to the members of Congress. Little coordination
seemed to be taking place between Carter's congressional liaison
staff and his cabinet. Less tangibly, the congressional Democrats
didn't feel they were part of a Carter team. Tip O'Neill was the
glue that held them together, not Jimmy Carter. Even some who
started as strong supporters of the president were feeling no alle-
giance or connection to him, Carter was told.

Carter remained the quiet listener. But, he said, he wanted to
know personally any complaint from a member of Congress about
the operation of any of his cabinet departments. He'd look into
it—just send him a handwritten note on a piece of scrap paper and
he'd take action. (What the president wants to be able to do, Frank
Moore explained to a Democrat, is embarrass a cabinet secretary
in front of his peers—this in the hopes of getting greater awareness among them all of the president's determination to exercise
control. That LBJ style of humiliation got results. No, Carter later
explained, he would only criticize a cabinet officer after checking
out a complaint to see if it were legitimate.)

Carter himself was fully aware of the many criticisms. He already had agreed with Hamilton Jordan's private critique and specific recommendations for change, but had not implemented
them. And he knew that some of the leading Washington insiders
had met to discuss his problems at the invitation of Robert
Strauss, then serving as his chief inflation fighter but becoming
more and more his political troubleshooter. Strauss was a beguil-
ing political pro from Texas with a mobile, expressive face and an

anecdote for every occasion, a protégé of John Connally's who practiced the art of maneuver with disarming, drawling effectiveness. As Democratic Party chairman, he was one of those in Washington who had been privately critical of the way Carter's presidential campaign was run; but now Strauss was becoming close to Carter personally, and indispensable politically. One night at his apartment in the Watergate, overlooking the Potomac, he brought together such close Carter confidants as Charles Kirbo, up from Atlanta, and Griffin Bell, the president's attorney general, along with other selected aides, to confer with what constituted a reigning "wise men of Washington" group—Clark Clifford, James Rowe, Harry MacPherson, Lloyd Cutler among them.

They agreed with Jordan's previous analysis—the president indeed faced trouble. He needed to demonstrate a sharpened sense of his public priorities, a better use of his time, people, and consultants. Jimmy Carter had to tighten his operation, and then show the public he was in charge and leading the way.

People on the White House staff also agreed about all this, but nothing had happened to correct the mistakes. "I don't think there was ever an attempt during our first year to sit down and analyze what our themes were, what our priorities were, how best to focus on effective legislation," one of them reflected to me then. "We allowed ourselves to be captives of deadlines. We didn't have foresight to see how it all fit together. I don't think we knew—I know I didn't—how important timing really was, that we really had to do our homework." That knowledge was long in coming, and painfully gained—for them, and the president.

In the middle of April, the president summoned the chief officials of his administration to the hideaway in the Catoctin Mountains of Maryland that FDR had mischievously called Shangri-La, but that Dwight Eisenhower more prosaically had renamed (after his young grandson) Camp David. No definable great crisis confronted the nation, or world, and no one could recall any previous president ever convening such a secret gathering on that mountain top. But Carter was attempting to set his presidential house in order. His convening of the Camp David meeting was a tacit admission that he knew he and his team had not been functioning well. Change was overdue, and weak spots had to be eliminated.

To one of Carter's closest aides, the meeting at Camp David was "kind of a confessional for the administration." Carter set the tone. He was candid. They had all made a lot of mistakes, he said, and he had made a lot of mistakes. The American people were giving them low marks, and he could understand why. The American people were disappointed in them, and should be. They had made many promises, and had failed to deliver them. They said they were going to do this and that, and didn't. It was time to straighten up, pull themselves together, and perform as they were capable. For they were capable, he had no doubts about that. They had been there a year and a half, and they had learned some expensive lessons. It was time to put them into practice.

To the cabinet members, President Carter said he wanted to continue giving them autonomy to carry out his policies, but he expected more political and substantive cooperation from them than he had received. He expected them to respond whenever Frank Moore or Hamilton Jordan called with a request. As for the White House staff, he expected them to pull together and behave differently. They were being bled to death on Capitol Hill by needless mistakes. Frank Moore had been taking the blame for all their sins. He cited examples from a long list prepared for the meeting. For example, when Secretary Vance talked to him about naming Elliot Richardson as ambassador at large and as the president's special representative for a major international law of the sea conference, Carter had concurred and the appointment was made. But neither Carter nor Vance had informed Moore or Jordan; the first *they* knew was when they read it in the papers. That was the first that Tip O'Neill heard about it, too, and he had been furious, for it appeared as if Richardson, a lifelong Republican of glittering credentials and national reputation, might eventually run for governor of Massachusetts—a seat O'Neill's son was seeking. When another Massachusetts appointment was announced shortly after—that of Evan Dobelle, to be the administration's chief of protocol—O'Neill erupted again. Dobelle had been twice elected as the *Republican* mayor of Pittsfield, Massachusetts, a point that Hamilton Jordan had overlooked—and neglected to discuss with O'Neill, who again learned of the appointment in the press. Carter aired other congressional complaints—about failure to be notified of federal grants in their various districts, about the unreturned phone calls, the missed signals, the lack of coordination.

Substantive changes came out of the Camp David sessions. White House task forces were established to oversee and follow through on specific issues. Personnel changes were made on the senior White House staff and in the congressional lobbying operation. Gerald Rafshoon, Carter's media adviser during the campaign, was brought into the White House to coordinate work, help establish themes, see that the administration spoke with one voice, and exert discipline. Whether these changes would make a difference was something else. The Carter White House had been aware of its mistakes for months, but the mistakes continued to be made.

When the president next met congressional leaders at a White House breakfast, he gave an abbreviated but candid appraisal of what had gone on at Camp David.

The president: We've had some problems that needed clarification after fifteen months in office. We were green. And so I spent two days at Camp David in very intimate, frank, brutal, discussions. And we've made some progress.

He realized, he said, that often when he made a decision Congress didn't know the reason for it. He wanted to set aside time with them, as he had with his staff and cabinet officers, to get away for a full day, talk, and clear the air. The more they could communicate the basic premises on which he made his decisions, the better. He also realized—and wryly acknowledged that he'd been told directly—of his tendency to raise public expectations. Yes, he'd made some campaign promises that were difficult to keep. And he knew, too, as he said, that trying for comprehensive solutions meant even if you achieved 85 percent of a package the public believed they had failed because they didn't get it all.

Through all his difficulties with Congress, Carter displayed a constant trait in his private meetings. He was a patient, attentive listener. Invariably, he would end his sessions by saying, "I've learned a lot." He appreciated their advice, he'd say. He appreciated their help. He was learning. He would concede his own failures, through lack of experience or personal misjudgment ("I had not worked in Washington until one year ago") but didn't offer easy excuses. He wanted them to continue giving him criticism and counsel. Rarely, would he express disappointment—and then usually by trying to counter it with a positive word. "At the cabinet meeting yesterday, I had to give a pep talk because everything seemed to be a problem or was negative," he said at one White House breakfast. And at another: "In closing, let me say that when I returned from the trip [in early April to the other countries he had not been able to visit, as planned, over New Year's—to Brazil, Venezuela, Liberia, and Nigeria], I had a sense that we have a tendency to despair. We must stay in close consultation with one another. I am eager to do it. Don't hesitate to call me at any hour of the day or night when you have a problem."

Despite their often strongly voiced differences, the congressional leaders sometimes came to feel almost protective about the new president. One morning in the family dining room of the White House, in the early spring of that second year, the president urged the group around the table to read Robert Donovan's book on Harry Truman—"a remarkable biography," Carter said. He had been struck, he added, to learn that Truman never got a major piece of legislation through Congress in his seven years as president. Tip O'Neill, touched, spoke up consolingly.

The Speaker: Mr. President, my own Jack Kennedy had the Bay of Pigs; Nixon had Vietnam and Cambodia; and Ford had Mylai. How many people understand what you have done in Somalia?*

The President: We have had some difficult times, but I am very

---

*O'Neill was referring to the view that Carter had wisely avoided involving the United States in a "proxy" war by military intervention on the side of Somalia (then receiving U.S. arms) in its conflict with Ethiopia, which had substantial Soviet military aid, some fifteen thousand Cuban troops, and the presence on the scene of a Soviet general. In a wide-ranging policy debate over what to do about Soviet-Cuban incursions in the Horn of Africa, Carter's national security adviser Zbigniew Brzezinski had advocated dispatching a U.S. naval task force if the Ethiopians crossed the Somalia border—a move opposed by Secretary of State Vance and Defense Secretary Harold Brown, and rejected by the president. Carter, briefing congressional leaders on the potentially explosive situation, described how Vance had been talking privately and frequently with Soviet ambassador Dobrynin and foreign minister Andrei Gromyko. Vance got what he and Carter believed to be a secret Russian commitment that Ethiopia would not invade Somalia. The best public account of this, as well as the best overall insight into the Carter Administration's foreign policy till then, was an article on Brzezinski by Elizabeth Drew in *The New Yorker* of May 1, 1978.

grateful for your help and don't hesitate to let me know if there is any matter you want to talk to me about.

Whether Camp David was the watershed Carter hoped for his administration could not be immediately known, but the president at least came out of those sessions with renewed determination. Within days he won a badly needed lift when the Senate gave final approval to the Panama Canal treaties, and he was pressing forward aggressively on civil service reform.

For more than a year the administration had been working on a plan to change the way the federal government worked. After laborious negotiations and consultations among labor and government groups, came a proposal to scrap the entire civil-service system. In the view of people like Alan Campbell, the new Civil Service Commission chairman, there was no other real alternative. The civil-service system had grown so complicated, rigid, and inflexible no one could live with it. Rewarding outstanding employees was almost as difficult as removing incompetent ones. Managers and employees alike were trapped in a maze of red tape. The rules and procedures that had been designed to protect merit hiring and remove the taint of political favoritism had become cumbersome and antiprogressive. And, as Watergate and the Nixon scandals had shown, the system could still be corrupted from the top down by cunning politicians and acquiesing civil servants.

The Carter administration sought a new system which would do two things: truly protect and encourage merit among government workers, and at the same time give government service more flexibility, more incentives, better management. In place of the Civil Service Commission would be an office of personnel management; it would operate as the president's supervisory agency to oversee the federal work force. An entirely separate Merit Protection Board would oversee and adjudicate reported political abuses and operate as an independent ombudsman for the federal service.

But the heart of the proposals—and by far the most controversial area—involved changes of the government's work rules and employee-status ratings. Some of the changes were radical—a senior executive service, for instance, would replace the present "supergrade" levels of federal pay. Job tenure and guaranteed fixed salary increases would be replaced by incentive bonuses, performance contracts, and deferred income—none of which had ever been a part of the federal government.

Other changes struck at other cherished chestnuts—certain kinds of veterans' preferences, labor practices, and long-established work rules that made it difficult to transfer or remove incompetent workers. Each of these proposed reforms threatened sacred-cow special-interest groups, especially veterans organizations and unions such as the American Federation of Government Employees that had built up political power in Washington over the years. Labor, for one, was not about to approve anything that would diminish the rights and protections of its workers. In particular, it shrunk from anything that would make it easier to fire employees. Before the program could be proposed and made into law, the Carter administration planners and the unions had to agree on general principles. Labor asked, and got, a number of concessions—a promise to expand the scope of collective bargaining, a pledge to create something similar to the National Labor Relations Board to oversee federal employee relations, et cetera. These private negotiations alone, in which the president was intimately involved, took exactly a year.

By March 1978 the Carter civil-service–reform legislation was ready for introduction on the Hill. Although it was backed by a number of national organizations—the National Civil Service League called it "the most important and positive civil service reform proposals since the Civil Service Act of 1883" (a measure drafted by the league itself)—it faced grave problems, for it would have to be cleared by the house Post Office and Civil Service Committee, which was considered one of the most ineffectual ("third rate," a congressional leader described it to me) of all committees, wracked with divisions and dominated by lobbying groups, unions and veterans organizations. Carter privately cited this committee on several occasions as a prime example of how some members of Congress are hostages of the special interests. The members of that committee would pick up big fees, he'd say, for speaking before a labor convention in the Caribbean and delivering a text written by the very labor lobbyists they dealt with on the committee.

After the Camp David meeting, Carter moved aggressively to put the power and prestige of his administration behind the civil-service reform fight. In one week he met separately with the Democrats and Republicans on the House Post Office and Civil Service Committee, with federal union employee leaders, conferred five times with Alan Campbell, and devoted forty minutes of a two-hour cabinet meeting to the issue. He told the cabinet officers this was one campaign promise he was determined to keep—and that he expected them to achieve results for him. Specific assignments were given to lobby key congressmen. The cabinet was instructed to report back with news of progress.

Some congressmen were surprised when no less an official than the taciturn secretary of state, Cyrus Vance, just back from a trip to Africa and the Soviet Union, telephoned them, and even more surprised to find that Vance wasn't offering insights into diplomacy but asking their support for the president's civil-service legislative package.

Unlike so many earlier administration efforts, the civil-service battle was well coordinated within the White House. The lessons gained from the lobbying operation that won ratification of the Panama Canal treaties—the first truly successful Carter-Hill operation—were invaluable, and were put into practice. A task force met regularly, first convening in the Roosevelt Room in the White House, and later shifting to a fourth-floor office in the Executive Office Building. There, for an hour or so in the evenings, in a room filled with charts and lists of senators and representatives, they planned their moves. The group included people from the president's congressional liaison and domestic staffs, the Office of Management and Budget, and Campbell, the civil-service chairman. For six straight hours one day the team met with staff personnel of the Senate Governmental Affairs Committee, seeking advice on how to pass the bill. Carter himself personally briefed important members of the House and Senate of both parties, and sought advice and support from others by phone.

And still, with all that, the civil-service bill faced continued opposition from labor and from Congress. In fact, the president and his people concluded that spring, it appeared doomed unless it could be rescued in the House Post Office and Civil Service Committee. Ironically, as they knew, only one person on that committee could help them, and he was no friend of Jimmy Carter's.

Tall and lanky, with an easy smile and an affinity for telling stories in a Western drawl, Morris ("Mo") Udall often was compared with Lincoln in the press. While he himself joked deprecatingly about linking his name that way, he had done nothing to discourage it, and, he knew, the Lincoln association helped him in his political career. Udall was from Arizona, and like his older brother Stewart, who served in Congress and then in John Kennedy's cabinet as interior secretary, he was a lawyer who had entered politics in Tucson. In the 1950s he had been an Adlai Stevenson Democrat and by 1976, after sixteen years in Congress, he had earned a national reputation as an old-fashioned liberal Democrat. He was among the earliest to announce his presidential candidacy that year, but, like the others, quickly found himself chasing Carter. In personal manner and political outlook, Mo Udall and Jimmy Carter were different; their contest for the nomination had been marked by bitter personal exchanges, and that bitterness remained. Udall was openly critical of the direction Carter's presidency had taken, and throughout Carter's first year in office his relations with Udall were distant and cold. Udall knew of unflattering remarks that had been made about him by certain people on Carter's staff, and once a cabinet officer told him that a federally funded water project proposed for central Arizona was targeted for elimination by the White House because of Carter's continuing hostility toward him. All through 1977 the ill will between them was compounded by the water projects controversy. Udall, as a major Western congressman, thought Carter had badly mishandled the issue, and said so. The water-projects fight had been particularly damaging to the president in the West. He had not carried a single state there, and his popularity was dropping even lower. Early in 1978 Carter's staff advised him it would be useful to repair relations with Udall. The Arizonan could be helpful to him.

Carter invited Udall to the White House for a private lunch. They'd had their differences, the president said, but he needed Udall's help. He asked about the political situation in the Rocky Mountain states, and what steps Udall thought the president might take there. In April, Carter asked Udall to come to the White House again for a special meeting about the civil-service bill. Would Udall take on the hard task of shepherding that bill through the committee and see if he could save it? At first, Udall demurred. He knew all too well about what he later described as "the vicious crosscurrents" at work in the committee, and had considerable doubts because of the attitudes of the other committee members and the union pressures they were facing that the bill could be passed under any circumstances. But Carter appealed to him personally, as an act of patriotism, for the good of the country and the government, to take it on, and Udall, who thought of himself as a Hubert Humphrey sort of Democrat, confessed to being "a sucker for that kind of appeal." He agreed to lead the fight.

They tell me you know how to handle that committee, Carter said. You're the quarterback. He'd do whatever Udall told him to, and back him all the way. If Udall wanted the president to make ten calls, just give him the names, he'd do it, Carter said once again, in his typical fashion. If Udall wanted the president to make a statement at a press conference, or speak out, he'd do that.

For the next four months Mo Udall poured his energies into that effort. There were many frustrations, for there were no tangible political gains to be had and almost no news value. The political operation remained difficult, and the pressures on the committee increased: on several occasions in the next months it seemed certain the bill was dead. But Udall persevered. He put together a fragile political coalition, spent endless days in mediating, patching, consulting, negotiating for an acceptable compromise. The bill that emerged from the committee wasn't the same that had entered it—the senior executive service had been cut back to an experimental phase and the labor-management section had been altered considerably—but it was nonetheless a potential landmark bill. It was scheduled for a vote sometime in September. "The single most important factor in that bill's success has been Mo Udall's unbelievable integrity, and the fact that he kept on pushing," a congressional lobbyist told me later. But Carter deserved credit, too. Udall found him as good as his word. He had done everything asked of him.

As a decision on the bill neared, Udall was meeting Carter at the White House regularly. They were going to get a bill because of him, the president told the congressman one morning. Udall had been splendid.

Then, almost as an afterthought, Carter wondered if there wasn't anything he could do for Udall. "Jimmy, I thought you'd never ask," Udall said. He took out a handwritten note from his pocket recommending a friend to be appointed to the Civil Aeronautics Board, and handed it to the president. He'd been carrying it around for days. The friend got the job.

When the House overwhelmingly passed the Civil Service Reform Bill, the phone range in Udall's office. It was Carter, with congratulations to someone, as he said, who might have been elected president in 1976.

At that point the presidential course was smoother and the performance record obviously improving. Carter's successes with the Panama Canal treaties and the Civil Service Reform Bill gave him greater credibility in his dealings with Congress, and it appeared as if some of the changes from his Camp David sessions were having effect: Rafshoon's White House public-relations operation, while sneered at as mere imagemaking in the press, focused much-needed attention on the president's plans and activities; and winning praise was the new effort to repair political damage by meetings with business, professional, and traditional political groups that previously felt ignored by the Carter administration. (This effort was headed by another new member of the president's staff, Anne Wexler, well known in Democratic circles for her campaign work in Connecticut and her work for Eugene McCarthy.)

And Carter had other successes and other demonstrated moments of political courage in the months that followed—he vetoed a defense money measure on grounds that building a nuclear-powered aircraft carrier was wasteful (and that from an Annapolis graduate and disciple of Admiral Hyman Rickover, the so-called "father of the nuclear Navy"); he rejected easy political appeals to support education tax credits; he vetoed a bill containing pork-barrel water projects, something he wished he'd done the year before, and sustained it. But nothing seemed to help him in the public-opinion polls, which gave him a dismally low rating. He was, evidently, as enigmatic a figure as ever.

Later in the summer, when I visited the same congressional leader who had taken to writing down his thoughts and impressions of Carter privately for his own files, I was struck by the contradictions between the Carter he saw and the one the public perceived. One day that summer Carter had conducted a White House briefing for leading members of Congress, and when the

politician returned to Capitol Hill he dictated another memorandum about the experience:

> He [Carter] impresses me as a person with an extra-sharp, fine
> mind. It is quick and facile. He did a tour of the world and all of its
> problems for about twenty minutes with no notes, good grammar,
> good sense of proportion. He still has little knack for getting humor
> into these things, but I was asking myself why he was so terribly low
> in the polls, in personal popularity, while at these gatherings he
> makes such good sense and is so effective. He spoke with feeling of
> the limits of U.S. power, of the end of the era when the U.S. and its
> allies and the Soviets could control most major matters. He spoke
> with feeling about one-half of the world being hungry and desper-
> ate, getting little help from anyone to become self-sufficient, and
> made a strong plea for more aid. It was a very impressive perfor-
> mance and I was asking myself, "How can this guy be so God-
> damned low in the polls and the object of so much ridicule when
> he's clearly in command and really quite impressive?"

☐ ☐ ☐

Early in this century Lord Salisbury offered a definition of effective diplomacy that is still as good today as it was then: "The victories of diplomacy," he said, "are won by a series of microscopic
advantages—a judicious suggestion here, an opportune civility
there, a wise concession at one moment and a farsighted persis-
tence at another—of sleepless tact, immovable calmness and patience that no folly, no provocation, no blunder can shake."

Jimmy Carter, at the peak of his presidency, in the moment that
will be remembered, exemplified those qualities. It was as surprising as it was successful, for Carter came to office with less background and preparation for foreign affairs than any president of
this century. In achieving a peace treaty between Israel and Egypt,
he demonstrated patience, tenacity, boldness, and the exemplary
skills of quiet statesmanship. Moreover, his success in bringing together the leaders of the two ancient enemies, and then mediating
between them until agreement was reached, was a personal triumph. It had worked because of his character, his faith, his insis-

tence on comprehensive solutions, his absorption in the minutiae of complicated issues, ironically, the very qualities that often gave him problems in dealing with the political world at home.

When Carter became president, the old international leadership was gone or ending. In Western Europe the era of the de Gaulles and Churchills had passed. West Germany's Schmidt was probably the dominant figure but in comparison to earlier leaders appeared weak. In Russia, Brezhnev's health was failing, and the entire Soviet hierarchy was old, and leadership succession uncertain. Mao and Ho Chi Minh were dead, and no equivalently powerful leaders had taken their places. In the previous thirty years, one hundred new nations had come into existence and the world's population had doubled. The stockpile of nuclear weapons was increasing, and being held by more and more nations.

Of all the explosive areas the Middle East was the most critical to the industrial world. The United States, then importing and consuming one-third of the world's energy resources, and more than half of its oil, was a hostage to the oil states of that region. In a very real sense, Americans were living by the goodwill of Saudi Arabia. Of the Arab states, Saudi Arabia was the closest to America; the Saudis believed they provided stability for the region, and for the international order; they had produced more oil than they wanted when requested (by America) and worked to keep oil prices down during a period of revolutionary change and resurgent nationalism all around them. But the Saudis were militarily vulnerable, and apprehensive about the threat of aggressive Soviet intervention. Egypt, the major Arab military power, and Israel, the alien dagger in the Arab world, had battled again and again since the Jewish state was created in 1948. Another war between them could easily involve all the Arab states.

It was nonetheless the president's view, and those of his senior diplomatic advisers, that conditions were right for resolving the Israeli-Egyptian dilemmas. Enough moderate leaders were in power in the Middle East to offer a realistic chance for successful negotiations: no matter how they acted in public, the Americans found them flexible in private. "Unless we do something in 1977, I don't think we'll get another chance in our lifetime," the president had said privately as his administration began. "We can't impose our will on the disputative nations in the Middle East," he said, "but we can search among them as a catalyst for grounds of agreement, particularly those that are expressed privately and confidentially to us. And when we see it, without timidity and without constraint, we will use our influence to bring together disparate ideas in nations which in the past have not been able to agree."

Carter was determined to avoid dominating Middle East events by force of personality, as Henry Kissinger had done in his years of "shuttle-diplomacy" as secretary of state. But in the end it was the personal equation that became most important.

Carter first met Anwar Sadat, the Egyptian president, early in April 1977, just after the failure of Cyrus Vance's mission to Moscow. From the beginning, Carter found Sadat compelling. Sadat was a visionary. He didn't think of himself as merely the leader of Egypt in the late twentieth century; he was, as he told the president, the spiritual descendant of the pharaohs, the heir to seven thousand years of Egyptian history. That first time they met alone, early one morning, Sadat talked about his background. He came not from a regal family, of course, but from a small village, he said, and a consciousness of those villagers had been a guiding concept in his own life—it was a religious commitment, an individual commitment, a pride in heritage that motivated him. Carter was struck: in this respect Sadat could have been describing Carter's own view of himself. After dinner that evening Carter and Sadat talked together for nearly *seven hours,* sitting face-to-face upstairs at the west end of the family quarters in the White House. This extraordinary session established the basis for all that was to follow between them.

Sadat asked Carter for his ideas on the Middle East and especially Egypt's relations with Israel. The president outlined the Israeli position: Israel wanted recognition of its right to existence by the Arab states, and then it wanted direct negotiations with them; it also wanted a real peace that included full diplomatic relations and trade, cultural, and student exchanges between Egypt and itself. They might possibly be able to achieve the first two, Sadat said, but genuine peace would never occur in his lifetime.

Carter had already conferred with the Israeli prime minister, Itzhak Rabin, but within six weeks of his meeting with Sadat, Menachem Begin was elected to take Rabin's place, signaling a radical shift in Israeli politics, for Begin's Likud Party represented the hard-line, right-wing Jewish view of the Arab-Israeli conflict. Begin and Carter met for the first time in mid-July in Washington.

Menachem Begin, then nearing his sixty-fourth birthday, looked like everyone's image of a Jewish uncle—balding, bespectacled, wide-eyed and smiling, rumpled in dress; he seemed mild and open. It was a deceptive appearance, for Begin was an entirely different sort, temperamentally and politically, from the urbane Rabin. Blunt, stubborn, suspicious, Begin had been shaped by a lifetime of activity as political insurgent and guerrilla-warfare leader. Born in Russia, educated as a lawyer in Warsaw, he had headed Betar, a Zionist youth movement in Poland, before World War II began with the twin Nazi-Russian attacks into Poland late in 1939. Begin was arrested by the Soviet Secret Police and sent to a concentration camp in Siberia (an experience he later said "made it possible for me to make harsh decisions"); then, after the Germans invaded *their* erstwhile ally, Russia, Begin was set free and enlisted as a corporal in the Polish resistance army. In 1942 he arrived in Palestine wearing the Polish uniform. He deserted and became commander-in-chief of the Irgun Zvai Leumi, a guerrilla force fighting British rule over Palestine, and began the career of underground-resistance leader that won him fame—and made him an object of protracted manhunts, living the life of a fugitive, moving from place to place, changing his identity, and continuing to fight. Begin's Irgun guerrillas raided Arab villages and blew up the King David Hotel in Jerusalem, killing ninety-five British soldiers. At one point he was being hunted by the British, the Arabs, and also the Haganah, the Jewish defense force, since he had opposed the more moderate position espoused by David Ben-Gurion on how to deal with the British. After the war, Begin founded the Herut (Freedom) inside Israel, and continued to take a hard-line approach to Israeli-Arab questions. His Herut movement merged with several other Israeli political parties after the 1967 war with Egypt to form the Likud right-wing opposition. An indication of Begin's intransigence had come in 1970 when he resigned his position as minister without portfolio (which had been given him in an attempt to reconcile the deep Israeli political divisions) in protest over the government's acceptance of an American proposal committing Israel to withdraw from formerly Arab territories it then occupied.

Begin was emotional. He could weep, and did, in recounting the anguish of the Jews. He spoke out of the Book of Job: of struggle, suffering, and persecution, of gloom, torment and haunted dreams. "We have had very few good days in our lives in our generation," he commented to Carter when they first met. "The days of solace are not many." Carter came to think of him as Jeremiah. In private sessions Begin also could be infuriating, inflexible, almost the opposite of Sadat. He had a tendency, Carter discovered, to harden his supposedly agreed-upon position from meeting to meeting.

Those early months of trying to mediate between the two sides were frustrating for Carter. It was a thankless task, he complained once. He was the target both of the American Jewish community and the Arabs; it seemed impossible to placate either side. The three main problems—withdrawal of Israel from its occupied territory in the Gaza Strip, the Golan Heights (the Biblical hills of Gilead), the West Bank of the Jordan River, and Jerusalem, all taken during the Seven Days War in June 1967; establishment of a Palestinian homeland granting Palestinian self-government in areas Israel controlled in the Gaza Strip and the West Bank; and guaranteeing defensible borders for Israel—remained as intractable as ever.

Carter established a private correspondence with Sadat, which continued as the Egyptian-Israeli stalemate lengthened and Middle East tensions increased. Carter attempted to break the deadlock with a personal appeal to Sadat. On October 24, 1977, he wrote Sadat a letter in his own hand urging him to undertake a bold stroke for peace. Carter sealed the letter with wax (the only time he ever did that in his presidency), and dispatched it via an Egyptian embassy courier to Sadat.

Sadat responded by urging Carter to ask all the Western leaders to a summit meeting in Jerusalem, where they would confer with the Egyptian, Israeli, Soviet, Chinese, Jordanian, and Palestinian Liberation Organization leaders. Carter immediately vetoed this; he knew that if Helmut Schmidt or any other major Western leader failed to attend, the summit would be fruitless, and agreeing to inclusion of the P.L.O., the organization pledged to the destruction of Israel, was then politically unacceptable. But Carter and Sadat continued to exchange many private letters.

Then, two weeks later, Sadat dramatically announced he personally would go to Jerusalem at the end of November in the cause of peace. No Arab had ever done this.

That Sadat-Begin meeting was a drama felt, via intensive live-television coverage, by millions of people all over the world. Deep emotions were tapped, ancient sorrows and tragedies uncovered, but the diplomatic dangers of such highly charged encounters were obvious: hopes were raised, and with such expectations any failure would assume greater proportions.

When Carter met with congressional leaders several days after Sadat returned to Egypt, he was asked what he could tell them privately about the trip. He mentioned that he and Sadat had exchanged many letters, but played down his own part in preparing for this breakthrough. It was better for Sadat and Begin to negotiate between themselves, he said. What the U.S. government was trying to do privately was to exert all pressure possible on the other Arab countries—and Russia—not to condemn Sadat. As for Sadat personally, the president had nothing but praise. Sadat was a tough, competent, courageous man, and Carter had gotten along better with him than any foreign leader he'd met. By going to Israel Sadat had put himself in danger—not only physically but also politically by risking his support in the Arab world, which stood united in vitriolic opposition to any direct dealings with Israel, and possibly jeopardizing $2 billion in economic aid from Saudi Arabia, a country bearing unyielding hostility toward the Jewish state. The United States was working hard on that last question of Saudi aid to Egypt, the president said. He believed Sadat's mission had been of great significance. Sadat and Begin were deeply religious men, and their religious convictions offered the best chances for peace.

The most significant achievement of Sadat's visit to Jerusalem was that the Egyptian head of state was publicly recognizing the right of Israel to exist as an independent nation. When Carter, on his round-the-world trip at the end of the year, met briefly with Sadat in Aswan, Sadat privately told him he had changed his mind about the prospects for genuine peace: he had never been so wrong, he told the president, as when he had said peace between Egypt and Israel could not occur in his lifetime.

Other changes had taken place: Egypt and Israel now agreed

that a comprehensive peace plan was advisable. The Israelis had agreed to abide by United Nations Resolution 242, requiring them to withdraw from occupied territories, and for their part, the Arabs had agreed that Israel's borders must be secured. And, despite the still immense difficulties in achieving it, the two sides had agreed that a genuine peace should be institutionalized by treaty. But encouraging though these developments were, grave problems remained—and new ones kept arising. By late January 1978 the diplomatic negotiations between Israel and Egypt had broken down. The most aggravating problem was Israeli settlements in the occupied territories. Not only was the Israeli government insisting on keeping them; it was expanding them.

At Carter's first meeting with Moshe Dayan, on September 19 in his first year, the Israeli defense minister had promised the president there would be only six settlements by the end of the year and no expansion of existing ones, which would be military and not civilian. With Dayan's permission, Carter had passed that promise on to the Egyptians. But since then thirteen more settlements had been established, and a fourteenth was under way. The settlements in the occupied areas were the point of most serious contention, particularly the civilian ones. Troops could always be withdrawn overnight; but homes, hospitals, and schools became permanent fixtures. The president believed, although he did not say so publicly, that Israel was violating its word. He felt, as he said at one White House meeting then, that the Arabs had met all the demands put upon them while the Israelis had escalated theirs. He and Sadat had each pledged their honor that there could be no separate peace without a solution to the Israeli-held lands on the West Bank and in the Gaza Strip. And over everything hung the confounding problem of the Palestinians. The 1967 war brought every acre of Palestine, as well as parts of Lebanon, Syria, Jordan, and Egypt, under Israeli occupation. For the second time in a generation—the first was in 1948, when Israel was created out of land on which the Palestinians lived—the Palestinians had been forced to flee. Tens of thousands lived in refugee camps. A generation of Palestinians had grown up in exile. But the questions surrounding Palestine, like those of the broader Middle East conflict, had far deeper and more tangled roots. Palestine had been a waif of war throughout much of recorded history. Its narrow strip of deserts and mountains was a central passageway of the great land-bridge between Mesopotamia and the Nile—the Fertile Crescent— through which armies from antiquity had moved in wars of conquest mounted against Egypt and the Nile. For more than three thousand years both Jews and Palestinians laid claim to the region: the Jews basing their rights on partial occupancy going back to the days of Abraham beginning about 1600 B.C.; the Palestinians asserting ancestral descent from the Philistines and Canaanites whom even Jewish history recognizes as living there before the first Jews. These cultural and religious disputes over territory and primacy are no more complicated than the common background and antagonisms of many Arabs and Jews (as Semites all—descendants of Shem, son of Noah). In the twentieth century Palestine had been a pawn of international politics and colonialism, finally resulting in the creation of Israel and the displacement of the Palestinians. Both Palestinians and Jews were determined to possess their land whatever the cost. Not the least of their tragedy was that the Jews, who had borne such suffering and injustice while searching for *their* homeland, were now in deadly opposition to uprooted Palestinians seeking *theirs*. President Carter's position was that he didn't favor establishing a separate Palestinian state but that he was for full recognition of Palestinian rights, a position he maintained was taken privately by most Arab leaders he had met. The issue was deadlocked.

By now, the president had a clear sense of the differences—and difficulties—in dealing with the Egyptians and Israelis. Sadat was interested only in the bold thrust. When Carter would start speaking to him about details, the president could see Sadat's eyes begin to glaze over. It was just the opposite with the Israelis, who were sticklers on detail, painstaking with every item. (There were other differences. Begin's opening words to the president would always ask that he expedite the sale of weapons to Israel. At the same time, Carter knew America couldn't leave the Egyptians defenseless.)

It was in the context of new problems that Sadat returned to the United States on February 4 for lengthy private discussions with the president. Carter found Sadat, in the president's words, extremely aggravated and on the verge of making a very disagreeable speech before the National Press Club in Washington. After hours of discussion with Carter, Sadat agreed to modify his speech and delivered what the president regarded as a more moderate one: he said he wanted to keep the doors open to resume negotiations with Israel, and that he was determined to continue the search for peace through diplomacy. But Sadat remained discouraged. He told the president he had been genuinely surprised when the Israelis announced they were keeping the settlements, and believed it was time for Carter to use his influence and intervene personally to persuade the Israelis to change. To Sadat, the settlements were the most important problem.

Carter was especially frustrated—and frankly expressed his feelings at another congressional breakfast after Sadat left.

The president, the morning of February 7, 1978: *I have just about reached the end of my rope. I don't like to be a messenger boy. In the next few weeks unless there is some major breakthrough, the whole thing will break down. In Sadat's view, he would be better off in the Arab world if it did.*

Subsequent events didn't increase his optimism. At the end of March he was more convinced than ever that Israel had not adequately responded to Sadat's bold initiatives. The question of the settlements had become more ominous. It now appeared as if Israel might renounce the UN resolution. If that were to be so, Carter was tempted to give up his mediating role. Four different presidents had operated under the principles of that resolution; if the Israelis would not withdraw from the West Bank territories the prospect for peace was gone.

The outcome of Carter's talks with Begin was worse than the president had feared. He was shocked when Begin told him that Israel took the position that UN Resolution 242 did not apply to the West Bank, that Israel was unwilling to suspend construction on any new settlements there (even while negotiations were taking place), and that Israel was unwilling to acknowledge that the Palestinian Arabs had a right to determine their own form of government through the ballot. There could be no progress until Israel showed flexibility on those issues, the president concluded.

Through the spring and into the summer, the peace prospects remained in flux, at times tantalizingly close, at others more distant than ever. Saudi Arabia, with the weakest military force of any substantial nation in the region and the most valuable treasure in

oil, was pressing Sadat to have Egypt rejoin the Arab block and renounce its attempted rapprochement with Israel. For his part, Sadat was urging Carter to offer a compromise proposal to break the
stalemate. And indeed Sadat, under attack throughout the Arab
world, now refused to have direct diplomatic negotiations with Israel. On all sides, bitterness and recrimination were increasing.

By August Carter believed time was running out. It was his concern, bolstered by information received in intelligence appraisals,
that if the situation wasn't resolved shortly, Sadat might feel
forced to take military action—October, it was suggested, could
see Egyptian troops moving into the Sinai. Sadat could be desperate enough even to take action that he knew would lead to defeat,
so as to save face at home and in the Arab world. Carter dispatched Secretary Vance back to the Middle East on August 6 for
one more attempt to reach agreement between the two nations.

It was then that Carter took his great gamble. He and his wife
had been to Camp David one weekend. The president had told his
wife that he was certain if he could just get Begin and Sadat to
meet alone, in the privacy of a place like Camp David, removed
from the intense political pressures that otherwise were exerted
on them, together they could explore and test the issues face-to-
face—and resolve them. Begin and Sadat both wanted peace.
They could achieve it if given the chance. Why don't you invite
them here? his wife suggested. The president decided to try it.

The next Friday after that Camp David weekend, when he met
with the advisers that regularly discussed foreign affairs each week
with him, the president brought up his idea of inviting Begin and
Sadat to Camp David. The advisers were uniformly opposed to it.
Peace prospects were gloomy at best, and to arouse public hopes
only to have them dashed again would be destructive to the president's own interests. He couldn't afford another public failure.
But Carter was not dissuaded. He believed he understood the
character of the men he'd be dealing with; he had faith in them,
and in himself. The summit was convened. It was, Sadat observed,
enroute to Camp David, "a last chance" for peace; but Carter was
more circumspect. "The prospects for complete success are very
remote," he observed. This was quite different from the sweeping
promises of his political past.

Much has been written about the thirteen days in September

1978 when the American, Israeli, and Egyptian leaders, accompanied by their ministers and chief aides, conferred alone in the Maryland mountains. The full story of Camp David will not be told until the participants give their own detailed accounts, but especially Carter. For from beginning to end, it was Jimmy Carter who held the keys to what occurred there. He conferred alone, for hours, with each opposing leader. For twelve straight hours one day, he and Vance met with one Israeli and one Egyptian high official, thrashing out the thorny questions about the Palestinians. It was Carter who drafted, in his own hand and with his own initiative, every word of a proposed agreement on the Sinai at a critical point midway through the discussions. It was Carter who set the tone for the discussions by asking that the three of them, Christian, Muslim, and Jew, pray together for world peace at the beginning of their deliberations. And, when the talks were in danger of collapsing, it was Carter who brought up religious factors for discussion.

Privacy permitted long talks, without the interruption of official schedules and obligations. Within two minutes Carter could walk fifty yards and confer, alone, with either Sadat or Begin in their separate cabins. And the conferring went on day and night. Often they didn't end until after three o'clock in the morning, only to resume again within two or three hours. It was a strain for everyone involved, but especially for Begin and Sadat. Both had suffered heart attacks not long before and had to watch their health carefully. Sadat followed a rigid daily regimen: he arose early and took a brisk, hour-long walk; then, returning to his cabin, he would perform calisthenics for another half hour. Carter, also an early riser, noticed Sadat passing by his cabin on his morning constitutionals, and several times he joined him—another chance for the two of them to talk.

For the first three days general discussions were held setting out the positions on each side. As Carter later said, Begin and Sadat disagreed violently on many issues, with quite a few vituperous exchanges between them in his presence. Each man told the president privately he could never resolve their problems, and each asked that the United States come forth with a compromise proposal. The president and his aides then came up with the first of what would be twenty-three draft agreements prepared during the thirteen days. But the rancor between Sadat and Begin was so destructive that Carter decided after three days that the only hope was to keep them apart from each other. For ten days Begin and Sadat didn't meet, and Carter was their mediator, going back and forth with proposals and counter-proposals between the cabins in which Sadat and Begin were housed.

The personal chemistry between the men was the key. Carter again found Begin difficult, given to long discourses on historic Jewish suffering and tending brusquely to interrupt either Sadat or Carter. (At one point when the three men were still meeting together, Carter attempted to break in on Begin. The prime minister said he should be permitted to finish what he had to say, and Carter for once lost his patience: "I'll give you the same consideration you've been giving us.") Yet in the end it was Sadat, whom Carter had counted on to respond positively despite the fact of frustrations and disagreements, who created the greatest problem—and who nearly wrecked the talks.

The summit was nearing its end and Sadat was becoming more pessimistic. Carter, thinking that Israel's Moshe Dayan might be more compatible with Sadat than the abrasive Begin, brought him to Sadat's cabin. They talked about the difficult matters of Israeli settlements. Dayan tried to explain that any agreement made now on removing settlements from the Sinai would have to be approved by the Knesset. Sadat, already suspicious that Begin never intended to make any concessions, misunderstood: he thought Dayan was saying Begin was powerless to negotiate *anything* without Knesset approval. He brooded. "Everything's collapsing," he said to Ezer Weizman, the Israeli defense minister.

Then he blew up. Sadat ordered his bags packed and a helicopter prepared to fly him to Andrews Air Force Base, where he would immediately leave for Cairo. Cyrus Vance, ashen, brought the news of Sadat's impending departure directly to the president in his quarters. When Carter saw Vance's stricken face, his first thought was that war had broken out. When he learned what had happened, he countermanded Sadat's request for a helicopter, ordering Vance and Brzezinski to do nothing about it unless he, the president, personally gave them written authorization. Carter felt betrayed. All along, he had trusted Sadat and Sadat had promised in advance of the meeting that he would see it through no matter how long it took. Now Sadat was breaking his word.

The president immediately went to Dogwood Cabin, where Sadat was staying. Those next fifteen minutes with Sadat were the worst of his life, he said later.*

The president told Sadat their own personal relationship, which he cherished, would be destroyed if he left then. But more than that was at stake: American-Egyptian relations would be seriously, perhaps irreparably, damaged. Egypt no longer could look to the United States for assistance. It would be isolated, vulnerable to any assault. He, Carter, had believed in Sadat, had counted on him, trusted him, and he could not believe the Egyptian would go back on his word.

Sadat was still emotionally wrought up—and still exasperated. Finally, he said: "You have imposed this and that on me, but okay. For peace, I agree." The negotiations resumed.

Begin had given Carter some photographs of the three statesmen to autograph, as Sadat already had done. Now the president had an idea. He asked his secretary, Susan Clough, to get the names of all Begin's grandchildren from an Israeli aide. Carter inscribed the pictures to each of Begin's grandchildren, and then took them personally to Begin's cabin.

In the last hours of the Camp David meeting, there were moments when it appeared as if everything would break down. Discussion of the status of Jerusalem was emotional, and threatened to tear apart everything else. At the moment of Carter's entry, Begin was talking about the likely collapse of the negotiations, when he looked down and saw how Carter had inscribed the pictures. He stopped, began telling Carter instead about his grandchildren—the characteristics of each, and which was his favorite. "He and I had quite an emotional discussion about the benefits to my two grandchildren and to his if we could reach peace," Carter recalled. "And I think it broke the tension that existed there, that

---

*I have relied here on the reporting of Jack Nelson of *The Los Angeles Times*, who interviewed Carter immediately after the summit. Other material in this section comes from a White House dinner with the president and his wife which I attended one week after the summit.

could have been an obstacle to any sort of resolution at that time."

Finally, groggy and numb from the long hours and days of negotiations, Sadat and Begin reached final agreements on a "framework for peace" between Israel and Egypt.

Rosalynn Carter could hardly believe it when she heard, and urged her husband to get Sadat and Begin to sign the agreements immediately. If you wait they might change their minds. Don't worry, the president assured her. It is all in writing, and each leader has initialed the documents.

The hatreds and animosities that plagued Egypt and Israel for thirty years, leading them to war four times in one generation, were not ended at Camp David. But the agreements reached there were more substantive than almost anyone would have dreamed possible. Nearly every contentious issue between the two nations seemed to be resolved. Israel acknowledged that United Nations Resolution 242 applied to the territory on the West Bank of the Jordan. It stated the right of the Palestinians to self-government, granting full autonomy free of military occupation for Palestinians living on the West Bank. Through their elective representatives, the Palestinians would have the right to accept or reject an agreement subsequently to be negotiated by the Israelis, the Egyptians, the Jordanians, and their own people. Israel agreed to an early, substantial withdrawal of its forces to specific encampments, in effect removing the Israeli military government and permitting the Palestinians to manage their own affairs.

Egypt, in the signing of an eventual peace treaty, would formally recognize Israel's right to exist. Full diplomatic relations between the two countries were to be established, and students and economic and cultural missions exchanged.

One outstanding issue remained—the Sinai. Begin emotionally insisted on keeping the settlements as a security buffer. Sadat, with equal passion, said that an agreement to restore Egyptian sovereignty to the Sinai was a prerequisite to signing the treaty. In a compromise, Begin agreed that the Knesset would determine the Israeli position on the settlements within two weeks, while the Egyptians pledged not to destroy any of the facilities after the Israelis had withdrawn. Begin further agreed that Israel would not establish any new settlements during the treaty negotiations to follow. A three-month limit was set for the final conclusion of the terms of the peace treaty, but all the parties hoped it would be achieved before that.

Peace wasn't guaranteed, but by any standard these results were extraordinary.

The president and his outsiders had had few occasions for cheer in Washington. Now they were ebullient. Before long, members of the senior White House staff began wearing large new buttons, bearing the initials FCBCD. When asked what that meant, they were happy to explain: "For Carter Before Camp David."

□   □   □

During the summer of 1978 the president had begun inviting small groups of people from newspapers and television—such network anchor people as Walter Cronkite and Barbara Walters, publishers and editors from *Time* and *Newsweek, The New York Times, The Washington Post,* and *The Los Angeles Times,* and other selected columnists, commentators, and journalists—to a series of informal dinners upstairs at the White House with his wife, Rosalynn. Other presidents had given dinners like this, but for Carter it was a departure. These were often long evenings with unusually frank conversations. (What had been the most difficult aspect of his job? I asked the president during the dinner I attended. He paused momentarily, and after his wife said, "Go ahead, Jimmy, tell him," he replied: "The intransigence of the Congress and the irresponsibility of the press.") The dinners would end after the president and his wife conducted their guests on a tour of the upstairs quarters, the Lincoln Room, the Cabinet Room (Carter's favorite, with the table at which Lincoln had signed the Emancipation Proclamation still in place), the Queen's Room (where his mother, Lillian, stayed), FDR's Map Room downstairs, and then said their farewells on the south grounds.

At such a dinner just after the Camp David meetings in September the subject of the recent negotiations understandably dominated Carter's mind. The Knesset was about to vote on the question of the West Bank settlements, and Carter was certain the vote would favor their being withdrawn. He had no doubts, either, that an Israeli-Egyptian peace treaty would be reached and signed.

The president appeared genuinely to welcome the chance to exchange views, to let others know what he was thinking and how he had arrived at his opinions. He wasn't stiff; his manner was relaxed, his mood philosophical. Watching and listening to him, I had the conviction there was nothing he wouldn't have answered if asked—and that here was the real Jimmy Carter speaking, not the Carter who labored alone over the briefing books for month after month in the White House, nor the broadly smiling candidate Carter, but a highly serious, well-informed man (with a certain wryness in manner that seldom appeared in public) who clearly wanted to engage in matters of substance. To me, he seemed the least politically minded president I had ever met. When he said he couldn't conceive of anyone's asking him to indulge in some of the practices he had heard others employed—Lyndon Johnson and Everett Dirksen sitting together and trading judgeships was an example—I didn't doubt his sincerity, although I wondered about his conception of the political process. At one point he seemed, unintentionally, to answer my unspoken question about his political creed: he wanted to do nothing improper, he said.

He recognized his mistakes, he said. He'd misjudged the Russians earlier, but now, when sitting at night in his room off the upstairs hallway, looking at the globe beside him, he tried to put himself in *their* place, to realize how lacking in true friends or allies they were. There had been some brutal private communications from Brezhnev, and Carter had firmly replied about violations of human rights in the Soviet Union and Russian sponsoring of Cuban military adventures in the Horn of Africa. He had been disturbed when he sat in his White House office and listened to Soviet foreign minister Andrei Gromyko lie outright: Soviet generals were not operating in Ethiopia, East German forces were not fomenting trouble in Angola, Gromyko had said to his face—although Carter knew, from unquestionably accurate intelligence, that these statements were false. (It was similar to the scene, sixteen years before, in the same office, when Gromyko boldly denied to John Kennedy that the Russians had installed missiles in Cuba.) Still, he was convinced that he and the Russians could fashion a realistic relationship. They would get a strategic arms limitation treaty, he was certain, fair to each side, practical and secure in its implementation.

A different era lay ahead, one offering a brighter chance for world stability, the president believed. The United States was even then privately exploring the possibility of establishing full diplomatic relations with the People's Republic of China. That would occur—altering the balance of forces in Asia, strengthening America's role there, and providing a counterpoint to the Soviet Union.

And there was the Middle East. They were going to get their peace treaty. In the president's view, there was no way it could fail. He knew Anwar Sadat would not let him down. Sadat was the greatest figure he'd ever met, truly a Biblical personage. It was almost embarrassing how much Sadat believed in Carter. If they came to an impasse in negotiating the peace treaty, the president was convinced that Sadat would go along with virtually anything he proposed; why, Carter said, he could draw the lines of the final map on the sands of the Sinai and Sadat would approve them without question!*

Events were falling into place. An assured president, with hopes of a more orderly world in the period ahead, bade farewell to his guests late that September evening.

As I walked through the grounds and to the gate beyond I thought that Jimmy Carter, after all the problems that had plagued his presidency, finally appeared to be fully in control of his job and at ease with his responsibilities.

□   □   □

In October a friend of mind in the State Department returning to Washington from a trip to Iran bore alarming news. He and a department intelligence officer had traveled throughout the coun-

---

*In preparing for talks aimed at completing the peace treaty, Carter obtained a huge map of the Sinai from the CIA, some twelve feet long and eight feet wide, and spread it out in his upstairs White House study. With the assistance of U.S. geographers, Carter then drew the interim withdrawal lines and final military zones for submission to Egyptian and Israeli negotiators.

try, and they had observed a genuine revolution sweeping Iran, one which no force could stop. They were convinced the shah of Iran would be overthrown in December. My friend was so alarmed at what he had seen that he called me several times in hopes that articles in the press would force U.S. officials to face the urgency of the Iranian situation instead of dismissing the rising turmoil as insignificant, as they did when he reported his findings. The American embassy in Teheran, confident of the shah, had seriously misread the situation; it was out of touch and had been so for years—so close to the shah and his regime, relying so heavily on information gained by the shah's brutal secret police force, SAVAK, which had been trained and supplied by our own CIA, that all the Americans' judgments about the state of affairs were skewed.

For months in Washington, there had been demonstration after demonstration against the shah mounted by some of the thirty-five thousand Iranian students then in the United States. Protests were familiar in the capital, but these had been different. They had a fearsome, primal quality: long lines of ardent young men and women, masked, many carrying clubs, marching in almost military procession to the accompaniment of drums, their shouted chants echoing off the downtown buildings at lunch hours. "Shah is a butcher." Boom. Boom. Boom. "Down with the Shah." Boom. Boom. Boom.

The shah, though, was regarded by most Americans as invincible. Since 1943 America had been deeply involved in Iran's economic and military development. American arms and assistance poured into Iran. The American CIA used Iran, with its twelve-hundred–mile–long border with the Soviet Union, as an intelligence staging area and sensitive listening post. And strategically, Iran was critical. Through the Straits of Hormuz, over which Iran had military control, moved 20 million barrels of oil a day, accounting for 37 percent of oil production consumed by the free world.

At the same time Iran was a nation subjected to massive internal strains and pressures. Since World War II its population had nearly tripled and by 1978 half of its people were under sixteen years of age. To shift from a semifeudal agrarian peasant culture to a Western industrial one would have been difficult under any conditions. In Iran the effort was especially dangerous. The shah dreamed of re-creating the grandeur of the Persian Empire. Under his autocratic hand, Iran had made its intensive industrialization effort. But the shah's regime was also brutal and corrupt, and his military might increased yearly. His armed forces numbered 420,000, backed by a vast store of modern weaponry.

The corruption of the regime, the clash of cultures, the lack of skills and education amid the pressures of change—all these came to a nation practicing a deeply devout brand of Islam whose traditions were fundamentally opposed to modernism in almost any form. Ninety percent of Iran's population were Shiite Muslims— led by, and believing implicitly in, leaders opposed to the shah, to industrialization, and to Western culture.

The internal warning indicators of trouble in Iran were there to be read by American policymakers. For a quarter of a century they were ignored. Throughout the 1970s the United States government handed the shah more and more blank checks: it was a "bastion of strength" and power in the Middle East.

My friend in the State Department wasn't the only one concerned about events in Iran that fall. He and others tried to convince White House policymakers that the shah was doomed. But they, and notably Zbigniew Brzezinski, were confident these reports of the shah's demise were inaccurate; besides, they were preoccupied by the Middle East peace treaty, by negotiations with the Russians on SALT, and by the secret talks with the Chinese. As opposition to the shah increased and news from Iran daily grew more ominous, the president maintained public optimism about stability there. In those months, whenever he was asked about the Iranian situation, his words were reassuring:

OCTOBER 10—My own belief is that the shah has moved aggressively to establish democratic principles in Iran and to have a progressive attitude toward social questions, social problems. This has been the source of much of the opposition to him in Iran.

NOVEMBER 30—We have confidence in the shah, we support him and his efforts to change Iran in a constructive way, moving toward democracy and social progress. And we have confidence in the Iranian people to make the ultimate judgments about their own government.

DECEMBER 7—The shah has attempted, in my opinion, while maintaining order in a very difficult period, to move toward social liberalization, sometimes directly in conflict with the desires of the more traditional religious leaders, and has on several occasions, increasingly lately, offered to form coalition governments encompassing his political opponents there. These offers have been rejected.

By then, the revolution had become bloody and CIA reports from Teheran had turned pessimistic. George Ball, a lawyer and foreign-policy analyst who had been under secretary of state during the Johnson administration (when his counsel against further U.S. military involvement in Vietnam had been ignored) was asked by the president to assess the shah's situation. Ball, too, warned that the shah's regime was about to collapse. But Carter continued to rely on contrary opinions offered by such as Brzezinski.

DECEMBER 12—I fully expect the shah to maintain power in Iran and for the present problems in Iran to be resolved. Although there have been certainly deplorable instances of bloodshed which we would certainly want to . . . see avoided, I think the predictions of doom and disaster that came from some sources have certainly not been realized at all. The shah has our support and he also has our confidence.*

Although the president cited Iran's history as cause for optimism—"I think it's good to point out that the Iranian people for twenty-five hundred years, perhaps as long as almost any nation on earth, have had the ability for stable self-government"—conditions inside Iran were now anything but stable. As the revolution spread, U.S. policymakers became concerned that the Soviet Union, already taking a newly aggressive position in the "proxy"

---

*Within a month, a special congressional panel, after studying the causes of the Iranian revolution, issued a strongly critical report of the U.S. government's performance. The president and his top advisers must share blame and responsibility with the CIA for failing to assess accurately the forces that finally toppled the shah, the group stated. (As late as September 28, just after Camp David, for instance, the CIA had advised the president that the shah "is expected to remain actively in power over the next ten years.") The entire administration's policymaking apparatus was faulted for not paying attention to the threatening events in Iran.

wars in the Horn of Africa, would be tempted to foment the Iranian unrest, and seek to seize the rich treasure in oil. Carter sent a "hands-off" message to Brezhnev, making it clear that the United States had no intention of interfering in the situation there—and, equally, had no intention of permitting others to do so.

Over the Christmas–New Year's holiday, the president went again to Camp David. He summoned his secretary of state, Cyrus Vance, to meet with him there secretly for two days. Like his first, his second year was ending with Iran. But now that "island of stability," as he had called Iran then, was disintegrating into chaos, and Jimmy Carter's vision of a new order in the world was dissolving.

7
THE PRESIDENT

LATE ONE afternoon at the end of May 1979, I approached the White House. The president had invited me and several others for dinner to discuss what Jody Powell had described over the phone as "important matters about the country" that were on his mind, but I arrived early and wandered around the Ellipse, watching the joggers and the softball players. Beyond the Washington Monument, over the slight crest of a hill on the Mall, I could see glimpses of sails along the Potomac. It was a perfect day, clear and soft, and the scene was so tranquil that it was difficult to imagine any problems intruding.

As I walked back to the White House, the foliage along the wrought-iron fence was at its most luxuriant, with rhododendron and roses in bloom, and inside the grounds I could see that each massive tree bore a small metal plaque stating in English and Latin its genus and age. What the plaques didn't say was that each tree had a presidential history dating back to the mansion's first occupant, John Adams, who had planted American elms and established a tradition followed by all his successors.

Jimmy Carter, the thirty-seventh president to live in the White House, had studied the trees, knew who had planted which—Andrew Jackson's magnolias, Benjamin Harrison's scarlet oaks, Grover Cleveland's Japanese maples, Franklin Roosevelt's little-leaf lindens, Dwight Eisenhower's black walnuts, Lyndon Johnson's darlington oaks, Richard Nixon's giant sequoias. Once Carter had greeted his guests he invited them to join him for drinks on the Truman Balcony, overlooking the grounds and emerald lawns and the sight of the athletes, the Monument, the Jefferson Memorial, and the river stretching beyond.

The president seemed to have aged. He had been jogging every afternoon, and had lost weight; the skin on his neck hung loose in folds, his hair was grayer, and little red marks dotted his face. Gesturing below, he pointed out to me the path he followed on his daily runs, first south beyond the Oval Office, through the trees and back, and then, on the east side of the mansion around the grounds and back again. He preferred running early in the morning, as he and his wife did regularly on weekends at Camp David, but his White House day was too tightly organized for that. He still got up at five o'clock each morning, had a CIA briefing, and began going through papers that he continued to consume voraciously—at least three hundred fifty pages every day.

On so splendid a day, removed from the dissonance of the city, amid such signs of solidity, calmness, and well-being, it seemed almost inconceivable that this president was deeply in trouble. He was, though, and he knew it.

Jimmy Carter's presidency had not been destroyed or disgraced. No great scandal had stained his administration. No great war-and-peace, boom-or-bust issue divided the nation. Yet his presidency had reached ever lower points in public approval and internal morale, and the office he represented institutionally was at its weakest in dealing with Congress and the federal agencies in perhaps generations. All of the federal government seemed to have come unraveled. On Capitol Hill, a sullen mood prevailed. Earlier congressional complaints leveled strongly against the president were now also being aimed at themselves, as Democrats were pitted against Democrats and the special interests grew even stronger. In the country, cynicism appeared to have worsened. No one believed anything or anyone—the gasoline shortage or the oil companies, the politicians or the president. For the president, it had been the cruelest spring. His third year in office had begun ominously. Iran's collapse into revolution, shutting off the flow of oil there, sent a shock through an industrial world dependent on Middle East petroleum. At home, hysterical cries that America "do something" had come from politicians of both parties and commentators of both liberal and conservative persuasions. Even normally circumspect citizens were apprehensive as events seemed moving out of control.

Carter had taken the greatest risk of his presidency, against the counsel of most of his advisers in private, and journeyed to the Middle East in a desperate last-chance attempt to gain a peace settlement there. He achieved what none before him had been able when Egypt and Israel agreed to peace terms, but there was little tangible public recognition of his triumph. And no sooner had the Peace Treaty been signed on the White House lawn on March 26, than Israel, willfully acting against its word pledged during the Camp David talks, began establishing new settlements on the West Bank of the Jordan, further complicating Anwar Sadat's already difficult and isolated position within an Arab world outraged at him for breaking the solid front of opposition to Israel by entering into a formal relationship with the Jewish nation. Carter's efforts to insure that Saudi Arabia and other Arab states not turn against Sadat, central to his hopes for real peace, had failed; the Saudis, whom he had extolled as the most stabilizing force for Middle East peace, were now moving away from the United States amid open criticism of American Middle East policy, what they perceived as Carter's ambivalent reaction to the Iranian revolution, and his seeming indecision as manifested by his order first to send a naval task force into the Persian Gulf, and inexplicably canceling it; and then ordering U.S. combat planes to fly over Saudi soil as a show of strength, support, and a supposed U.S. warning to the Soviets to keep hands off the ill-protected Saudi state (and yet planes took to the air without ammunition, something the Saudis could not understand, and said so).

New concern about American impotence in foreign affairs, particularly in the Middle East, made prospects for winning Senate ratification of a strategic arms limitation treaty with the Russians more doubtful.

Carter's standing in the polls continued to slip, plunging him to nearly as low a mark as Richard Nixon's lowest. As always, the polls didn't really address what people *thought* or *felt* about Carter personally. By measuring his political performance in simple black-and-white terms—"Do you approve or disapprove of the way President Carter is handling his job?": Approve, "X" percent;

Disapprove, "Y" percent—it was possible for those polled to like, or even admire, Carter's character but to be recorded as holding negative views about his presidency and the manner in which the issues he was confronting were being solved. But the constant repetition of his unpopularity in the polls contributed to a general belief that he was weak. The press was as critical as ever, indeed writing Carter off as hopeless. Political cartoonists, who always reflect the popular assessment of a president's standing, had arrived at something of a collective judgment on how to portray Carter: his figure grew smaller and smaller, his manner more and more befuddled, his gaze more frequently raised upward, as if praying for fortune or the Lord to extricate him from his problems.

His announcement during an April 5 energy speech that he would begin lifting price controls on crude oil, a move intended to spur domestic production and which some in his administration admired as his most courageous, set off a bitter political controversy. Carter coupled the price decontrols decision with a proposal to impose a two-tier windfall-profits tax on the oil companies— but he had *not* made his decontrol decision contingent upon congressional approval of the windfall tax. Carter's plan was to use funds from the windfall-profits tax, if enacted by Congress, to create an "energy security fund," part of which would be used to give rebates to families with annual incomes under $7500. His proposals, though, were assailed by liberals as a bonanza for the oil companies and a "rip-off" of the poor.

The controversy over lifting controls and then seeking a windfall-profits tax was among the most intense of his presidency on two main grounds: serious doubts existed whether lifting oil price controls would in fact cause the oil companies to increase production, a point publicly conceded by Treasury Secretary Blumenthal; and the burden of the increasing energy costs would fall largely on those Americans least able to afford them. In Congress, his fellow Democrats, meeting in party caucus, administered a humiliating rebuke by going on record overwhelmingly against his decontrol decision; then, in an action that Congressman Richard Bolling of Missouri described as unconscionable cowardice, the House refused by a vote of 246 to 159 to grant him stand-by authority to ration gasoline, even in a national emergency.

Inflation roared on, nearing a 14 percent annual level with no end in sight and no one, anywhere, it seemed, with the means to curb it. Carter's voluntary anti-inflation program was dealt a mortal blow when a federal judge ruled that he didn't have constitutional authority to deny government contracts to those abusing his wage-and-price guidelines. It was a toothless program to begin with, and Carter had evoked unflattering comparison to Gerald Ford's unsuccessful campaign to "Whip Inflation Now" through voluntary efforts and the wearing of WIN buttons, when he had addressed the nation early in February to urge, once again, a voluntary effort to honor the speed limit, turn down home and office thermostats, cut back on driving, and shift to car pools. But gasoline consumption—and prices—continued to rise as dollar-a-gallon charges were recorded for the first time in the country. At the same time recession loomed, raising new doubts about economic stability and arousing more fears.

In the midst of all these disturbing events, Carter's friend Bert Lance was indicted in Georgia in a massive criminal conspiracy case, which charged that he and other associates repeatedly violated federal banking laws to obtain more than $20 million in loans, including acts that occurred during his White House service.

Internally, the administration was showing signs of disintegration. Senior officials were leaving important government posts, and it was expected that more would go. Talk of the inevitability that Ted Kennedy would be the next Democratic nominee dominated Washington and political circles across the country. Kennedy for President groups were forming in the key primary states, and in every poll Kennedy rated as the overwhelming favorite among Democrats, usually topping the president by two or three to one. As Carter continued to slip, Kennedy continued to maintain he would not run, but he was watching every poll and every new event. (One day in the Senate he launched into what amounted to a long soliloquy before an old Senate colleague. He was going to go away to Hyannis Port later in the summer, Kennedy said, and assess where everything was coming out politically: events might doom Carter by the fall, in which case he would declare— not a question of if, but when. The conversation was so frank and so intimate that it made Kennedy's colleague uncomfortable; he had heard Robert Kennedy express nearly identical thoughts, in the same searching way, when *he* was deliberating whether to run against Lyndon Johnson in 1968.)

Through the turbulent spring of 1979 the president remained apart, as distant a figure of a chief executive as any in memory. "He hasn't a single friend up here," a Southern senator said to me at lunch one day in the Capitol. "Not one soul." It wasn't that Jimmy Carter was hated or feared. He didn't seem to stir any emotion at all. It wasn't that he failed to speak out. He did, but he wasn't being heard.

His personal pollster, Patrick Caddell, had been taking national political soundings. Every survey showed that people were rapidly turning pessimistic about their own, and their country's future. Disbelief in the ability of politicians or the government to solve problems was growing. Governance was breaking down. Caddell was convinced that the national disillusion with politics and the presidency had grown even worse during Carter's tenure, and that only a dramatic change in Carter's political approach could begin to win back necessary public support.

As Caddell studied his own survey data, and the writings of several contemporary Americans dealing with the changing nature of political leadership and the new values and attitudes of American citizens in the 1970s, he began to see the difficult conditions as both political curse and blessing. More than inflation, more than normal political cynicism worried Americans, he concluded; a majority believed that nothing was working; and if these attitudes continued, U.S. society literally *would* become ungovernable.

Even as Caddell was forming a political approach to deal with these intangible matters of the American spirit, American pride in its vaunted technology suffered a series of blows that spring. Commercial airplanes cracked and were grounded after a DC-10 crashed in Chicago on April 25. Nuclear plants became suspect after an ominous accidental "bump in the night" at a Three Mile Island, Pennsylvania, installation touched off alarms and sent radioactive clouds into the atmosphere at the end of March. The nation's largest orbital space endeavor, *Skylab*, began plunging toward the earth late in April and no official or scientist could say for certain where it would land. Here, it seemed, was proof that at least part of Caddell's thesis was correct, for surely these events, coming as they did immediately after the civil war in Iran and amid the new gasoline shortages, would intensify national doubts.

But Caddell was also persuaded that if Carter could address these underlying problems, and the attitudes that compounded them, he could rebuild confidences, regain credibility as a leader, and move the nation in new directions. He took his poll data about declining national confidence and rising pessimism to Rosalynn Carter. She was impressed enough to call in others among the top Georgia group to discuss them. By the end of April Caddell had committed his findings to paper, and he and Mrs. Carter met with the president then to discuss the points raised in his memorandum and their political implications. From these conversations flowed a number of other small meetings within the White House inner circle, and the beginnings of a new approach to Carter's presidency, both in the way it was managed internally and in its approach to the public and to the national questions.

It was in this context that the president invited me and the others in a small group to the White House at the end of May, along with Caddell and Jody Powell—to discuss what he described to us as Caddell's "apocalyptic findings" and what they meant for the nation.

Serious as Caddell's implications were for the political process, for Jimmy Carter they were especially disturbing. He came to office believing he and his wife had a special understanding of the American people. He wanted to create a government as good, and as compassionate, as the American people, he had said during his campaign. A slogan, certainly, and politics, to be sure; but he sincerely believed it. He felt closer to the American people than anyone in the room, he had said behind closed doors that day shortly before his inauguration when he discussed foreign policy with the congressional entourage at the Smithsonian. It was an extraordinary—and arrogant—thing to say to a group of veteran politicians, each of whom had been judged by the people longer than he. Considering how he reached the presidency, though, Carter had reason enough to believe it.

Now, with another presidential year approaching, here was evidence of a dismaying national cast of mind. Willingness to sacrifice for the national good appeared absent. Suspicion, self-indulgence, and selfishness apparently reigned.

Carter and his wife had read Christopher Lasch's *The Culture of Narcissism* and found it raising many doubts. If Lasch was correct, if the pollsters were correct, then something alien to their experience was at work in America. The lessons of Washington—of dealing with Congress, the lobbyists, the press—had been difficult enough. But if basic American attitudes were changing from traditional optimism to pessimism, that posed the most profound of all political questions. In so fractious a time, how could a political leader lead? In so fragmented a society, with citizens withdrawing further from the political process, how could you even reach them? No matter how correct a course, would anybody listen, would anybody care, would anybody follow?

The president and his wife discussed the questions at length. They had taken to reading about travails of other presidents, Lincoln and Truman among them, and they raised all these and other questions that May evening in the White House before people whose views they said they respected: John Gardner, the former head of Common Cause, cabinet officer, and author of *Morale*, a book about political leadership; Daniel Bell, the Harvard sociologist, co-editor of the magazine *The Public Interest* and editor of *The Cultural Contradictions of Modern Capitalism*; Lasch; Charles Peters, editor of *The Washington Monthly*, whose article on a political agenda for the 1980s had impressed the Carters; Bill Moyers, Lyndon Johnson's press secretary and protégé (and also friend of Robert Kennedy) and television commentator; Jesse Jackson, the black civil-rights worker from Chicago.

Part of the problem, we told Carter that night, was that Americans were *correct* in reacting gloomily to events. The news *was* bad. They had good reason to believe they weren't getting straight answers—or that anyone had the answers at all. And part was Carter's own fault. "The good preacher" in him, who had touched people during the campaign, wasn't being heard or felt, someone said. Another told him something else had been missing from his presidency: he owed his election to the belief that he was an unconventional politician who promised to be an unconventional president; yet his presidency had been a most conventional one. It was fifty-fifty or less that he would be returned to office, Carter was told.

The power of his office had been eroded. Experts on public

opinion and television believed that people would listen to a president only in times of demonstrated dire emergency, and they told him so. Carter's own speeches were proof of the dramatic decrease in his national audience: when he gave his first televised fireside chat (the "cardigan sweater" speech two weeks after his inauguration), 80 million people had watched. By that April 5, 1979, when he delivered another, his third major speech on energy, his audience had fallen to only 30 million (four times as many tuned in to the Super Bowl). Even if the president could command at will the nation's airwaves (a doubtful premise in the post-Watergate era), the audience would be small. Fireside chats, even if delivered with Roosevelt's verve, an impossibility for Jimmy Carter, probably no longer would work, his PR experts believed.

In times of a diminished presidency, it was suggested to him, perhaps the most effective thing for a chief executive to do was to act as a mediator between opposing groups on vital issues—energy, inflation, arms reduction. That meant convening the representatives of various influential groups—in the White House, or perhaps at Camp David, and then attempting to hammer out agreements on the difficult issues. The president was doing this; he had not closed himself off, as others before him in times of trouble; he *was* reaching out, he *was* listening, seeking advice, soliciting varied views. But it seemed to make no difference. He was holding on to a patch of sand; nothing bound the grains together. To Washington, and to the country, he appeared irrelevant.

In adversity other presidents railed at their enemies, plotted revenge, became self-righteous and defensive, brooked no dissent. Carter sat, quietly listening, weighing what was being said, even if most critical of him personally. He encouraged frankness, he said at dinner that night, smiling faintly; he felt no sense of paranoia and recognized the need for tough examination. He freely acknowledged fault. If the message was right but was not being delivered, there must be problems with the messenger. That the message *was* right, the approach to the issues correct for the long-term, was an unshakable conviction with him. Nor—acceptance of mistakes and misjudgments aside—was there a feeling of personal failure.

Carter, no less than previous men in his position, clearly wished to be vindicated, and returned triumphantly to power. But, to what seemed to me a remarkable degree, the personal search for answers to these political questions seemed genuinely removed from a win-or-lose political context. Jimmy Carter gave the impression of being driven by selfless motives, of truly putting national interests above personal ones in ways uncommon to many presidents. Around the dinner table that night his wife said she remembered how they felt, in 1961, when John Kennedy became president. They were in Plains then, with their three boys. Kennedy brought a surge of pride to America. She felt it, they felt it, and that's what they'd like to recapture. How did you make Americans feel better about themselves and their country? That consideration seemed more important than any discussion of political strategy, of bills won and lost, campaigns run and fought.

Jimmy Carter's life was a testament to belief in all the cherished virtues—thrift and frugality, hard work and integrity, self-improvement and decency. Perhaps more than any president in a lifetime, he believed in, and was motivated by, a kind of mystical faith in the People. Lincoln could speak, over a century ago, in a different age and different America, of "the mystic chords of memory, stretching from every battlefield and patriot grave to every living heart and hearthstone all over this broad land" and of "the better angels of our nature." But few politicians now share so spiritual a vision of the country. Carter does, there seems no doubt. For him to entertain serious concerns about the governability of the people, and perhaps even deeper ones about the national character, had to be as disillusioning as it was poignant.

To feel America had become ungovernable wasn't to prove it was true, of course. Nor did his doubts begin to address how much was his responsibility, how much the political process, or how much beyond solution. For the moment, he seemed, as one of those who saw him in that cheerless spring said, to be "a good and decent man about to go down in flames."

□   □   □

During the first two years, whenever serious mistakes were made, one of the president's aides had always blamed the acolytes instead of the priest. But that spring, he finally concluded, responsibility for problems could no longer be neatly separated. The priest also had to bear the burden for failure. "What drives people here crazy, and why so many people want to get out, is that we have the notion there are still useful things to do," he said to me. "We know that in today's political climate they're hard—but they're do-able if we take advantage of all the resources and use all the levers at our command. I'm willing to give people the benefit of doubt and the time to learn. But when we're three years into it, and we're *still* making the same mistakes, it drives us all absolutely nuts."

At the time he was speaking, in June 1979, one-third of the National Security Council staff had resigned. Over at Health, Education and Welfare, in only a few weeks five officials had announced plans to leave—the under secretary, the education commissioner, the food and drug commissioner, the National Institute of Education director, the general counsel. Similar departures were under way at other agencies, and at the top it appeared as if virtually every cabinet officer would be gone by the end of Carter's first term. Even among the very close and small circle of presidential advisers, some were making private plans for other work after the 1980 election.

Individually the reasons varied—fatigue, disenchantment, difficulties complying with a new ethics law, personal complications—and it is also true that collectively every administration experiences a third-year slump. But the Carter administration's problems went beyond this.

The Georgians around the president grew more protective and defensive. Privately, you heard them express contempt for the cabinet. ("We've been a lot more loyal to them than many of them have been to us.") And even a murmur of disappointment about Vice-President Mondale, whom Carter had gone out of his way to praise publicly as having taken a more significant part in his administration than anyone who ever held that difficult position. The weekly senior staff sessions on congressional relations no longer included Mondale or anyone outside the Georgians, a presidential aide observed bleakly. "That little group's feeding off themselves," the aide said. One night, in a moment of frustration, a cabinet officer confessed to me he wanted to leave desperately, and speculated that political events might doom Carter before the first 1980 primary. To hang grimly on until the four years were up, and to keep as far away as possible from the White House group—those were the cabinet officer's personal intentions.

At the Executive Office Building, a circular making its way from office to office was drawing private laughs and adding to the cynicism. This anonymous parody of the condition of the administration went as follows:

> Six Phases of a Project
> 1. Enthusiasm
> 2. Disillusionment
> 3. Panic
> 4. Search for the Guilty
> 5. Punishment of the Innocent
> 6. Praise and honor for the nonparticipants

Another presidential assistant remarked on the change in the sense of personal involvement in politics:

> I'm much more cynical about brave new beginnings that are not founded on a very careful analysis of what people have tried before and of what has some chance to work. You have to look at the inter-est-group dynamics, at the congressional dynamics, and if you get over all those hurdles you still have to have some rough calculation of whether it's worth it. Even if you're very good and lucky, what-ever you achieve is going to be discounted by the cynical atmo-sphere. For a lot of people, the result is to decide to be sort of fast and loose with the substance of whatever they're doing. They tend to feel it's all symbolism, all show, so they make the best and tem-porary case, because they're not going to get credit for achievement anyway.
>
> All of us have the sense that the times are not very generous to reform efforts, and that we're going to have to pick our targets very carefully and not overpromise. We're guilty of the rationalist fallacy that a good idea will carry its own weight—that it will not have to appeal to a selfish group to survive. Well, that's just not true. In to-day's climate, there's a me-first attitude on almost everything.

In Boone, Iowa, those spring weeks were hard. Prices kept rising and bills increasing. Interest rates were soaring, home building had come to a halt, construction loans were almost impossible to obtain, and Fred Doxsee was finding money to run his real-estate business "very, very tight." It was unsettling, frightening even; no one seems to be running the country, Doxsee thought.

There was a "whole new feeling, a deep feeling," about the country, Doxsee told me in May. You could sense it in what people said everywhere. Part of it involved the president, for Doxsee and his friends had changed about Jimmy Carter. Disappointment wasn't the right word; Doxsee wished he could think of another. There was something about Carter that made you feel sorry for him; you wished you could do something to help; but Carter's presidency hadn't, as he said, "washed down." Now it was hard to find anyone who admitted to having voted for Carter—it was that bad. "It's just like having someone in town that you know's a nice guy, but he's never done anything, and you just put him out of your mind," Doxsee said. "I voted for the nice guy, and he *has* been a nice guy, but he isn't coming over. He doesn't get us excited. I wouldn't ask people over to listen to him again the way I did. He doesn't let us know what kind of a human being he is. A little cold, maybe. I don't know, he hasn't humbled himself. I don't think he's a guy I could talk to. He's got the powers, he should have the powers, but it doesn't seem like he's used the powers of the president."

Doxsee recalled again how his doubts about Carter began when Carter dropped the fifty-dollar tax rebate exactly two years before. "It was something he didn't have to do, and he said he was going to do it, and then he wasn't going to do it. I know that's a small thing, but sometimes small things are important. It makes you wonder." As for the Middle East peace efforts—well, yes, Carter had done a good job, but that was what he was supposed to do. "I know that's not much in-depth thinking, maybe, but we're worried most about our own family, being swallowed up by inflation and our bills and our heating costs and our gasoline."

Carter had evidently not persuaded Doxsee just what his policies and programs were, or how they were going to work. Doxsee also suspected that "he doesn't seem to have his people behind him in Washington." He tried listening to the president's energy speech of April 5, two years after that first one in April 1977, "but he just didn't come up with the answers." He believed ever more deeply that no one was going to make sacrifices voluntarily: something stronger was needed. Carter couldn't whip a pussycat right now.

"One person made the remark the other day—and I feel this way, too—that, 'Well, what I'm looking for now is a stronger, older, ward-politician type.' If I had the opportunity now I'd take the old hard-nosed politician who could get something done. We need an old war horse in there." An old man, a friend, had said something disturbing the other day that struck home: he hoped he wouldn't live until the next election, the old man said, because he wouldn't know how to vote or what to believe. "What can we do to get back something good in the country?" he asked. Fred Doxsee didn't have the answer, but next time he'd take experience over the outsider.

□   □   □

Dismal as the readings were, Jimmy Carter's political demise was not assured. Other presidents had faced deteriorating political conditions and survived. Truman had been low in popularity, and won his famous victory over Dewey in 1948. Nixon at a comparable point in his first term was regarded as a certain loser, trailing far behind Democratic presidential rivals; he came back to win in 1972 by the greatest of all landslides. And the fact is that no incumbent president in the twentieth century who actively sought renomination has been denied it. In the age of instant mass-media attention, a president's ability to get public credit for taking strong, surprising action is a powerful political asset.

Nor was Carter's record barren. He had not fulfilled all his promises, notably in tax and welfare reform, consumer protection, and national insurance, but no president had worked harder in trying to achieve them and few brought a better mind to bear on national problems. His successes were, perhaps, negative ones— he had not dishonored himself, his office, or his country: he had not led the nation into war; he had not made the kinds of blunders that precipitated a crisis, at home or abroad. Given the history of what had gone before, these were significant by themselves. The ethical tone remained high. Lance notwithstanding, his administration had not been sullied by the kinds of cronyism and corruption that had occurred during the Truman and Nixon administrations. His closest aides may not have been the wisest and most experienced of counselors, but they were refreshingly free of self-importance and hunger for power; to an unusual degree they kept a sense of humor and wore their titles well. And it could not be said the president had failed to tackle the great issues; he was no reclusive Coolidge. He had brought many excellent people, many of them young, into government, and notably among the regulatory agencies. Overall, the quality of his appointments was outstanding. He had proven much less stubborn than expected, and he seldom let ideology get in the way of cool appraisal of facts. Christianity shaped his values and his beliefs, certainly, but he was no prayer-spouting, Bible-thumping, simpleminded fundamentalist in the White House. His religious convictions were normally separated from his temporal dealings.

Yet Carter received credit for almost nothing. By the middle of 1979 any public praise of him was so rare as to be noteworthy. Philip Geyelin, editorial-page editor of *The Washington Post* and a Pulitzer Prize winner who had written a book on Lyndon Johnson's foreign policy, began studying Carter's foreign affairs record, and, on June 10 in an appraisal with which I, for one, agreed, wrote:

> By about this time in his presidency, Dwight Eisenhower had approved CIA-supported coups in Iran and Guatemala. John Kennedy had bungled the Bay of Pigs and so misrepresented his will and resolve to Nikita Khrushchev that we had, in quick and frightening succession, a Berlin crisis and Soviet missiles in Cuba. Lyndon Johnson had dispatched combat troops to South Vietnam and the Dominican Republic, dealt inconclusively with riots in Panama, intervened in the Chilean elections by not-so-covert CIA activity, begun bombing North Vietnam. Richard Nixon had widened the Vietnam war to Cambodia and Laos. Gerald Ford had suffered 40 U.S. Marine casualties, directly or indirectly, in order to rescue about an equal number of crewmen from the *Mayaguez*. Saigon had fallen; the frantic American evacuation was a humiliation.
> And Jimmy Carter?

To begin with, no war, no military involvements and, so far as we can tell, no abortive, covert CIA activities. And on the plus side, in terms of his purposes if not necessarily everybody's, a Panama Canal treaty that four predecessors tried unsuccessfully to achieve. Similarly, the lifting of the Turkish arms embargo does not pave the way, necessarily, for a settlement, but it does remove an insurmountable obstacle, and Carter fought that issue successfully in Congress, as well. I am not going to get into the interstices of SALT II, but here again Carter has brought to fruition a diplomatic enterprise that eluded his immediate predecessors. And he did the hardest part of normalizing relations with China, on terms Congress accepted—and this time the Chinese came to see us. Finally, in the Mideast, Carter [achieved] far and away the most substantial advance in the direction of a comprehensive Mideast settlement in the entire thirty-one year history of the Arab-Israeli conflict.

Yet even Geyelin felt constrained to explain his praise. "If this is beginning to sound like an apology, so be it," he wrote. "It is intended as a balancing of the account."

The domestic side of Carter's ledger was less favorable. An energy bill finally had passed, but only after what was probably the most laborious and heated lobbying in U.S. history drawn out over eighteen long months. In the hours just before dawn, on Sunday, October 15, 1978, the last day of the 95th Congress, the National Energy Act of 1978 became reality when House members passed the bill which their Senate colleagues had approved only hours earlier; but the legislation that made its way back to the president's desk bore little resemblance to what Jimmy Carter had first proposed. The energy bill had been compromised, truncated, and altered dramatically: its heart—taxes on crude oil and on industrial use of oil—had been cut out. Originally, the bill contained four separate systems of tax and rebate, put together in so tangled a fashion that even veteran legislators were aghast at its complexity. By the time the lobbyists and special-interest groups were through, the gas tax had disappeared in the House and the other three taxes (on crude oil, industrial use of gas and oil, and inefficient cars) had vanished in the Senate. By the most generous estimate, Carter had got about half of what he had wanted. After he signed the act three weeks later, he said, almost plaintively: "I have not given up on my original proposal that there should be some constraint on consumption, and thus on oil imports." But there was a bill, and for the first time the United States had taken a tentative step toward making a national commitment to conserve its energy.

The other great domestic item on the president's agenda, the drive to reorganize the government, a central theme of Carter's 1976 campaign, had become an issue scarcely perceived by the general public; but progress *had* been made in government reform. The civil-service system had been scrapped, and although it would take years to see how effectively the new personnel management worked, the changes already were the most sweeping in almost a century. Reduced paperwork was being encouraged diligently, and efforts to make the governmental legal and regulatory processes more open *and* less formal were under way. A new system of independent inspector generals had been created which unquestionably would help police mismanagement scandals such as those that had occurred at the General Services Administration. On balance, probably more had been accomplished inside government than at any time since the Hoover Commission reforms of a generation ago. But the record of change in no way matched the president's goals or the public expectations, and the Carter people knew it. "It's not very sexy," observed one of them ruefully, who had worked full time on government reorganization. "It's clearly not what people expected when they listened to the campaign."

Lack of success clearly wasn't all Jimmy Carter's fault. Party loyalty, discipline, and power had eroded even further during his tenure. The new Congress elected in 1978 brought more new faces and new attitudes: half of the members had served less than five years, a figure unmatched since the days of the Founding Fathers. An ugly air of negativism, powerful and destructive, prevailed. Being a disbeliever was so fashionable it was becoming even more difficult to convince people that government had done positive things in the past, was more necessary in the present, and would have an indispensable role in the future. Cut back, dismantle, and reduce were the political order of the day, as the antigovernment mood he had appealed to during his own campaign inspired new groups organized nationally to advocate cutting property taxes, limiting government spending by constitutional amendment, and altering the existing governmental structure by calling for the first constitutional convention since the one that originally adopted the Constitution in 1787.

Ideologically, the nation was in a state of transition. But to what? The old certainties had crumbled. The new consensus had not formed. Ambiguity reigned. Everything was complex. No true causes remained. Cries for leadership were continually heard, but no one was certain where the leader was to lead. Or, once there, if it had been the correct course. Sail against the wind, Edward Kennedy urged. Perhaps that was what the people wanted, although they and their representatives were reacting differently: they were retrenching, withdrawing, following the safe route. Affixing blame was easy, though; it was all the president's doing. *He* hadn't solved the problems.

But that begged the question, and the question, in the end, was personal. It was the riddle of the priest, the president, Jimmy Carter himself, that had to be answered.

A veteran of government service, who had held high rank in both the Ford and Carter administrations, reflected on what had gone wrong for Carter in a conversation we had in mid-1979. "It struck me the other day that there's an interesting contrast to be drawn between Ford's administration and Carter's," he said. "Both suffered from an inability to communicate a sense of direction, priority, purpose, goals, strategy—but for very different reasons. Ford operated by what I used to call the rosary-bead method—problems went through his hand like somebody saying his beads: one problem was the same size and shape as another, and he took them in the order in which they were strung. This was an approach he evolved over years as a congressman, especially as minority leader. Carter's problem is the problem of a person who had a clear sense of the importance of preserving his diet, but who gets to the smorgasbord and just can't resist eating everything. What might have been his strategy or set of priorities is overwhelmed by his eagerness to do many, many things."

Carter's young chief speechwriter, James Fallows, was similarly disturbed. Fallows resigned at the end of 1978, and we talked at length then about what he thought of the Carter White House and

Carter himself.* There was a good reason why Carter had failed to inspire people as president, Fallows believed. Carter didn't want to alter his speaking style: they had talked about that "a million times." The president wasn't going to change himself. But that was only the surface problem. The main reason had to do with personal conviction, with philosophy, ideology, or their lack. And in Fallows' view, Carter had no coherent political philosophy. "You can't inspire people with a jigsaw puzzle," he said. "You have to tell them what you want them to do, and say, 'This is where we're going.' And you can't say where you're going in this administration. That's why there's all this floundering around trying to find a theme."

Fallows was a young aide without previous government experience and little exposure to politics. Yet his criticisms were shared by many people with national political experience. On Capitol Hill, a Democrat, himself a presidential prospect, who felt he had a good fix on the strengths and weaknesses of Carter, said to me,

Jimmy Carter is an engineer without deep philosophic roots, and that explains a lot. If you're Hubert Humphrey or Franklin Roosevelt or Harry Truman—or even Jerry Ford—you develop certain basic feelings and beliefs. They're part of you. Nobody had to ask how they were going to come down on the issues. Nobody had to ask Hubert Humphrey how he was going to come down on civil rights or education or health—you knew damned well. Carter is one of those super-achiever types you see in any high school—very intelligent, very ambitious. His whole life, its strong points and its weak points, revolves around this. He's a quick study. He's got a good mind. He absorbs information as quickly as anybody I've ever seen. But he's also the engineer who wants a comprehensive solution.

I remember when Carl Albert [House majority leader from 1962 to 1971 and then, for five years, Speaker] had a wall with sixty pens on it that Lyndon Johnson had given to him after signing bills. LBJ didn't say, "I have a comprehensive Great Society program—pass it all in one bill." Shit, he'd send up a cancer bill today, and an aid-to-education bill tomorrow, and an arts-and-humanities bill the next

---

*Later, in successive issues of the *Atlantic Monthly* in May and June 1979, Fallows wrote a critical, incisive, and careful analysis of the president and his administration.

day, and a poverty program the next. Some got passed immediately, some got watered down, some got defeated. But at the end, the mosaic of those pens was the Great Society. It was the same as Franklin Roosevelt with the New Deal. They were masters at sending up those bills. And they overlapped. They weren't neat and comprehensive, which is what Carter wants.

Presidents are largely creatures of their time. In the long run, they're judged at most by half a dozen things. You don't remember everything Franklin Roosevelt did. Carter started out with a zero-defects concept. He was going to read all the papers in all the departments, and then make all the changes. His campaign promises were sacred covenants, while other presidents view their political promises as political bullshit. I think he took seriously this idea that his cabinet was going to be different from others—yet it's just like any other. A president must learn to concentrate on a few basic things, and that has been a real problem for Carter.

Criticizing Carter was simple enough—and certainly done often enough in Washington. The idea of improving an administration by giving cabinet officers more autonomy, for instance, was nearly unanimously regarded as foolish. The most difficult problems of government were not those that a single cabinet officer could resolve, but those requiring recognition of an entire set of considerations that went beyond any one, or several, cabinet departments. The presidential problem was to devise a mechanism to identify those issues, to sort them out, decide where they should be funneled—which went into the Office of Management and Budget, which into what areas of the White House staff, which into intelligence, and, finally, which ones, and only the *toughest*, actually went to the president's desk. That meant congregating within the White House and in the cabinet the most capable, knowledgeable, experienced group one could find. And that meant a true staff director to insure that the mechanism worked, that the priorities were maintained, and that, once made, decisions were carried out.

The cabinet had not worked, as Carter had hoped, nor had his own staff ever really performed as crisply as he needed. It continued to lack strong central direction. Gifted people worked for the president, but the White House remained thin on experience, and often equally so on talent. "There is no way you can say, 'Why not the best?' without a horse laugh about the staff there," Fallows said to me in his conversation. "If you ask whether anybody there is absolutely the best suited to do the job, the answer is ninety-nine percent likely to be 'no.' Most people are competent, only a few are galling incompetents, but you can think of someone who would be better in almost any job—not because they are Georgian, but because they are not all so able or so experienced as they should be."

This harsh judgment was shared by others in the White House. As one person there said, for a variety of reasons the president had not brought in experienced people, "and we paid a terrible price for it." Another observed: "I simply don't find the president enlarging his confidence in very many people. My impression is that of a man who is quite bright, who does a lot of reaching out for pieces of information and viewpoints, but then keeps his own counsel with a very small group of people. The president feels, as many of us do, that he can do it better than anybody else, and he finds it hard to hand over something to somebody and say, 'It's yours.' Nobody I know of has broken through that circle around him. What's it all come to? Here's a man who's capable and strong in his own right, but he has not enlarged his own capabilities by using other people well."

By 1979 people began wondering if the president's refusal to change the basic cadre of Georgians around him didn't express a basic insecurity on his part, an underlying fear of surrounding himself with independent, experienced advisers. One of his aides had another view, which he shared with me: "He is measuring himself by internal standards so high and strict he'll never meet them," he said of Carter. "They'll always fall short, and that's what determines his outlook and attitude. He is always feeling sinful, falling short of the ideal standard. It's not a good public personality." Perhaps this was closer to the mark, for Carter himself, in a revealing remark to Bill Moyers at the end of 1978, had expressed this frustration: "I feel my life now is one massive multiple-choice examination, where things are put in front of me and I have to make the difficult choice." Yet his insistence upon the rightness of his decisions and his stress on the difficulties of his work hinted at some sort of underlying insecurity.

Whatever Carter did, it wasn't working—or was said not to be working. Washingtonians wanted him to be more like a traditional

politician, an operator and manipulator, a Lyndon Johnson, for-
getting that the country had elected him precisely because he
seemed different from that. And Carter tried to accommodate
both expectations, employing the skills of both the outsider and
the insider. But it didn't quite come off, more for personal than
political reasons. Carter's distance, what was taken to be his aloof-
ness, now became another Washington cliché, and, like all clichés,
it became more confirmed as truth the more it was told. In interviewing for this book, I found a number of people who had been
storing up impressions about Jimmy Carter that by 1979, in the
season of despair about his leadership, they were anxious to share.

A congressman went to a White House state dinner for a visiting
Arab potentate, and showed me the impressions he had jotted
down of the president: "He's very much in command, but has a
withdrawn way about him that is vaguely troubling. He's all very
much business. When the dinner came to a close, he walked out
without showing the camaraderie that one learns to expect from
political types. He just doesn't have the traditional politician's
need for the warm kind of personal bond you feel with people you
work with a lot. This may explain why he doesn't have close
friends."

At the House of Labor, the white marble AFL-CIO headquarters overlooking Lafayette Park and the White House, it was said
over and over that the old man, George Meany, had complained
that talking to Carter wasn't like talking to other presidents. "Carter listens. Period," someone said. He then recalled an example,
from Carter's second year, which they often cited to themselves:

One day Meany was invited to lunch with the president. He was
delighted, for he thought it would be an opportunity for a serious
talk. When he came back, he told his labor aides that it had been
nothing but a pleasant social luncheon upstairs with the President
and Mrs. Carter. He was not impressed, and said so. Going to the
White House to see presidents was old hat to him; he wanted to
have a direct exchange of views.

When the two men did have a serious exchange, however, the
outcome wasn't always productive, sometimes hostile. For example, the president had called the labor leaders into the White
House on May 10, 1978, to urge them to support his wage and
price guidelines to keep down inflation. Already, the union people

had told the White House people they could not pledge to keep down wages, as Carter wished, and their individual member unions would have to make that decision. Nonetheless, the president repeated his plea to hold down national wage-contract demands. Carter "finished his little sermon to us, and started to leave," said one labor official who was there. But Meany spoke up. He'd appreciate it if the president stayed because he had something to tell him: organized labor *could not go along* with his request. The president should do his best to keep prices down, and they would do their best to keep wages down. But they could not and would not *promise* anything.

"You could see the president's face throughout this," the labor official said. "When Meany said he wanted to speak, Carter was a little cloudy. Then his face got progressively colder. When George finished, Carter got up and said, 'Well, I hope you'll stay and talk with these men [his aides]. They've got a number of things they want to discuss with you. I'll only say this: I won't condemn you. But if you make that statement publicly the press will condemn you as a man who is trying to kill the effort to stop inflation.' With which he shook hands with everybody and walked out of the room."

This was a very typical encounter. Surely no president had been addressed so bluntly, so critically, (and sometimes disrespectfully) so often as he. "It got to be kind of the 'in' thing to tell him off," one congressional leader observed. But Carter rarely showed anger or emotion; when he dressed down a cabinet officer one day in the dark year of 1979, the story quickly passed to other cabinet officers because it was so unusual. He showed none of the famed Eisenhower explosions of temper, or the bawdy profanity of John Kennedy. Only once in public had he shown a flash of real anger: that came during a press conference on July 13, 1977, when he was asked whether it was fair for women who could not afford abortions to be denied federal funds for them, while wealthy women continued to obtain them when they wanted. (The question came several days after the Supreme Court had ruled, 6 to 3, that neither the Constitution nor federal law required cities and towns that had public hospitals to spend Medicaid tax money for abortions.) With Carter's blue eyes turning icy and his face freezing, he snapped, "Well, as you know, there are many things in life that are

not fair, that wealthy people can afford and poor people can't."
(Why Carter responded with such fury remains pure speculation,
but it struck me then, and later, that he resented any suggestion
that he was partial to the rich—and, in fact, I can find nothing in
his record or his behavior to indicate he ever courted the wealthy
and powerful at the expense of "ordinary" people.)

His wife said he didn't let criticism bother him. What concerned
him was that he do what was right. "He doesn't make snap judgments," she said. "People accused him of that in the campaign,
but he does not do that. He reads and he studies and he consults
with all sides and then he finally decides. . . . I don't know how you
decide what's right except that you study and you make a decision
based on what you learn and what other people think." But obviously Carter and his wife—and their political partnership was un-
precedentedly close—reacted to the mounting criticism, she often
more strongly than he. "They won't give us credit for anything,"
she said in the spring of 1979, when citing how the polls had
dropped—even after her husband's successful Middle East trip
that ended thirty years of war between Israel and Egypt.

Still, Carter didn't show any of the bluster and rage of an LBJ or
a Nixon. In private as in public, he was courteous, gracious, and
self-possessed. "It may well be that his incredible self-possession
is as much a liability as his meticulousness is," an administration
official said. Whatever disappointments he felt remained private.
On at least two occasions he had been hurt deeply—over Bert
Lance and over the breakup of his son Chip's marriage—but he
never let it show.

"Carter does good things badly," an administration official told
Don Oberdorfer of *The Washington Post* early in his presidency. It
was—and is—a devastating assessment. But the assessments grew
even harsher. By mid-1979, when Carter the populist seemed to
have been supplanted by Carter the conservative, he was referred
to disparagingly as a Democratic Coolidge: like Coolidge, he was
personally thrifty, a close watcher of his and the nation's money
(he charged even his closest advisers for the breakfasts they ate
with him in the White House). But there the resemblance ended,
for he was at least as much a progressive as a conservative—if indeed those terms could be said still to have any political relevance.
Some people found Woodrow Wilson a closer parallel with Carter

the Southerner, the Christian, the highly intelligent student, the political moralist who sincerely wished to do "right" in the best interests of the country. Arthur Link, the noted American historian and editor of Wilson's papers, drew the lines sharply:

> Carter I would call a managerial type: He believes that all problems can be solved by intelligence. He was educated as an engineer, and he clearly believes that when a difficult problem arises, you sit down and solve it. Carter is not widely read in history, political science, the social sciences, literature, the humanities, as Wilson was. The comparison is not entirely fair, though, because Wilson was the best-educated president we have ever had, except perhaps for Jefferson and Madison. . . .
>
> Carter is unable to communicate great ideas and to formulate great programs in language that will capture the hearts and inspire the minds of the people, as Wilson could. Carter can say the most important things in the dullest way, particularly in public addresses. He is much better in unrehearsed encounters, press conferences and the like. But on the whole, he has so far a miserable public style. I want to emphasize that I have enormous respect for Carter as a man, but I do feel that his leadership so far has been inept; he has not been able to rally the country.
>
> Wilson, by contrast, along with his great knowledge, had an unparalleled grasp of the English language. He could change history through rhetoric. He was probably the greatest orator since Edmund Burke. The majesty of his prose could and did rally people to a cause . . . and he had a very warm working relationship with Congress.*

Wilson—like Lincoln, or the Roosevelts, or Truman, or Johnson, among strong American presidents—was successful in large part because he was a skillful politician. These men studied the process, understood it, mastered it, employed its techniques, and grew in stature and success. *They enjoyed politics.* Jimmy Carter gave the impression that he found politics ignoble and the practice of it faintly distasteful. This was a common American view—"They're all crooks, you can't trust any of them"—become more pronounced in recent years. Yet, as J. William Fulbright said in 1943, his first year in Congress: "It is a mistake to sneer at the word 'politician.' In fact, we should accord to the word great respect

---

* From an interview published by *The Princeton Alumni Weekly,* September 25, 1978.

and honor. We should transfer to the politicians some of the honor and reverence which we have so generously bestowed upon the Lindberghs, the Fords, the Edisons, the Morgans, and the Babe Ruths." What Fulbright meant was that chemistry, banking, engineering, or manufacturing were, as he said, "child's play compared to the science or art of government." Scientists can control their methods or subject matter; politicians must deal with personalities, issues, and events they cannot always control.

Carter is an excellent politician, his top aides would maintain. Given his remarkable run for the presidency, they were right. At the same time, they would say, Carter took almost perverse delight in not being political.

"He will always look better from a distance than close up," one of his senior aides told me in May 1979. "He came here to be a good president, not a popular one." The great challenge of his presidency was a moral challenge—whether he could point the country in a different direction, whether he could establish a different tone so that democracy could continue to function. "Twenty years from now people may say his greatest achievement was the Middle East peace settlement," the aide remarked. "I would hope it would be said that he created a different political dynamic in a country in a time of trouble." The question was: Could a president like Carter confront the big issues and show results?

But in the difficult spring of 1979, as conditions continued to deteriorate and the public mood grew angrier, that outcome appeared doubtful. The question was now, no matter what action he took could Carter possibly survive?

□   □   □

The president's schedule called for two foreign trips in mid-June 1979—to Vienna to sign the Strategic Arms Limitation Treaty, and then to Tokyo for an economic summit meeting. His trips came at a time when he was privately musing about the country's declining confidence in the future, and, judging from the attitudes he encountered among other national leaders, Americans were not alone in their pessimism.

From Carter's discussions with Brezhnev and other Soviet officials in Vienna it appeared that in Russia, too, a general malaise existed. An increasing fragmentation of society, compounded by growing energy shortages and sharpening conflicts over ethical and moral standards, led to rising competition among citizens for use of the limited supplies of natural resources.

Days later, in Tokyo, as the leaders of Japan, Germany, Great Britain, France, Italy, the United States, and Canada met, this global crisis worsened when news came of another serious blow from OPEC. The oil-producing countries again dramatically raised prices on crude oil. Figures given the president to measure the effect of this latest increase on the United States showed it would cost a million jobs due to unemployment layoffs and raise the inflation rate some $2\frac{1}{2}$ percent within a year. Already the OPEC nations were threatening to pull out their vast investments in Western economies—as a retribution for the peace drawn up between Israel and Egypt—and every Western leader recognized how vulnerable his nation was and realistically how little any of them could do about it. OPEC had the power to incapacitate Japan, Italy, and France, each of which imported nearly all of its energy sources.

At home in America, the political situation worsened overnight. Gas lines grew across the country, and with them came explosions of anger, frustration, and disbelief about this latest energy "crisis." (The newest gasoline shortages came at a bad moment, as a strike of some thirty-thousand independent truck drivers shut off the delivery of produce and other goods from California, Texas, Florida, South Carolina, and other states, threatening urban food shortages and driving up costs everywhere. The administration had attempted to respond to the truckers' demands by making available more diesel fuel, but still the strike continued.) The political firestorm sweeping the country threatened to remove the last vestiges of public goodwill for Jimmy Carter. The polls showed Carter's standing had dropped to an approval rating of only 25 percent—lower than Nixon's just before his resignation, lower than *any* president's fortunes ever recorded.

Pat Caddell sent the president an urgent message in Tokyo: he had to return swiftly and address the political conditions at home.

And on June 28, Stuart Eizenstat, the White House domestic affairs chief, sent the president an unusually blunt memorandum:

> Since you left for Japan, the domestic energy problem has contin-
> ued to worsen:
>
> □ The actions taken to help the truckers have not yet broken the
> back of the strike. Jack [Watson, secretary of the Cabinet] and I are
> continuing to review the problem. As you know, the vice-president
> will today announce a series of actions to help improve the situa-
> tion.
>
> □ Gas lines are growing throughout the Northeast and are
> spreading to the Mideast.
>
> □ Sporadic violence over gasoline continues to occur. A recent
> incident in Pennsylvania injured 40.
>
> □ Gasoline station operators are threatening a nationwide strike
> unless DOE [Department of Energy] grants an emergency profit
> margin increase.
>
> □ The latest CPI [Consumer Price Index] figures have demon-
> strated how substantially energy is affecting inflation—gasoline
> prices have risen 55% since January.
>
> □ Congress is growing more nervous by the day over the energy
> problem. The Moorhead Bill [to explore formally the feasibility of
> producing synthetic fuels] was pushed through the House yester-
> day, so members could go home for the recess claiming to have
> done something about the problem. It is fair to say that in normal
> times, a bill as significant as Moorhead's would have been consid-
> ered much more carefully. Despite that vote, and the forthcoming
> vote on Thursday on the windfall tax, members are literally afraid
> to go home over the recess, for fear of having to deal with very an-
> gry constituents. That fear was expressed to the vice-president and
> me yesterday when we briefed members on the Tokyo summit.
> They were almost completely uninterested in the summit, and spent
> all of two hours talking about gasoline and related problems.
>
> □ Press accounts are starting to appear about the administration's
> inability to deliver on the commitment to have 240 million barrels
> of distillate in stock by October [a pledge the administration had
> made to Northeastern governors to assure an adequate supply of

home heating oil for the winter]. The Northeast will soon be pressuring us to clarify whether we still believe 240 is possible.

□ The continuing problem of conflicting signals and numbers from DOE persists. The DOE gasoline allocation formulas are now coming under particularly heavy attack. Yesterday, the state of Maryland sued DOE for misallocating gasoline. Other states can be expected to shortly follow that politically popular route.

In sum, we have a worsening short-term domestic energy crisis, and I do not expect to see (with the possible exception of a break in the truckers' strike) any improvement by the time you return.

Eizenstat's assessment was unsparing:

I do not need to detail for you the political damage we are suffering from all of this. It is perhaps sufficient to say that nothing which has occurred in the administration to date—not the Soviet agreement on the Middle East [to hold a joint conference in Geneva, a move roundly criticized and then dropped in the early months of the administration], not the Lance matter, not the Panama Canal treaties, not the defeat of several major domestic legislative proposals, not the sparring with Kennedy, and not even double-digit inflation—have added so much water to our ship. Nothing else has so frustrated, confused, angered the American people—or so targeted their distress at you personally, as opposed to your advisers, or Congress or outside interests. Mayor Koch [of New York] indicated to me (during a meeting the vice-president and I had with the New York congressional delegation on their gas problems) he had not witnessed anything to compare to the current emotion in American political life since Vietnam.

While the Vietnam analogy is a strained one in many ways, it is one which this week press accounts are beginning to make. The similarities between problems of credibility and political opposition from the left are real, though clearly undeserved. We can expect to see repetition in coming weeks of the analogy, which was prevalent at the ADA [Americans for Democratic Action] convention I addressed over the weekend.

All of this is occurring at a particularly inopportune time. Inflation is higher than ever. A recession is clearly facing us. (Indeed, when our July budget forecast comes out with a zero GNP [Gross National Product] estimate we should not attempt to avoid the obvious, as Ford tried to do, but we should be honest and admit a recession is likely.) OPEC is raising prices once again. The polls are lower than they have ever been. (The latest Harris poll shows something never before seen—a Republican opponent, Reagan, leading you by several points.) Kennedy's popularity appears at a peak. And the Congress seems completely beyond anyone's control.

In many respects, this would appear to be the worst of times.

But it didn't have to be that way, Eizenstat concluded; it was also a time of political opportunity, perhaps the last, at this late hour, that could come to Jimmy Carter. He proposed that Carter shift the blame for inflation and energy problems to OPEC, thus enabling Carter himself, in Eizenstat's words, "to gain credibility with the American people, to offer hope of an eventual solution, to regain our political losses." The memo spelled out steps the president should take—cut short, or eliminate entirely, his planned vacation over the Fourth of July in Hawaii on the way back to Washington from Japan; issue a "tough statement" attacking the OPEC cartel, which would buy time before giving the country more specifics for action; hold a series of White House meetings with energy experts and political advisers, and then go to Camp David to prepare a report to the nation, in part "to demonstrate your continuing commitment to solving this problem": every day deal with "and publicly be seen as dealing with" the major energy problems. The two or three weeks after his return from Japan were crucial, Eizenstat believed: if the president's attention to energy wasn't total during that time, he would be unable to stem the tide of events, or "convince the American people that we now have a firmer grasp on the problem than they now perceive." Strong action around a real crisis and singling out a "clear enemy"—OPEC—could mobilize the nation and restore Carter's prospects for political leadership.

Carter followed the script. He canceled his Hawaii vacation, issued the tough statement in Tokyo attacking OPEC, flew directly back to Washington, and immediately plunged into a round of highly publicized White House meetings on energy. Then he left for Camp David after announcing he would deliver a major televised address to the nation on Thursday night, July 5.

Once again, Jimmy and Rosalynn Carter went off to Camp David, and once again without consulting any aides or advisers, the two of them together made a fateful decision for the presidency and set in motion events that might either extricate Carter from his political problems or quite possibly destroy him.

The president and his wife were alone in the living room of their cabin early in the afternoon of the Fourth of July. Carter was about to start work on his speech, and the draft text from his speechwriters lay on the coffee table. He asked Rosalynn to look at it and see what she thought. Mrs. Carter picked it up and began to read. There was nothing wrong with the speech as a speech, she finally said, but who would listen to it when he gave it? It was just another speech. They began to discuss the subject that had been at the center of their concern since their private sessions with selected guests and advisers earlier in the spring—how to reach the public at a time of growing cynicism and preoccupation with self, how to convince people that a genuine energy crisis did exist, and how to persuade them to alter their lives in ways that ran contrary to all their experience and attitudes. They also had with them another Caddell memo, this the longest of all, completed while they were in Tokyo, urging a breakthrough in the way Carter conducted his presidency.

Carter himself was convinced of three things: that the basic proposals he was prepared to announce—calling for a major national effort to produce synthetic fuels in the next decades—could succeed in diminishing American dependence on foreign oil; but that given the fact that with each of his previous energy speeches the television-viewing audience had declined, it was highly unlikely many people would listen to him; and that it was quite likely Congress would see his latest proposals as merely another attempt to put himself in competition with them, thus leading to new difficulties with the Hill. But more important to himself and to his wife was his belief that the drafted speech didn't address the larger issues about growing pessimism and willingness to sacrifice for the national good.

The more the Carters talked, the stronger their conviction became that this planned approach and prepared speech would not work. It was the wrong way and the wrong time. He decided to cancel the July 5 speech, seize the moment to dramatize the present energy threat, and build a national consensus for action.

Instead of merely producing another package of legislative proposals, once again he would use Camp David as a symbolic means
to broaden the scope of his message. He would convene another
Camp David summit meeting—Camp David III, really, coming
after Camp David I with his cabinet and staff in April 1978, and
Camp David II, the celebrated days with Begin and Sadat—with a
wide range of national leaders who would meet privately with him
on the mountain. That way, whatever evolved after consultation
with members of Congress, governors, mayors, economists, representatives of religious, educational, and other citizens' groups
would be seen as a *national* effort, not just as Carter's. In Carter's
mind, the energy issue could be the device to restore American
confidence in the future, heal some of the wounds that remained
from the divisive Vietnam-Watergate years, and develop common
resolve to attack complex problems going beyond energy itself.

It was a bold move, and it was probably Jimmy Carter's last
chance to save his presidency and restore some of the power and
prestige of his office. Failure almost certainly would make him the
fifth straight president unable to survive in office.

Given these circumstances, the manner in which Carter carried
out his great gamble was extraordinary. Other than his wife, he
didn't consult with anyone on the steps he was about to take.
About three o'clock that afternoon, a sultry, overcast holiday when
the life of the capital had stilled and its governmental leaders were
scattered, Carter picked up the phone in his Camp David cabin
and instructed the operator to get him Vice-President Mondale,
Hamilton Jordan, Jody Powell, and Gerald Rafshoon on a conference call. The operator reached all but Powell, who was out
buying a watermelon for his children to eat during their July 4
celebration later in the day. Carter told the three men he was canceling his speech. He didn't yet have a clear idea of what he wanted to say to the public and what form the new Camp David summit
would take, but he was certain it would be useless to go through
with the speech as planned.

No explanation was given in public for the president's cancellation. He had instructed his aides to say nothing. This abruptness
created consternation in Washington and, after the press reported
the mysterious nature of the way it had been handled, in the coun-

try. Inevitably, speculation about a major White House crisis, or even personal illness, spread. (Later Carter conceded that if he had to do it over again he would have accompanied the cancellation with a clear explanation of why and a brief word about the process he was about to start at Camp David.) Again, the president had compounded his problems by his own actions; it was reminiscent of the way he had handled the first energy proposals early in his presidency—keeping everything close to himself and then acting suddenly and catching even top aides by surprise.

The reaction was worldwide: the dollar declined on international money markets the next day and the price of gold rose, setting off more concern about instability at the head of the American government. Finally, after urgings by such people as Treasury Secretary Michael Blumenthal, the White House issued a brief reassuring statement. The president was well, he was in charge, and he would be giving the nation a detailed report later not only about energy but about questions going beyond it.

On July 5 Carter brought the key members of his staff up to the Catoctins to work out a schedule of whom to invite to Camp David and when. He also set out to build a larger national audience for the speech he would eventually deliver. Each day helicopters left the White House lawn carrying new visitors to confer with the president, and each day his press secretary refused to explain what was taking place—other than to say Carter was examining the energy question in "a broader context" than previously studied. And each day as visitors returned from the mountain they told waiting reporters tidbits of the mysterious events taking place in secrecy. The president was described as listening patiently, both he and his wife taking notes on yellow pads, encouraging those present to give frank opinions on what actions should be taken.

As planned, the so-called Camp David "domestic summit" came to have a life of its own: the longer the silence from Carter, the greater the suspense; the more people consulted, whether in or out of government, the greater the public anticipation of the final result. This was political stage-managing on an unprecedented scale. Carter had the country's attention now; this time, he would be heard.

Carter hoped his speech might, as he put it at Camp David, re-

vive the spirits of America. Caddell's polls earlier that spring,
showing growing pessimism over the future, plus what he had
learned on his foreign trips had convinced him of a fundamental
change in national attitudes. Whether he was correct about this
was something else, however; I was only one of the people present
when he discussed these alleged gloomy new trends and wondered aloud what to do about them; but it seemed to me then
there was little that was new in the attitudes he had "discovered."
Public pessimism had been around for years, and it was based on
quite specific causes, not just a general "malaise of the spirit" as
the president described it. The Vietnam war and the Watergate
scandal and the failings of government were facts, just as the long
gas lines and rising prices were facts. What citizens were looking
for, it seemed to me, were specific actions taken by their president
to cope with very real problems.

But Carter certainly was correct in one respect: prior to Camp
David, he wasn't being listened to, or heard. Already that spring
he had tried to express some of his convictions, and the substance
of his message was hardly reported. A speech he had made at the
end of May before the Democratic National Committee in Washington had shown a marked departure in tone and theme for him.
He said then, reflecting some of Caddell's themes:

> The American people are disturbed, the American people are
> doubtful, the American people are uncertain about the future, the
> American people do not have automatic trust in you or me or other
> Democratic officials.
>
> Too many Americans today are watching the spectacle of politi-
> cians grappling with the complex problems, for instance, of energy
> and inflation. They see the demagoguery and they see political tim-
> idity and they wonder if we who are in office are equal to the chal-
> lenge.
>
> The American people are looking to us for honest answers, not
> false claims, not evasiveness, not politics as usual. But they look to
> us for clear leadership; for they often see here in Washington and
> elsewhere around the country a system of government which we
> love and which we are sworn to protect which seems incapable of
> action; they see a Congress twisted and pulled in every direction by
> hundreds of well-financed and powerful special interests. They see
> every extreme position imaginable, defended to the last breath, al-

most, to the last vote, by one unyielding powerful group or another.

They often see the balanced and fair approach that demands sacrifice, a little sacrifice from everyone, abandoned like an orphan without support and without friends. Often they see paralysis, stagnation, and drift. The American people don't like it and neither do I.

This country was not founded by people who said, "Me first, me last and always." We have not prevailed as a free people in the face of a challenge and crisis for more than two centuries by practicing the politics of selfishness. We have not continually enlarged individual liberty, freedom, responsibility, opportunity, human dignity for all the people by listening to the voices of those who say, "We must have one hundred percent now or nothing, and I will not listen to other voices who are seeking a common goal for our country. . . ."

The question today is not whether government reaches solutions which any of us support one hundred percent. The question is whether government, on these extremely difficult questions, can reach any acceptable solution at all. The issue is not one of political philosophies, but a failure of will and a failure of the political process itself.

These were unusual things for a president to address, and acknowledge, but they had made virtually no impact on the press or public.

Six weeks later, by the time of the Camp David summit, he said he believed the United States had reached a turning point in its economic and social history. Could Americans find the strength and ability to solve this highly publicized and specific problem—energy—and, through a marshaling of the national will, work together to solve even larger problems: lack of trust in government and institutions, lack of faith in the future? That was what he was going to try to talk about when he spoke to the nation on Sunday night, July 15.

On the eve of his speech, in a long "background" conversation with a group of journalists flown to Camp David, Carter conceded he might fail in arousing public support for his new proposals. He also was unrelenting in criticizing his own failures as president: he acknowledged he had not done as good a job as he should in governing the people. He had not stayed as close to the people. He knew he needed to present his programs more clearly and effectively, and he needed to make some basic changes in the structure of his cabinet and White House staff. Whatever the outcome of his own effort, he had no doubt the energy problems would grow worse, year by year. By the year 2000 Americans would be experiencing a lower standard of living. There would have to be a reduction in the amount of energy they used, and that process would require a reorientation of what people valued most in their lives.

Sunday afternoon, several hours before Carter's speech, Caddell telephoned me to say he'd never seen anyone change so much as the president had during his ten days of soul-searching at Camp David: the president recognized past weaknesses and had emerged from his self-examination stronger and more confident. This clearly self-serving view was repeated by others in Carter's inner circle. To Hamilton Jordan, Carter had come back to Washington from Camp David with a different attitude about his presidency and a different approach to government and governing. More than anything else, Jordan said, Carter's attitudes had changed. Perhaps so, and perhaps not.

Still, the president who spoke to the country that summer night obviously had worked at presenting himself in a more forceful manner. His delivery was brisker than usual, his pace faster, his gestures more assertive as he gave what amounted to a sermon on the new national approach to energy. The sermon involved what he called "a fundamental threat to American democracy, the erosion of our confidence in the future [which] is threatening to destroy the social and political fabric of America," he said, restating the theme he already had explored in his speech at the end of May. (Indeed, Carter's "crisis of confidence" speech repeated almost *verbatim* central passages of that earlier Washington address, a fact that went unnoticed in the lengthy commentary and analysis that followed.)

This curious address, a pastiche of old phrases and new themes with echoes of his campaign days ("Looking for a way out of this crisis, our people have turned to the federal government and found it isolated from the mainstream of our nation's life; Washington, D.C., has become an island"), judged merely as oratory was his most successful since he had accepted his party's nomination exactly three years before in Madison Square Garden. The general reaction to his speech, on Capitol Hill and in the press, was favorable. One opinion poll taken immediately after showed his popularity had risen by 9 percentage points. It was just possible Carter might have won his great gamble and gained public support for himself and his program. Sixty-five million people had watched him that night—more than double his last televised speech audience.

Aside from giving a general outline of his energy proposals— a limit on oil imports and a fixed goal to cut 4.5 million barrels a day from what the United States would be expected to import in 1990, establishment of a new corporation to spur production of oil and gas from coal and shale, and creation of an "energy mobilization unit" with authority to cut through the red tape in the construction of important energy projects— Carter left the specifics to be spelled out in the days ahead. The next day he went to Kansas City and Detroit and gave more details: the United States would spend $140 billion over the next decade to assure its independence from foreign energy sources. And again his speeches were well received.

Then, just as it appeared that the public was beginning to rally around Carter's new bid for leadership, once again his administration was shaken.

On Tuesday afternoon, July 17, immediately after the stock exchanges closed for the day, Jody Powell announced to the press that *all* the cabinet officers had offered the president their resignations, and, immediately following that, eighteen of Carter's senior White House assistants had also offered to resign. This astounding bulletin was unquestionably the most stunning White House news since the end of the Nixon days. Again, no explanations were given—only that the president was studying which resignations to accept, and that major governmental changes would be made.

In the next few tumultuous days, as once again the value of the dollar declined abroad and the price of gold soared to an all-time high and criticism of the president intensified, the serious purpose and tone set by Carter's Sunday speech dissipated. What was this inexplicable crisis in government? It was a shakeup, unparalleled in more than a century, for which no clear reasons were given, and those reasons that *were* advanced seemed to contradict Carter's presidential promises. Many within the White House were dis-

mayed by the sudden moves. Even so high an adviser as Stuart Eizenstat told me he knew nothing about the "mass resignations" of
the cabinet until after they had occurred.

Each day brought new evidence of turmoil, as changes were
made at the Treasury Department, the Health, Education and
Welfare Department, the Justice Department, the Housing and
Urban Development Department, the Transportation Department, the Federal Reserve Board. Each day the press reported
acrimonious accounts of internal controversy, and new gallows
political humor made the rounds. ("What do you do when Jimmy
Carter comes at you with a pin?" went one joke passed around the
House Democratic cloakroom. "You run like hell. He's got a grenade in his mouth.") Several cabinet officers reported that the
president in their presence had sternly administered a tongue-
lashing to United Nations Ambassador Andrew Young, accusing
Young of "crippling" his administration by his repeated controversial statements.* These and other reports were denounced on
the instruction of the president as untrue. There were even uglier
rumors, including intimations of lying: Publicly HEW's Joseph
Califano said the president had praised him for having done a superb job, perhaps the best in the department's history, even as he
fired him (a statement the White House strongly denied); privately, Califano told friends that Carter had said he would pray for
him, a statement which Califano, a devout Catholic, deeply resented.

Gone was the Carter celebration of cabinet-style government.
Gone, too, the spokes-of-the-wheel theory about equally important workers on the White House staff having equal access to the
president. Hamilton Jordan was now appointed White House chief
of staff, and he immediately handed cabinet members and top
Carter aides evaluation forms on which they were to give assessments of their highest-ranking assistants. Supposedly, many of
these administrative problems had been addressed at Camp David
II in April 1978. Now, it appeared, they had not.

---

* Four weeks later Young "resigned' (in fact, was fired) after he met privately with
Palestine Liberation Organization members against State Department policy and
after misleading department officials about that meeting. His departure touched
off nasty public exchanges between American Jews and blacks.

In his speech the president had given a broad hint of what was to come when he quoted someone as telling him at Camp David: "Some of your cabinet members don't seem loyal. There's not enough discipline among your disciples."

The effect of all this was to suggest that the president had placed political loyalty over independence and competence. Nothing on the record indicated that the officials he dismissed had been fired because they failed to manage their departments well, or failed to seek the best-qualified people to work for them. Tremors swept through the bureaus and agencies, exposing old fears about the federal work force being politicized by presidential fiat. Carter's promise to measure performance by the highest standard of excellence—Why not the best?—had been, it appeared, broken. In some of the departments, activity ground to a halt. It was months before the management teams serving the old officials were replaced and confirmed.

Within a week of the purge of his cabinet, Carter's popularity dropped even lower than it had been before his heralded speech: one poll showed him down 3 points in only seven days, and three weeks later Lou Harris, who had been John Kennedy's personal pollster in 1960, sent me what he called "rather drastic results from our latest polls" and was reporting to his national clients that

> President Carter's overall rating with Americans has dropped again to 74–25 percent negative, the lowest he has yet been accorded and the worst standing for any president in modern times. Even among Democrats, he comes up with a 68–31 percent negative rating. Basically, these results indicate that after all the Camp David meetings, the dramatic speech on Sunday, July 15, and the cabinet firings, he is back where he began—essentially a chief executive who is rejected by his ultimate constituency, the American people. . . . In his specific task of rebuilding confidence in himself as the national leader, he has struck out.

In Congress, the Democratic party leaders were openly critical, and in a matter of days George McGovern and Henry Jackson, representing ideologically opposite wings of the party, suggested it was time for Carter to abandon hope of a second term in favor of Edward Kennedy.

In the midst of the battering the president was taking, I spoke to one of the top officials in HEW. He felt, he said, "an overwhelming sense of sadness because of the waste—the waste of so many people who have worked so extraordinarily hard for thirty months." To me, it all seemed both sad and familiar. The hopes of the early summer, for a new start and new direction, were dissipated; the Congress—in what amounted to a gesture of contempt—failed to respond to any of the president's pleas on energy set forth again in his speech, closed shop, and left on vacation; the political reading of the country, mulled over for so many months by the president and his aides and shaped, I believe, as much by the Carters' small-town American heritage and beliefs in community spirit, volunteerism, and old-fashioned patriotism as by Caddell's data about national pessimism, had proven incorrect in leading to a regeneration of public faith in the political system; the calculated strategy to show a strong president firmly in charge, firing many of his top echelon and shaking up the entire governmental command structure, had created almost the opposite effect—of desperate action, ill-considered and hastily implemented, that bespoke more the maneuvers of public relations than of presidential leadership.

And there was, in each of these events, a recurring strain: it was the little mistakes, the personal misjudgments, the failures to understand how actions might be perceived publicly that had bedeviled the Carter administration from the beginning, and they were still being made. The handling of earlier problems had raised doubts about the Carter group, particularly about Carter's handling of his associates—the clinging to Bert Lance until the end, in face of the evidence, during that summer of 1977; the reluctance the next summer to remove Dr. Peter Bourne (one of the earliest and closest of the original Georgia group who urged Carter to run for president) as the White House drug-abuse adviser after Bourne became involved in a sordid drug case (he had written a prescription for a White House aide for quaaludes, a hard "street drug," using a fictitious patient's name, and after he was reported in the press to have used cocaine at a Washington party, issued a statement saying many others in the White House regularly used illegal drugs); the quick and gleeful firing of Bella Abzug in January 1979 as head of the president's advisory group on women, amid chortles from the White House Georgians, who believed her ouster would demonstrate presidential decisiveness and thus reap political benefits but accomplished just the opposite. And in dismissing half the cabinet without touching the core of the Georgia group many of these old doubts were stirred anew. Once again Jimmy Carter's presidency had been damaged not so much from events outside but from actions within. The wounds were self-inflicted.

EPILOGUE

EPILOGUE

THE NARRATOR

IN HIS opening words the historian Herodotus is straightforward in style and grand in theme: "Here are set forth," he writes, "the researches of Herodotus of Halicarnassus that men's actions may not in time be forgotten nor things great and wonderful, accomplished whether by Greeks or barbarians, go without report."

I had no illusions about recording great and wonderful historical acts and noble deeds in Jimmy Carter's Washington. It was as a detached observer, watching one president struggle with the unyielding problems of his times, that I began research for this book. The questions were important, the outcome worth pondering for lessons about governing in the future, but I did not have vested feelings in the matter. Now, however, I feel I've witnessed a tragedy.

Jimmy Carter was probably intellectually better prepared than any recent president to deal with the complex issues that will dominate the rest of the century—the finiteness of natural resources and the rapid squandering of them, the advantages and danger of advancing technology, the spread of nuclear weaponry, the rising population worldwide, and the heightened tastes for more material comforts amid increasing shortages, the growing pessimism about the ability of governments to solve problems. Carter was a technocrat, an interpreter of blueprints and systems, but he also brought to office fine moral purpose, uncommonly high ethical standards, and a tempered view of the presidency that suited, I thought, the realities of his political period. He was, as that shrewd Washington counselor had said early in the administration, a brighter man than the political system usually offers up to the American people. Three years after his election I see a capital more cynical, a country more disaffected, a political system more incapable of responding even to day-to-day crises, to say nothing of long-range planning. If attitudes about public service improved, in or out of government, I can't detect them, and obviously anger with Washington has risen. For his presidency to create such disillusionment after so much effort—and promise—is dismaying. Whether Carter wins renomination and reelection becomes insignificant beside those larger concerns.

It was Jimmy Carter's fate to preside at a time when events seemed dangerously out of control and destined to grow worse; when a new generation had come to maturity doubting that government could make a difference in their lives and lacking confidence that any attempt to effect governmental reform would do more good than harm; when the best times appeared behind us; when the glorious boom of the postwar period had passed; when public faith in the political process had dropped to new lows; when the presidency had been weakened and the political consensus shattered. He had been elected as a reaction to these circumstances, the only true political outsider of the century, and now there was a feeling of deep disappointment in him. In Washington, Jim Fallows expressed it best: "I think Carter is a good president, and I will vote for him again," he said to me. "I think he is doing a lot of good things. But I just expected so much more. Everybody hoped he was going to be more remarkable than he is."

As I write, another presidential campaign commences. Once again, with countless other reporters, I'll be attempting to report the race from primary to election, but I look forward to this work with less enthusiasm than ever before. On my desk are reminders of how much we in the press have become a part of that electoral process and a source of political controversy—letters from readers around the country that express dislike of what they see as a "negative" press. "What is the effect of journalism, of media, of the current state of the art of reporting on the ability of [a] president to lead?" writes a man from Mission, South Dakota. "I am sure that many serious journalists weigh and consider the changes that have occurred within their profession, the effect that these changes have on the nature of reporting, and the effect that a more sensitized reporting has on the public's ability to believe anything positive. This is not a diversion. Is the determination not to be lied to or used by any public official (a determination that is crucial to a free press) something that can—not does, or will, but *can*—create false impressions? No president or presidential action can survive skepticism when that skepticism is combined with simplicity and superficial reporting." And a woman from Mendocino, California, comments: "I carry no torch for the president, and am strong for a free press in America, but it seems to me you, the media, are doing him in for the whole population, and I'm sure we'll thank the press for this in the long run."

I have no way of knowing how prevalent these views are nationally, but from the number of such letters and from the remarks of people I meet, I believe them to be both substantial and significant. The press didn't destroy Jimmy Carter—the worst damage done the president was at his and his own people's hands, creating for the public the impression of incompetence and blundering—but the following opinion of one political scientist strikes uncomfortably close to the truth. "The news media, except for a few weeks after Camp David, has been unremittingly hostile to Mr. Carter," Professor Reo Christenson of Miami University at Oxford, Ohio, wrote in *The New York Times* in March 1979. "It will continue to be so. In forty years of close president-watching, I have never seen a president treated so unfairly." Part of Carter's problems with the press derived from his background, his lack of familiarity with Washington, and from plain mistakes; but part stemmed from the more critical tone of *all* press reporting after Vietnam and Watergate. The "pictures in our heads" have been uniformly unflattering about all politicians. *Any* president would have faced—and any president *will* face—suspicion and harsher criticism from the press. That is now one of the new realities of presidential life, and one of the new problems of governing.

A destructive state of mind is only one reason for me to be wary as another campaign begins. Another is that instead of being more manageable, our system of choosing presidents becomes more disorderly. Even greater effort has to be expended in campaigning, leaving still less time for planning on what to do once in office. Following Carter's winning example in 1976, more candidates are starting earlier. They are preparing to contest in more primaries, cross the country more often, and, everywhere, promise to return the government to the people and straighten out the bureaucratic-political mess in Washington.

Proliferation of the primaries continues. Democratic presidential aspirants who labored through seventeen costly state primaries in 1968, then endured twenty-three in 1972 and thirty-one in 1976, have to run in thirty-five of them in 1980. The day of the regional or national primary—a useful reform that would shorten the debilitating process, better enable attention to be focused on issues, and perhaps generate public interest and participation in the campaign—remains as distant as ever. Though every recent president, including Carter, has come to favor the idea of a six-year term, prospects of such a constitutional amendment making that possible are remote. (The same is true of raising the congressional term from two to four years, allowing House members to spend more time in Washington.)

Television even more strongly dominates the electoral process, and the power of the national press in selecting—and rejecting—the leading figures consequently increases. Candidates scramble all the more to be seen and heard, fleetingly, over the national networks. In the resulting cacophony, one voice cancels out another. During the campaign days the press will follow behind them demanding to know how they will "solve" inflation and "solve" energy and "solve" the recession—and the candidates will give their "solutions." We, in the press, look for *the* issue, and *the* typical voter, when no one truly exists: each relates to another, and together they are filled with contradictions.

In the age of television, the politics of personality has replaced the politics of party. Though some people in Washington think a rebirth of the political parties will regenerate the process, on what ideological grounds do the parties now stand? Around what issues will they coalesce? If political consensus exists, it revolves around a politics of reality, of pragmatism, not party slogans and platforms. In the absence of a true expression of the national will, the powers of the special-interest groups gain. Increasingly, *they* become the force that actually governs. It is a system that breeds superficiality and confusion, wearies the public, leads to further decline in voting, and makes the task of national governing more difficult. Obviously, such a system is inadequate to the demands of the times—and to the greater strains about to be experienced by citizens and government alike. Dealing with complex economic and social issues is difficult in the most harmonious of eras, and harmony does not exist as the new decade begins. The presidency stands weakened; the Congress remains fragmented; the press becomes more critical; the public grows more distrustful.

It's almost no-win politics, Max Cleland was telling me one day as the 1980 election year drew near. For Cleland, the first of Carter's outsiders to meet with the new president in the White House, the triple amputee from the Vietnam war who was going to give the Veterans Administration a new birth of energy and direction, the experience in Washington had been harsh. I had seen him from time to time, had followed his record, and knew no one could have worked more diligently, but for Cleland the job had been "a voyage into reality," he said, and worse. Vietnam veterans' groups had accused him of betrayal, of failing to stand up for them in the face of budgetary constraints in the austerity mood of the Carter administration. Cleland wondered whether government was capable of governing. More than interest-group politics was at work in Washington; we now almost had interest-group democracy. There were mornings when he came to his tenth-floor office, overlooking Lafayette Park, feeling beaten up; then he'd gaze out the window toward the White House seven hundreds yards away and think of Jimmy Carter. How could anyone bear up under the pressure of such problems? "I keep hearing the critics, I keep hearing the negatives," he said of the president. "But then I look at the man. Can a good man govern? What do the American people want and expect from a president?" To Cleland, a loyalist, the true colors of the American people would be measured in how they responded to the kind of president Jimmy Carter had been. People had rejected the imperial presidency and sought honesty and simplicity in the White House. They got it, he said. Now they seem to hunger for an omnipotent father from Washington.

Cleland was both right and wrong, I was thinking. Carter seemed to personify the contradiction of the times, the sharp conflict between placing limits on government and increasing the demands for more government. His own energy proposals, on which he staked the success of his presidency in the summer of 1979, showed this vividly: as he took his political case to the people outside the capital he complained about red tape and the workings of Washington—and at the same time he wanted them to support the idea of more federal tax money and new bureaus in Washington to work on the energy problem.

Carter was contradictory in other ways. I remember listening to him in April 1978 when he delivered a speech about inflation, the scourge of the age. Along with energy it was the issue on which he would be judged. He was going to do what he could about inflation, he said, and was determined to set the government's own house in order as an example for the nation. At the same time the idea that government could do it alone was a myth. "No act of Congress, no program of our government, no order of my own can bring about the quality that we need: to change from the preoccupation with self that can cripple our national will, to a willingness to acknowledge and sacrifice for the common good."

The idea that a president doesn't have all the answers, doesn't possess all the powers necessary to alter events, was a refreshing statement of fact. Millions of Americans understood it. They had been attracted to him because, in such words as these, he was different from the political norm. At the same time they rightly expected him to tell them what he wanted them to do, to lead by offering a specific agenda. Too often, as in his address on inflation, he spoke only in the vaguest generalities. Jimmy Carter, it seemed to me, often had the right approach—and, for a brief time, the right audience—but was incapable of marshaling support to carry out his policies. Carter the technocrat could diagnose the problems, but Carter the politican could not summon the emotions necessary to make people work for him.

Yet ironically the very qualities that political Washington complained so loudly about were the ones the nation found most reassuring when a genuine crisis developed at the end of his third year. Once again, it was over Iran. The storming of the U.S. Embassy in Teheran early in November 1979 and the seizure of American hostages after the President had reversed himself and permitted the exiled and previously barred Shah to enter the United States for cancer treatment brought together in one explosive moment nearly every major issue Carter had grappled with as president—the challenge from the Mideast oil states, highlighting American dependence on them and the American failure to implement an effective energy policy; the frustrations of citizens at home about sudden threats to their accustomed life-styles and their doubts about the nation's future; the new presidential dilemmas of dealing with infinitely more complex problems requiring delicate combinations of diplomacy and strength—all at a time when the president was operating in the absence of power enjoyed by his predecessors in the recent past. Carter behaved with quiet firmness as he refused to capitulate to blackmail and yet struggled to preserve peace and national honor, and Americans, for that moment at least, responded to his brand of leadership more favorably than at any point during his presidency.

Bill Moyers once reminded Carter, during a televised interview in November 1978, of T. S. Eliot's remark that every imposing new figure in literature changes our perceptions of literature itself. The same is probably true of the presidency, he said, and he wondered what change Carter would most like his presidency to create. Carter replied that he'd like people to believe progress had been made toward restoring an accurate image of a good nation with integrity and purpose and of a president who spoke accurately for the people themselves. Again, those were worthy thoughts but, withal, generalizations. I suspect that Carter's presidency will be seen as a transitional one from the traditional political patterns of the past, the presidencies of promises, to the more difficult and demanding presidencies of realities, as exemplified by the dangerous and unstable conditions in the Mideast.

Before Carter even became a candidate, Jay Forrester, the futurist at MIT, gave a prescription for presidential leadership in the new decade. "It's inherent in a system like ours that the leaders don't lead," he told me, during a long conversation early in 1975. "They really follow. They can't lead if there's no constituency. By the very definition of the process they are following the accepted ideas, therefore the past, and they will continue to do so until those ideas are reversed. Now it doesn't need to be this way. A leader who has a clear image of the future can mold public opinion, but he has to have a very clear image. He has to be very sure of himself, and he has to be willing to lose an election or two while he makes his case." To provide such leadership in these times of cynicism about politics requires the greatest gifts of public expression and public persuasion—the gifts of a politician in the best sense of the word, the gifts expressing a vision of a future that people can understand and believe.

The most difficult challenge for a president in the 1980s and beyond is to persuade the country what it can't do, as well as what it can; to accept less materially, not more; to believe that fundamental changes in patterns of living do not necessarily mean a more unrewarding life, personally or nationally. Choices are going to be painful. In the past, long-term questions always could be set aside in the press of daily political events, but the luxury of avoiding hard decisions no longer becomes possible. Only a president can articulate a national purpose and explain national issues, and in our system only a president can serve as public educator for the nation.

It's not surprising, given the disappointments surrounding another presidency and the fears engendered by new threats to the nation's economic stability, that the new decade begins in a climate of doubt. Our present political system faces perhaps its greatest test as assumptions about the future are changing. A nation for two hundred years built on the belief that cheap energy abounds in limitless supply now finds the sources scarce and the cost extremely high. A people proud of their history of hard work now rank toward the bottom of the Western world in productivity. A governmental system designed in large measure to prevent abuses of power, with all the careful constitutional checks and balances firmly established over the generations, now sees its processes slowed and often stymied by competing groups. The lesson of Jimmy Carter and Washington, the clash between the outsiders and the insiders, shows *neither* side has been functioning effectively.

I began this book with a confession that, like Lippmann, the "pictures in my head," based on where I had been and what I had seen, had not prepared me for the political world I was about to enter. If that personal journey has been confounding, I find, at the end, that it's not the uncertain future that attracts me now, but a certain reassuring quality about the past. Lippmann could say, at the end of World War I: "If amidst all the evils of this decade, you have not seen men and women, known moments that you would like to multiply, the Lord himself cannot help you." And I would say, that the capital city I entered twenty-two years ago has changed for the better, that the country has matured, and that the people I've met along the way more often are less intolerant and better informed. America always has been an uncomplacent culture—a critical, self-searching society where every flaw is held up to the view of all. And a society that effectuates change, not perhaps as fast as it should or could, but change nevertheless.

Perhaps our politics grows more distasteful. Perhaps the quality of our leaders remains a disappointment. Perhaps our governmental and economic systems need overhauls. Perhaps Socrates has been right all along: that the art of politics, of making men good citizens, cannot be taught and perhaps cannot even be achieved. And perhaps what matters most is not whether *they*, those divine leaders we seek but never find, can educate *us*, but whether we are educable at all and if so (as I believe we are) whether we can act upon what we learn. The promise of Jimmy Carter's presidency hasn't been fulfilled, but the political challenge remains the same. It is to lead America into an understanding of the realities of late-twentieth-century life.

ACKNOWLEDGMENTS

I owe a debt to many more than can be acknowledged here, but I especially wish to thank these people: my *Washington Post* colleagues Benjamin C. Bradlee and Howard Simons, its executive editor and managing editor, who allowed me a leave of absence and were understanding as I extended it, and extended it; Professor Edward H. Sullivan, chairman of the Humanities Council at Princeton University, who backed me in my appointment to the Ferris professorship there in 1978 and helped make my time of teaching and book research pleasant and profitable; John Fox Sullivan, publisher of *The National Journal*, who made available a special set of every issue his magazine published during the Carter presidency, a resource I found indispensable; Kathleen McBride, my editorial assistant, who deserves far more credit than the passing word given here; and Elisabeth Sifton, of The Viking Press, whose personal encouragement and editing skills contributed immeasurably to this project.

H.J.

INDEX